VIKING SOCIETY FOR NOR
TEXT SERIES

GENERAL EDITORS
Peter Foote and Anthony Faulkes

VOLUME IX

THE WORKS OF SVEN AGGESEN

THE WORKS OF
SVEN AGGESEN
TWELFTH-CENTURY DANISH HISTORIAN

TRANSLATED
WITH INTRODUCTION AND NOTES

BY

ERIC CHRISTIANSEN

VIKING SOCIETY FOR NORTHERN RESEARCH
UNIVERSITY COLLEGE LONDON
1992

© Eric Christiansen 1992

Printed in the University of Birmingham

ISBN 0 903521 24 5

The cover illustration is based on part of a mural, painted c.1200, in Ål church, 8 miles west of Varde, W. Jutland (cf. p. 41).

CONTENTS

PREFACE	vii
INTRODUCTION	1
(i) The Author	1
(ii) The Text and its Congeners	4
(iii) Lex Castrensis	7
(iv) Historia Compendiosa	18
(v) The Lost Genealogy	26
(vi) Translations	27
THE LAW OF THE RETAINERS OR OF THE COURT	31
SUPPLEMENT TO LEX CASTRENSIS	44
A SHORT HISTORY OF THE KINGS OF DENMARK	48
NOTES	75
To the Introduction	75
On the Law of the Retainers	86
On the Supplement to the Lex Castrensis	103
On the Short History	104
APPENDIX — SVEN'S FAMILY	141
ABBREVIATIONS AND BIBLIOGRAPHY	146
INDEXES	165

GENERAL EDITORS' NOTE

The forms of early Danish personal names in this volume usually follow the spelling of them found in the headwords of *Danmarks gamle Personnavne*. Patronymics have been normalised throughout in *-sen*. West Norse names and other words appear in conventional Old Icelandic form.

The printing of this volume is made possible by a gift to the University of Cambridge in memory of Dorothea Coke, Skjaeret, 1951.

PREFACE

But where is the text? To publish a book in a Text Series without one seems perverse. The excuse is that Sven's own words can never be established with certainty, because they have been transmitted along two very defective conductors. One was a scholarly scribe of the late thirteenth century, who improved, clarified and paraphrased the text he was copying. Even his manuscript is lost; a version of his version was printed in 1642 and was accepted as Sven's own work until the late nineteenth century. The other copyist was a post-Reformation student, who barely understood the early manuscript he had been commissioned to copy and misinterpreted about one word in ten.

As a result, the best text is a reconstruction published in 1915/16 by the great Svendborg *filolog*, Martin Clarentius Gertz. It was a masterly reconciliation of two flawed versions, but it is always open to further imaginative emendation, or to pedantic criticism. There seems no point in reprinting the work of Gertz when it has appeared three times, and part of it four, this century.

Consequently I have not attempted a general discussion of Sven's latinity, which would be futile without the concurrent versions of what he wrote and would add little to the critical commentary of the 1915/16 edition. I offer only a halting English translation, with an introduction and notes, hastily compiled, treating some of the problems presented by Sven's works in their surviving form.

Sven is bound to be of interest to students of medieval Scandinavia, but his writings may also be of interest to students of medieval historiography and legal apocrypha. The 'Military Law' of King Canute has been an irritating shadow on the fringes of Anglo-Saxon history for some time, and has been of more substantial importance in the discussion of the development of the Danish state. Sven's *Historia Compendiosa* is a tempting fruit of the international culture of the twelfth-century Western church, and in the notes I attempt to explain this connection rather than probe at length the possible Nordic antecedents of the work. Sven borrowed from the Icelanders, but it was his classical and legal schooling which taught him his art.

I am most grateful to Professor Peter Foote for suggesting and nursing this book, and to Dr Anthony Faulkes, his fellow-editor, for trenchant criticisms. The Revd D. H. N. Carter has been generous with his help, and I am indebted to the Warden and Fellows of New College, Oxford, for the expenses of research in Copenhagen.

Eric Christiansen
New College
July 1990

INTRODUCTION

(i) *The Author*

Nothing is known of Sven Aggesen other than what he wrote of himself in the works attributed to him. He mentioned Saxo, the more famous of the two medieval Danish historians, as his associate; but Saxo never mentions Sven by name, even though he often mentions members of his family and made use of his work.[1]

Sven came from a great dynasty, which had played a leading part in Danish politics for nearly a century until 1176, when five of his cousins were implicated in a supposed conspiracy against King Valdemar I. Not long afterwards the chief of the clan, his uncle Eskil, archbishop of Lund, resigned his see and retired to Clairvaux, where he died in 1181. The metropolitan see, held by the family for nearly 90 years, passed to Bishop Absalon, who established his authority in Scania after a period of open revolt and civil war. Eskil's heir presumptive, Asser Svensen, provost of Lund cathedral, was dead by 1194, after a long exile; Sven's other cousins were no longer a force to be reckoned with. (On Sven's family see the Appendix, pp. 141–5.)

So who was he? A nephew of Eskil, son of Eskil's brother Aggi, and a man who was alive in 1185, when he witnessed the surrender of the Pomeranians to King Knut VI, Valdemar's son. That much is certain; and his own pride of ancestry reveals more. It suggests mixed feelings: pride in his father, misgivings about his grandfather and great-uncles, and complete silence about the great Eskil.

Kristiarn Svensen, the grandfather, had been a powerful and highly respected man, along with his brothers, in the first third of the twelfth century; but he had set a bad example of lawless violence to others. His son Aggi (not the same name as Aghi and Aki but already confused with them in Sven's day) had fought heroically against the forces of King Nicolaus in 1132. According to Saxo, he was still fighting 25 years later, for King Sven III against Valdemar: he gave the advice to attack which led to the annihilation of his own side on Grathe Heath.[2]

It is possible that Aggi was on bad terms with his brother the archbishop. The Cistercian memoir of Eskil[3] tells how the old prelate saw one of his dead brothers in a vision:

He had fallen slain under the sword of an enemy, and had not been shriven before he died. While he lived, he had once offended the archbishop for no just cause, and had not been reconciled to him or made amends before he died.

The brother is not named but he is called both 'uterine' and 'by the same father', and must thus be either Sven Kristiarnsen or Aggi; and Aggi was still fighting for Sven III in 1157 when Eskil had abandoned the king in 1153.[4] If this connexion could be substantiated, it would be significant: it would make Sven Aggesen the son of a casualty, as well as a hero, in the sword-play he hoped to curb in his Law of the Retainers. It might help to explain why he ignores his uncle in his Short History.

There is another story, only in Saxo (GD, 436–7; EC, 454), of how King Valdemar threatened to hang one of Eskil's nephews, who was being educated at Esrom abbey, unless the garrison surrendered one of Eskil's castles. That was in 1161/2. The castle was handed over to the king, but the archbishop was very angry, for his response had been 'that he was more concerned for his castle than for his *nepotes*, and that their lives were on no account to be put before its safety.'

It is tempting to identify this boy with our Sven, but the odds are against it: *nepos* means both 'nephew' and 'grandson', and at the time Eskil had two young grandsons and at least three young nephews. We cannot conclude that Sven's education involved nearly being hanged by King Valdemar, but his work suggests that it included the study of classical *autores*, the art of composition, civil and canon law, and the Bible and liturgy. Gertz concluded that he went to Paris for at least part of this education, like other well-connected Danes;[5] again, the possibility exists, but there is no sign that his acquaintance with any of these branches of learning was deep or detailed, or evidently the result of attending Parisian lectures, or of reading whole works rather than florilegia and compendiums.

He described Saxo as his *contubernalis*, which means they had some kind of association or fellowship at the time of writing: that is, post 1185. It has often been pointed out that Saxo was probably much younger than Sven. His grandfather had fought for Valdemar I, perhaps after 1157, while Sven's father had been a leading warrior as early as 1132. Therefore this *contubernium* is unlikely to have been a school.

The primary meaning of *contubernalis* is military: 'tent-companion'. It has often been assumed that Sven and Saxo served together as knights or clerks in the households of the king or Archbishop Absalon.[6] Sven drew up a version of the king's household laws, and he witnessed the surrender of the Pomeranians on the campaign of 1185: he must therefore have served as a retainer of the king, and the same must be true of Saxo.

The fallaciousness of this deduction has been demonstrated more than once, most recently by Karsten Friis-Jensen, who summarized the many reasons for not making soldiers or royal retainers out of either historian. Their interest in military and political affairs is fully compatible with what we know of the outlook of Danish clergy at the time, and their historical vision is no more secular than that of other twelfth-century clerks in the rest of Europe. The obvious conclusion to be drawn from their language and learning is that they were both ecclesiastics. Educated laymen existed but they did not at this period compose Latin histories, unless they were Italians.

Friis-Jensen goes farther and identifies Saxo with the canon of Lund who witnessed charters in 1180/3 and 1197/1201[7]—or at least he presents the argument for a probable identification. If he is right, Sven's identity is not lost. A *Sveno archidiaconus* is eighth in the list of canon-deacons in the Lund necrology, between Esbiorn, who was in office from *c.*1174, and Provost Asser, Sven Aggesen's cousin, who was exiled in 1176/7 but remained titular head of the chapter.[8] It appears from a document summarized by Hamsfort in the sixteenth century that Archdeacon Sven attended Absalon's great synod of July 1187, along with Andrew, deacon, and Martin, priest, as representatives of the Lund chapter. The post he held had been instituted by Archbishop Eskil in 1145 'for the lawsuits and administration of episcopal rights in the city',[9] and he may have been effective leader of the canons in the absence of the provost. When he died he left the community property worth half a mark—less than his cousin Asser, who made a bequest of at least two estates, in Scania and Sjælland.[10]

A necessary knowledge of law; membership of a *contubernium* to which Saxo may also have belonged; high rank in a chapter once dominated by Sven Aggesen's family. That may not seem enough on which to base an identification, even if we add the well-known propensity of archdeacons to write history. However, Lund is the obvious place for Sven. Danish annalists were at work there as early as the 1140s, and historical writing persisted there for over two centuries, as Anne K. G. Kristensen has demonstrated. So obvious is the connexion that it was made in the eighteenth century, by Lagerbring and Langebek, and later by Velschow in his introduction to Saxo (1858).[11]

The hypothesis was abandoned for lack of positive evidence in its favour, and in deference to the view that Sven must have been a rough diamond, the voice of the lay nobility rather than of the clergy. In my reading of his work I have found nothing to support this view and much that is consistent with the career of a learned clerk with legal responsibilities and a comfortable prebend in the chapter of Lund. As a survivor of the régime of Eskil who had made his peace with Absalon, he could put his legal expertise, such as it was, at the service of the new archbishop in an endeavour to tame the royal household; and employ the records of Lund to supply the new Danish monarchy with a rather topical history.

I believe that Sven has been misrepresented by those who suppose that he wrote for a particular social or political group: for the traditional values of the war-band, for aristocratic privilege, or for the 'Valdemarine establishment', all three of them very nebulous concepts.[12] He was evidently a witty, humane, and slightly pretentious pioneer, who supplied the Danish king with three types of composition commonly used to glorify other twelfth-century monarchies: a law treatise, a political history in outline, and a royal pedigree. This hardly makes him a propagandist, unless the term be used to cover any work in which a political tendency is discernible. None of his work is openly dedicated to any patron, even if he compliments his king and his metropolitan in the Law of the Retainers.[13] He claimed to be writing spontaneously, and I can find no internal evidence with which to contradict his claim. An archdeacon of Lund (if such he was) and a scion of Denmark's highest nobility, he was entitled to express his own views on matters of public interest, and on the beauty of the Queen Mother too, if he chose.[14] He was no ideological purist, but a man with an interesting mind.

(An excellent summary, in English, of all that is known about Sven Aggesen may be found in Joaquín Martínez-Pizarro's 1988 article listed in the Bibliography, p. 158.)

(ii) *The Text and its Congeners*

Sven's works survive in two versions, neither of which is an accurate copy of what he wrote.

A is AM 33 4to, an inexpert copy probably commissioned by Claus Lyschander (1558–1624) of an early and authentic manuscript.

S is the improved and corrected version of another early manuscript by a scribe of the late thirteenth century and by Stephan J. Stephanius, the editor of the first printed edition, published at Sorø in 1642. The manuscript was lost in the great Copenhagen fire of 1728, and it is therefore impossible to be certain whether the improvements and omissions were made by the medieval scribe or by Stephanius or by both. This version was reprinted by Langebek, the Short History in SRD, i (1769), the Law of the Retainers in SRD, iii (1774), with useful notes, and by Gertz as one of parallel texts in 1915/16 and in SM, i 56–143 (1917/18). Although the superiority of this text was challenged by Waitz in 1887, it remained the commonly accepted version down to 1915/16.

Then M. Cl. Gertz published *En ny Text af Sven Aggesøns Værker* with four parallel texts:

(i) An almost perfect transcription of A, AM 33 4to, as it stands, blundered and obscure.

(ii) His own reconstruction, with conjectural abbreviations and sigla, of the original appearance of the manuscript travestied by the A scribe.

(iii) His reconstruction of X, the lost manuscript behind A.

(iv) The S text.

An exhaustive critical commentary and comparisons between the two versions established X as the 'best' text, and Gertz reprinted it with amendments in SM, i.

The X version of Sven Aggesen's *Lex Castrensis* (LC hereafter) reappears with critical apparatus and some further emendation in DR, 6–24. The text used for the present translation is referred to as X, and any deviations from the Gertz 1915/16 version are noted.

Saxo Grammaticus also included a version of LC in the tenth book of his *Gesta Danorum* (GD hereafter), and this is most conveniently printed in DR, 34–41, as edited by Erik Kroman. It is translated into English from the 1514 *editio princeps* of GD in EC, 36–44. Saxo's LC is almost certainly later than Sven's, and differs in scope and style; on which see Riis, 31–47.

This leaves the Danish text entitled *Witherlax ræt* (WR hereafter), which is preserved in at least fourteen manuscripts of the period 1400–1650; it was published from two lost manuscripts in 1672, 1740, 1774, 1827 and in 1971 in DR, 1–5. An English translation from this last print is given on pp. 44–7 below.

In the following I use the well-known Danish word *Vederlov* as a general term for the body of regulations reflected in Sven's LC, Saxo's LC, and WR.

WR cannot however be allowed any independent importance. It consists of a set of eight regulations, with proem and epilogue, purporting to be the original rules drawn up by Knut VI and Archbishop Absalon for the *hird*, a work to which Sven also refers as his source (see p. 31 below). According to Jørgensen, 56–7, WR is a later version of that Absalonic code, and in 1971 Kroman thought 'there can scarcely be any doubt but that its provisions were really once the law of the Danish *hird*' (DR, 1).

It has however often been pointed out that this cannot be so. Firstly, all the regulations but one in WR coincide with those in Sven's LC. Sven has more, but still admits that his work is incomplete. So WR must be even more so. Secondly, WR omits the passage on outlawry by sea which is also missing in Sven's LC, although present in Saxo. Thirdly, the proem and epilogue simply condense Sven's own proem and commentary on the infraction of the old law.

For these reasons WR must be rejected as anything other than a neat historical reconstruction, based solely on Sven's LC, or on the Saxo version in one detail. It was probably made in Scania at some time in the thirteenth century (the language and style are believed to suggest a comparatively early date; Diderichsen, 55-7). In 1974 Gordon Albøge attempted to vindicate the status of WR as a version of Absalon's code rather than a précis of Sven's, but his mainly philological arguments cannot dispose of the three objections listed above. Nevertheless, others agree with him.

The table below shows the order in which Sven, Saxo and WR deal with the various regulations. The differences are discussed with the utmost delicacy in Riis, 31-47.

Regulation	*Sven*	*Saxo*	*WR*
On horses' work-loads	1	2	–
On horses' fodder	2	3	–
On seating in hall	3	1	–
On watering horses	4	4	–
On the king's patronage	5	–	–
On the king's duties to men	6	–	1
On transfer of homage	7	9	4
On prosecution for insult	8	–	–
On jurisdiction of court	9	–	6
On cases of land-right and theft	10	–	7
On choosing jurors	11	–	–
On killings and woundings	12	5, 7, 8	5
On blows	13	–	–
On purgation	14	–	–
On accidental woundings	15	6	–
On treason and outlawry	16, 17	5	2, 3

Saxo also gives regulations on wrong seating, on annoying jests and drink-splashing, on sleeping sentries, and on the inadmissibility of counter-oaths.

The transmission and survival of Sven's text were discussed most fruitfully by Karsten Christensen in 1978.

(iii) *Lex Castrensis*

> Although it is in the king's power to issue or change laws, we do not issue this law as a new one; rather, as a law established from ancient times, which has been obscured by the clouds of ignorance, and which we are recalling to the memory of man, darkened over by the passage of many years, which is the mother of oblivion.

So runs the conclusion of the earliest surviving example of royal Danish law-making, the decree on homicide issued by Knut VI for the benefit of the province of Scania on 28 December 1200.[15] The device of law-making by rediscovery was well suited to the Northern world, where law remained largely unwritten until the twelfth century. It was what the good men at the provincial law-meetings could remember. Here, the king is remembering for them.

Hitherto kings had played little part in this business. At their accessions they may have sworn to uphold 'the good laws of King Harald' (i.e. Harald Whetstone, d. 1080), and they attended some law-meetings and trials. They were entitled to fines for aggravated forms of homicide, and to a redemption payment for outlaws (*frithkøp*); but the system recorded in the earliest provincial law codes depends on collective responsibility and private prosecution, not on royal attempts at peace-keeping.[16]

Under Valdemar I (1157–82) there are signs of change. He may have had some part in the codification of the Sjælland laws which goes by his name,[17] and he held a meeting in 1171 at which laws were revised and improved.[18] Before 1161 he had eased restrictions on mortmain bequests, at least in favour of Tommerup abbey.[19] He conducted prosecutions and a show-trial for treason (1167 and 1177). Nevertheless, when he died, the kingdom lacked any official law-making body, and the king was peripheral to the execution of the laws. Even ecclesiastical law was a matter of negotiation between bishops and the provincial law-communities;[20] the bishops, not the king, seem to have initiated the recording and mending of law.

It was left for Valdemar's sons, Knut VI and Valdemar II, to begin issuing royal ordinances and to move, by way of tentative reforms, towards the great Jutland code issued by the king in 1241.[21] Meanwhile, laws had to be found somewhere, preferably in the past, to deal with the problems created by the assertive monarchy of the Valdemarine kings, who appear to have had ample private resources but somewhat undeveloped public powers. Thus, by 1230 Valdemar II enjoyed an income comparable with that of the king of England;[22] but until the 1190s his father and brother had faced open defiance by magnates and commons in peace and in war. They had no formal exchequer, no royally appointed judges, and no tenurial hold on their upper classes.

The only central institution which the king controlled was his own household, the staff of followers who travelled with the royal family. Saxo usually calls it the *clientela* of the king; modern historians call it the *hird*, using a word not often found in Danish sources but common in Norway. By c.1270 the Norwegian *hirð* was a three-tier organization of knights, officials, and servants, described in *Konungs skuggsjá* and governed by the surviving *Hirðskrá*;[23] but the size, composition and nature of the Danish *hird* remain uncertain.

Twelfth-century sources indicate several sorts of people who might be found attending the king as part of their duties. They included his immediate family and kinsmen; intimate counsellors, lay and clerical; chaplains, plain clerics or doubling as scribes and physicians; stewards, bailiffs, and officers with outside duties; household officers, the stallers, a chancellor, a treasurer, a chamberlain, a marshal, a butler; knights or guards; servants, grooms, huntsmen, technicians, and presumably the musicians and 'mimics' denounced by Saxo.[24]

The witness-lists of charters single out the more important of the king's followers. The 'suitable witnesses' are named in Valdemar I's privilege to St Knut's, Odense (6 Feb. 1180; DD, i:3, no. 89); but at Ringsted in 1177 there were 'many other knights and priests and monk-brothers' (DD, i:3, no. 62). In 1145 a grant of Erik III referred to seven named witnesses and 'many of my *curiales*' (DD, i:3, no. 91). The four 'stallers' (*stabularii*) of Knut VI must have had some authority over other curials, if not over the clerics, who would have looked to the notary or chancellor. There must always have been bishops in attendance, but the military following was presumably the most indispensable: the royal knights were the only force at the king's disposal all the year round.

He could count on the occasional use of the public levy (*lething*) and of the retinues of bishops and magnates, but his own guard provided the core of the army in wartime and the only police force in peace. (Jutland was already a famous horse-breeding peninsula, and the Saxons had taught the Danes their knightly skills.) The battle record of the king's knights over the twelfth century was good. Their performance as a security force was not. In 1134 King Nicolaus and his knights had been mobbed and murdered by burghers in Schleswig. In 1137 Erik II had been assassinated at a law-meeting when surrounded by his escort, and all but one of his *aulici* had run off (GD, 370–1; EC, 355). According to Saxo, Erik III had paid too highly for the services of his followers: they helped him win a civil war but proved useless against the Slavs (GD, 374; EC, 360). Sven III had recruited upstarts and foreigners to attend him, and had been loyally served up to a point; but in the crises of 1153 and 1157 his knights were out of control.

Valdemar's knights were suspected of favouring a conspiracy against the king in 1174–6: according to confessions extracted from the principals, some had known about the plot without revealing it (GD, 503–12; EC, 549–64). In 1180–2, when the Scanians defied both the king and Archbishop Absalon, some courtiers sided with the rebels, until the king sent them away (GD, 528–9; EC, 588–90). When the Scanians rebelled against Knut VI in 1182, several of the king's knights preferred 'to feign ignorance and stay at home' (GD, 538; EC, 604).

Reading Saxo, we find it difficult to believe that this volatile assemblage of paid fighters, officials, and clerics formed the law-bound corporation of Sven's treatise on the *Vederlov*. When Saxo dealt with those laws in his tenth book, he placed the system he described back in the time of 'old' King Knut, for 'the princes of our own time have thought it no shame to break this rule.'[25] The only time the king's knights appear as a self-regulating body in his narrative of twelfth-century history falls during the troubled 1150s, when there were two rival royal followings. Sven III's men refused to arrest his rival, young Valdemar, when ordered to do so; and when Sven gave up the struggle in 1153, the loyal remnant of his followers attempted to change his mind with strong words, and finally condemned him, perhaps as a *nithing*, and resolved to fight on without him.[26] After his defeat and death in 1157, the warriors of Valdemar and Knut V attempted to decide the fate of the defeated Sven's adherents and to deter the king from showing mercy; a compromise was reached between their 'law' and his, but only after Ulf of Ribe had virtually been lynched.

None of these examples suggests that the laws and privileges of the household were an important political fact in the time of Valdemar I. There is no suggestion that the supposed conspirators of 1176/7 were tried or condemned according to the processes of Sven's LC; the chief of them, Magnus Eriksen, was threatened with the ordeal, which plays no part in these processes. He stood trial before the nobles and bishops of the whole kingdom, not before any *huskarlastefna*; then, and at a second hearing in private, he was convicted by written and verbal evidence, and escaped sentence by confessing. The procedure seems to have been entirely at the king's pleasure.

By contrast, there is evidence that something like LC was applied in the thirteenth century. Three royal ordinances attributed to the 1250s (King Abel's, King Kristofer's, and *Super Crimine Lese Maiestatis*) and King Erik Glipping's Treason Law of 9 October 1276[27] indicate that there actually existed a body of courtiers (*hofmæn*) and magnates (*høfthinge(r)*), known collectively as the *Witherlagh*. They were liable to pay triple fines, as well as compensation, for injuries inflicted on each other, after a hearing before the king, at which they were entitled to the support of twelve oath-helpers chosen from among their fellows. A third of the fine was distributed among the 'community of the court'. In cases of treason, a fifteen-man oath was to be selected by two respectable residents of the *syssel* from which the accused came. In 1276 this oath was reduced to twelve men, selected in threes from each of four *worthæl* ('wards, watches', ON *varðhald*). In such cases, conviction meant capital punishment and the forfeiture of lands and goods.

The details are not dissimilar to those found in Saxo and Sven, and it looks as if LC was dealing with the same institution at an earlier period, with intentions that were not quite the same as the royal legislation after 1250. The code in Danish on which it was based seems to have been an attempt by the archbishop to introduce writing and royal authorization into what had previously been a self-regulating, if not autonomous, system of house-rules. As with the Scanian ordinance of 1200 (p. 7 above), the attempt was justified by an appeal to the past.

But why to the days of 'old' King Knut? The English code known as II Cnut did contain one law, ch. 59, for the royal household: 'If anyone fights in the king's court, he is to forfeit his life, unless the king wishes to spare him' (Liebermann, i 350–1). It was a repetition of Alfred, ch. 7, remote in date, scope and intention from anything in LC, and Absalon was almost certainly unaware of its existence. It was a law against fighting in the king's vicinity, not a law for the king's following.

It is possible that the whole story of Knut's law-making originated with Sven, but it is more likely that Absalon, whose historical interests are well attested by Saxo (GD, 3, 5, 459–60; PF, 4, 6, EC, 486–7), attached the name to the new code to justify whatever innovations it contained. No other Nordic source of the twelfth or thirteenth century gives any hint that 'old' Knut was remembered as a legislator, although Sven's contemporaries in Iceland attributed a fictional law-code to Pálnatóki for the regulation of the Jómsborg Vikings (and a later Icelandic source associates Knut's father, Sven Forkbeard, with similar rules).[28] Saxo went even farther back and presented the mythical kings, Frothi and Regner, as lawmakers. If Nordic tradition played a part in the subterfuge, it was most probably derived from Norway, where Hákon Aðalsteinsfóstri was remembered as the originator of the Gulathing law and St Olaf was credited with giving laws to his subjects and, by Snorri, to his own household as well.[29]

On the other hand, Knut was respected in twelfth-century England as the compiler of English law in the 'pandect' form of the *Consiliatio Cnuti*, and as the imagined author of the Forest Law.[30] His wide conquests and his large professional army were a living memory, at least in London, and the influx of Englishmen to Denmark in the reign of Valdemar I will have brought the tradition to Absalon's notice. However, what Sven Aggesen made of this connection was a historical olio which had nothing to do either with the laws of the Danish king's following or with the ascertainable facts of Knut's military arrangements in England.

This last point would not be worth making if it were not so frequently asserted that Knut's army was a legally autonomous institution or gild, regulated by its own *husting* in accordance with rules similar to those of LC.[31] Sven Aggesen's text cannot be allowed as evidence: it depends on an absurd presumption of continuity between a paid army, not exclusively of Scandinavians, stationed in England before 1050, and a small force of knights serving in Denmark over 130 years later. As for the gild, there is no evidence from the time that Knut's *þingamannalið* was organized in a gild-like way. Nor, despite the *þing* element in its name, that it was governed by an autonomous assembly or court.

Husting is a loan from ON *húsþing*. It was used by the Anglo-Saxon Chronicler to describe the meeting of Thorkel's army which tried to intimidate Archbishop Ælfheah in 1012, but it reappears in the twelfth century to describe the normal Monday Court of the leading Londoners who met at the royal hall. Neither of these usages proves that there was a gild.[32] Nor is there any implication in the Scandinavian sources that the word connotes any form of civil or military gild-meeting. References in prose are too late to be relevant, but early Norse poetry makes it clear that a *húsþing* was a council between a leader and his chief men and usually, it appears, when they were on a war footing.[33] If Knut's London army was governed by a *húsþing* (and there is no evidence that it was), it was because it was governed by Knut.

But why was it called *þingalið* or *þingamannalið* or, in Sven's LC, *Tinglith*? The names are well attested, and in calling its members *þingemanni* the *Leges Henrici Primi* (ch. 15, 1; a collection completed by or in 1118) agree with Þórðr Kolbeinsson's term, *þingamenn*, in *Eiríksdrápa* (st. 11; c.1015).[34] The word *þing* usually means a law-moot, an assembly at which a court might be constituted, but it is not usual to name an army or its members after an assembly or law-court, quite apart from the difficulty posed by the first element in the early compounds, *þinga*, which can hardly be counted as anything but a genitive plural. The problem has produced some strange answers but no convincing solutions.

One is that the word *þingamenn* is a borrowing of OE *þeningmenn* (see Bosworth-Toller, s.v. *þegnung-mann*), or even that the first element is from OE *þeg(e)n*.[35] *Þeningmenn* are servants of a lord or king, or nobles attendant at a court. It is unreasonable to assume that members of Knut's army would be known by the same name as the courtiers of King Ethelred; in the circumstances, some distinction would have to be made. Any connection with the word *þegn*, as used either in England or in Scandinavia, can be ruled out by the difference in sound and meaning between *þegn* and *þing*, and the supposed compound, *þegn-maðr*, is unattested and extremely unlikely. The word *þing* has other meanings than 'assembly', ranging from 'encounter' or 'muster' to 'object' and 'contract' or 'agreement', and one of these must lie behind the compound *þingamaðr*.[36]

By the time Sven Aggesen and the authors of kings' sagas were writing the original sense of the compound will have been obscured by the much commoner usage of *þing* as law-moot or assembly for public affairs. Hence the prominence of the warriors' court in LC, a court which allowed Sven to interpret the puzzling term *tinglith* (older *þingalið* = *þingamannalið*) and provided a dignified origin for the domestic assembly, the *huskarlastefna*, of the late twelfth century. Sven employed this misunderstanding to good effect. His *tinglith* was an army ruled by law, and the law had been made by the greatest of Danish kings. The warriors of Knut VI might therefore be expected to obey it, as an inheritance from the more glorious days of Danish empire in Western Europe.

Nevertheless, LC is a strange production. It purports to be a Latin rendering of a code of rules in Danish recently rediscovered and written down. But it isn't. It is a legal-historical *tractatus*, which explains how these rules originated and underwent modification in the course of time.

The emphasis is on methods of trial and punishment and on the ethics of the system; not on the regulations themselves, which appear only in part and virtually in parenthesis.

Those rules which the author singles out are for the most part obsolete or fanciful.[37] Most carry conviction neither as ancient nor as modern. The stated aim, in the proem and the conclusion, is to edify young students of Latin composition, and to inspire them to improve and consummate the work. It is not made clear why they should wish to do this.

The regulations, whether ancient or modern, are intended to curb indiscipline and brutality. Yet, in effect, they confer rights, privileges and status on the trouble-makers. The only penalties they have to face for offences short of wilful homicide or treason are loss of dining-rights, self-abasement, or fines. Traitors can be ceremoniously outlawed, but not executed unless they attempt to return or happen to meet any of their former comrades.

The ancients are commended for their keeping of the good old law, and infractions of it are attributed to the work of the Devil. Nevertheless, the chief law-breakers are 'old' Knut himself and the author's own grandfather, Kristiarn Svensen, whom he appears to admire. He seems to endorse the old commonplace of modern degeneracy, and then to draw back: to commend Archbishop Absalon and the king for reviving ancient customs, and then to demonstrate that the ancient customs no longer apply. When Saxo came to deal with the same subject, probably during the period 1201–16, he produced a simpler and more rational picture, of a good system which had been followed in the remote past and abandoned in modern times, to the detriment of the king's service.[38] By contrast, Sven appears to be confused and equivocal. Whose side is he on?

I cannot explain these difficulties. Too little is known about Sven himself, or about the court politics of the reign of Knut VI, to allow more than speculation. LC relates to a lost text in Danish, and to an ill-defined body of litigants over an uncertain number of generations. All that can be attempted is description.

LC is a *tractatus*. Not in the usual sense of a treatise about one aspect of law—penance, evidence, judicial privilege—but about a particular system of law; not extensive enough to justify a *summa*, but sufficiently important to deserve analysis and comment.

It is not a military law in any sense recognized by Roman or twelfth-century legists, that is, a disciplinary code concerning the waging of war and the duties of a soldier.[39] Such codes were applied by later medieval

Danish kings, and appear in the form of 'the old *gaardsret*', i.e. laws of the king's residences,[40] which are immediately recognizable as serious garrison orders:

> If a man slays another man, then he shall give life for life ... if a man beats or strikes or stabs another man and draws blood, he shall lose his hand ... if a man calls another thief, he shall lie in the tower for a month with bread and water ... if any man steals as much as two øre's worth, he shall hang for it; and if he steals one øre's worth, he shall be flogged and fined one øre.

This is not the language or outlook of LC. When Sven called it *militaris*, he must have meant 'knightly' rather than 'military', and if it was *castrensis*, the *castrum* was not the camp but the king's *hof*. This is a form of civil law, and the way he handles it is consistent with some knowledge of Justinian's Code and the methods of twelfth-century law students. To begin with, he imitates the proem of the *Institutes*. Knut's legislation, like Justinian's, comes as the sequel of his imperial conquests—'Imperial Majesty should not only be graced with arms but also armed with laws'—and Knut sets to law-making *invicto conamine*, like Justinian after *bellicosos sudores*. In the same way as Justinian, Sven claims that he brings to life many old laws that have fallen into disuse;[41] and he ascribes the framing of the old code to a committee of Knut, Øpi and Eskil, just as Tribonian, Theophilus and Dorotheus were the named compilers of the *Institutes*. He also insists on the unifying effect of Knut's code on the differing nationalities and customs of his warriors.

The usages he then describes are of course wholly un-Roman. He uses some terms of art that show he was familiar with at least the vocabulary of the civil law student;[42] since he was writing in Latin, these could hardly be avoided. He begins with the legist's interrogative style, 'who ... why ... where?'; refers to his own work as 'enucleation', from a verb characteristic of the civilian;[43] and in the course of it he poses several *quaestiones*. Even so, the influence of the canonists is stronger.

Sven has usually been described as a resolutely secular author. He seldom mentions a priest or bishop by name in his Short History, which has been summarized as 'a brilliant, occasionally hyperbolical, panegyric of princely power' (Johannesson, 313). However, Johannesson has also demonstrated how thoroughly Saxo and to a lesser extent Sven were immersed in the learning of the church, and how they applied it to their own ends. Whether Sven was educated in France or not, his only way to the study of jurisprudence was through canon law, which was a living system in Denmark as elsewhere.[44] When Birgit Sawyer (1985b, 689) writes that his 'conventional style does not obscure the secular nature of his work, but it made it easier for leading churchmen to read,' she seems to overstate Sven's detachment from clerical concerns.

Indeed, he had little choice in the matter. Phrases from the Codex were ornamental, but esoteric. Not only the language but the concepts of canon law were a force that touched the lives of all the clergy and many laymen. Writing about law without using this force would have been virtually impossible, as the framers of Valdemar II's Jutland code were to demonstrate, even though they wrote in Danish.

According to Sven's more accomplished younger contemporary, Archbishop Anders Sunesen, Hex., 2982, 'it is just that the lesser handmaiden should obey the greater lady, and that the civil law should yield to the canon.' Sven would probably have agreed. In the civil law the principles and application of laws were studied outside the political system where they had originally prevailed. This was useful in explaining procedures that were supposed to have evolved over a period of 150 years; but the treatment of issues raised by these procedures owes more to the reforming impulse of the canonists than to the strict equity of the civil lawyers.[45] It is as if penalties were devised to avoid or minimize the rigour of the law; to prevent rather than punish wrongdoing; to inspire fraternity rather than impose discipline.

Breaches of the *Vederlov* in earlier times are twice attributed by Sven to the work of the Devil, once to the 'human condition', which is always prone to error. To defeat Satan and repair human frailty, LC offers 'remedies', 'antidotes', and the possibility of relaxing their rigour by formal emendation, by 'new constitutions'. This is canonist teaching: law as physic, and the view that 'penalties may be changed if the commutation be more acceptable to God' (Damasus, no. 97; cf. p. 92, n. 44, below).

The reservation of all suits between retainers to the household muster, *in colloquio, quod dicitur Huskarlestefne*, resembles the *privilegium fori*, which Danish clerics had enjoyed since the early twelfth century. Like church courts, this meeting had to be dignified above the level of other secular assemblies, and so the erring legislator, King Knut himself, prostrates himself before it, begging for *indulgentia*, for a *dispensatio* to 'expiate' his crime.[46]

The *huskarlastefna* was entitled to shed blood, unlike church courts. But Sven almost rules out the possibility of capital punishment by dwelling on the more 'temperate' alternatives of outlawry and public disgrace. Even disgrace is mitigated in the case of Kristiarn Svensen: for him the principle of atonement or amends, *satisfactio*, is introduced—not the routine *bot*, compensation, of the provincial laws but a massive apology to the whole association and its lord. In his case, as in Knut's, the sequence of *lapsus—poenitentia—satisfactio—reconciliatio* replaces the rigour of simple crime and punishment. For lesser offenders the clerical penalty of kneeling becomes a *satisfactionis formula*, and for small incivilities the table-rules of the monastic refectory are the rods of discipline (cf. pp. 90, 91, nn. 33 and 37, below). Inadvertent wounding is assessed by the confessional criterion of intention rather than by the extent of the injury as in ordinary law (cf. p. 99, n. 91, below). Only the traitor appears to be denied the possibility of redemption, but his is not the plain *svik* of secular life. It is the 'crime . . . of Judas the traitor', first specifically identified with political treason in the report of the papal legates to Pope Hadrian I, after the English synods of 786:

> Let no one dare to conspire to kill a king, for he is the Lord's anointed, and if any . . . bishop or anyone of the clerical order take part in such a crime, let him be . . . cast out . . . as Judas was ejected . . . and perish in the eternal fetters of anathema . . . associated with Judas the traitor.[47]

When Saxo came to deal with this code, he recognized only two grades of crime and punishment: minor, subject to demotion at table, and major, subject to expulsion and outlawry. He recognized neither monetary compensation (except in the case of Knut himself) nor kneeling as suitable penalties. He aimed to describe not an actual system of law but an ideal code in the past, which modern indiscipline had breached (see pp. 77-8, n. 25). Saxo's LC was adapted to fit into the tenth book of his national history, and to remind the unruly moderns of what they had lost.

By contrast, Sven's laws relate to modern conditions, even if they are not equally valid. In the light of school jurisprudence they justify a system of restraint which the king hoped to apply both to his retainers within the household and to his homagers outside it, be they magnates or bailiffs. They could thus not be Draconian: that would wound the sense of honour which acted as the spur of knighthood.[48] This could not be a comprehensive code (*pace* Holberg, 130), because the sovereignty of *lex scripta* was not yet established. It could still reinforce, albeit in terms which may not have meant much to most royal retainers, what Kai Hørby calls 'a special legal condition which was different from and stricter than that which applied to the rest of the king's subjects'.

Peter Kofod Ancher's pioneering history of Danish law, published in 1769, carried on the title-page a symbolic engraving of the leafy tree of the law, fed by four tap-roots with LEGES CANUTUM inscribed on the first. The grammar may be questionable, but the message is not entirely fanciful. Sven's *Lex* was an important step towards the creation of a unified rather than a diversified legal system.

Was it also a statement of aristocratic privilege, as Niels Skyum-Nielsen insisted? Hardly, for while it dealt tenderly with the rights of the rich and the powerful, it concerned men who were apt to escape the rigours of the ordinary courts in any case—as Knut VI's homicide decree put it:

> locupletes quos sibi consanguineos annumerant, licet extraneos, rapinis et depredacionibus violentis ad satisfaciendum secum quantum exigunt compellentes (DGL, i:2, 775).[49]

The *Vederlov* was meant to control them, even if the controls were moderate. The only way they could enjoy this moderation was by serving the king.

Insofar as it concerns less distinguished retainers, it certainly freed them from the care and expense of suing each other in provincial courts; but it trebled their liability in cases of wounding, humbled their pride in the punishment for plain assault, and brought them under a heavy-handed treason law. This is not aristocratic privilege, unless we assume that more popular courts had been less tender with the great and the unruly—an unwarranted assumption.[50]

However, I stray from Sven's text to the text that inspired it. We shall never know exactly how Absalon disciplined the royal following, or whether irony and subversion lie hidden in Sven's treatise. It seems clear, however, that in LC he envisaged a cure for the *malheur du guerrier*, which had dogged the makers of Danish history whom he celebrated in his other work, and which made his own century a period of mutual slaughter for kings, bishops, nobles and knights. Holberg (267 and 130) argued that he took an essentially antiquarian law code from Archbishop Absalon and the king, and added modifications made after the time of 'old' Knut and further 'new constitutions' to turn it into a statement of current practice. I would prefer to align LC with other spurious law codes, as a text aimed partly at the reinforcement and partly at the amendment of the prevailing system, with its historical dimension justifying its newness. The evidence cited above of a properly functioning *Vederlov* in the thirteenth century indicates that Sven's LC, aided by Saxo's and the earliest vernacular recension, met with some success. The lack of evidence that such a system prevailed before 1185 indicates the solid worth of pseudo-legislation.

(iv) *Historia Compendiosa*

The title appears in the Stephanius edition of 1642: COMPENDIOSA REGUM DANIAE HISTORIA. It is lacking in A, and may not be Sven's own. However, since he referred to the work in his preface as written *sub compendio*, he probably used this or a similar title. I have translated it as 'A Short History of the Kings of Denmark' but commonly use HC as the abbreviation for it.

Historical abridgements were common among the clergy of England and France in the twelfth and thirteenth century. They were not necessarily short. William of Malmesbury described his five large books on the kings of the English as a 'compendium of histories', and Radulphus Diceto called his substantial annals 'abbreviations'; in the 1230s Roger of Wendover was to promise his readers that his immense historical compilation would be brief and concise. This was partly because such abridgements embraced whole libraries of earlier sources; partly because the affectation of brevity was a rhetorical *topos* employed by nearly all historians of that period.

Sven's brevity was not affected. It reflects the fewness, not the abundance, of his sources. It comes also from the deliberate narrowness of his aim: to trace the survival of one royal dynasty, with few ramifications, over many generations, and to summarize notable royal achievements which his colleague Saxo was to elaborate. He relegated the full genealogy of his kings to an appendix, now lost.[51] His geographical and chronological references are rudimentary. All he offers is a rapid review of some 35 reigns, enlivened by two good anti-German anecdotes, a kidnapping, two and a half royal martyrdoms, and concluding eulogies of the king and the king's mother and father.

Sven was not the first historian of Denmark. He was merely the first to say he was the first. Adam of Bremen's fundamental work on the two centuries before his own time was completed outside Denmark, in the 1070s. Within Denmark the pioneers were English monks, using their alien craft to honour or admonish their patrons.

At Odense in the 1120s the emigré Canterbury monk Ælnoth had written the life of the martyr-king, Knut IV. He surveyed the reigns of all the kings from 1047 to 1086, and so began recording the Danish past in the medium of hagiography. Sven made use of his *Gesta Suenomagni regis*, up to a point; he must have found his 'high style' enviable, if old-fashioned, and both he and Ælnoth put kings foremost, even in spiritual matters. After Ælnoth and the other English hagiographer, Robert of Ely, came the anonymous author of the so-called *Chronicon Roskildense* (CR or the Roskilde Chronicle hereafter), completed in 1141: a highly original history of the Danish church and kings from 826 to that date, with an emphasis on the bishops of Roskilde and the tribulations of the clergy. Not a congenial tutor for Sven, and he may only have known the work at second hand. He certainly knew the equally original *Chronicon Lethrense* (CL; the Lejre Chronicle), which was composed under Valdemar I (1157–82), probably as a retrospective introduction to the Roskilde Chronicle. It is a brief collection of legends and names from the pre-Christian past, the work of an eccentric entertainer with slight intellectual ambition. However, if it were not for his simple narratives of Dan, Ro, and Raki the Dog-king, neither Sven nor Saxo could have written as they did.

Other kinds of historical writing were practised before Sven, if only in a small way. The first annals and king-lists were drawn up, probably at Lund, and a set of Lundensian annals was carried over to the new Cistercian house of Kolbacz in Pomerania.[52] It has been claimed that passages of Danish history found chiefly in the first universal chronicle by Ralph Niger (*c.*1200) were borrowed from a full résumé of Danish history, and this putative lost work has been given the name of 'The Chronicle of Knut Magnusen',[53] because the unlucky Knut V, murdered in 1157, was treated sympathetically in Niger's source. Knut's son, Valdemar, became bishop of Schleswig in the early 1180s, and such a chronicle could have been dedicated to him. It is conjectured that its somewhat critical treatment of Valdemar I may have led Sven to reply in kind, in defence of the monarchy. It is possible that such a text existed, but as its exact date, shape and wording are unknown, Sven's reaction to it is doubly difficult to define. He may have used it as a source for earlier periods, rather than going directly to Adam of Bremen and the Roskilde Chronicle.

Thus a Danish historical tradition of sorts existed before 1185, and Sven made some use of it. He was not the lonely retriever of half-forgotten deeds portrayed in his preface. Nevertheless, he broke new ground in two ways.

First, he wrote a history of the Danish monarchy as an inheritance from very early times which had been vindicated by the courage and wisdom of most of the present king's ancestors. To our way of thinking, this was an obvious distortion of the past for the purpose of supporting current political arrangements. To Sven's contemporaries it was nothing of the sort. The past was expected to reflect the present. It was also expected to reflect, or at least to match, the better recorded pasts of other monarchies, also interpreted as inheritances through ruling dynasties. It was in the nature of kings to avoid sharing power, as Sven observed in his account of the murder of Knut Lavard; the ensuing civil wars of 1131–57 were contests for supremacy over the whole people, not for liberty or justice. Valdemar's emergence as sole king in 1157 was God's verdict on the right political order.

Sven's second new departure was his bringing pre- and post-conversion history together into one continuous sequence, with no dramatic break. The Lejre Chronicle had apparently introduced Latinists to a 'lost world', or vice versa: now it was possible to reconnect this lost world to the present, as the Icelanders did, by the device of linear genealogy. Sven's unbroken line from Skiold to Knut VI owes much to the learned pedigree-fakers of the Oddaverjar,[54] who had increased their own standing in the early twelfth century by claiming descent from Danish kings. Sven introduced his monarch to a less confident version of the spectacular ancestry that had been fabricated for the Knýtlingar by Sæmundr hinn fróði: less confident because influenced by the Lejre Chronicle and by Sven's own anxiety not to be caught 'stringing together the reigns of kings' in too neat a fashion.

The king may have been amused to discover how long his pedigree had grown. If so, he made no use of the discovery when in 1193/4 he had to commission an official genealogical tract to exonerate his sister, the queen of France, from the charge of consanguinity with her husband, King Philip Augustus. This work by Abbot William[55] begins with a brief list of pre-Christian kings, mostly not in Sven's history. The principle of hereditary monarchy, which Valdemar I had introduced for his son's benefit, had no practical need of the roots in primeval Denmark which Sven supplied. Rather the contrary: unbroken descent from heroic antiquity glorified all who could claim it, including many of Knut VI's potential rivals.[56] Here, Sven's inspiration was more likely to be the fashion for ancestry in Iceland and elsewhere than the aspirations of his king.

He also claimed that his stories from the remote past were supplied by 'aged men' and ancient traditions. This claim has often been taken at face value, and some of his tales have been accepted as native Danish legends handed down independently of the materials used by Icelandic saga-authors. This was a natural assumption for most nineteenth-century scholars, and both Axel Olrik and H. M. Chadwick wrote memorable works on the strength of it: *Danmarks Heltedigtning* (1903) and *The Origin of* the *English Nation* (1907) use Sven and Saxo as terminals connected with the fifth and sixth centuries by a process of oral transmission.

Scepticism about the nature of oral transmission has undermined this belief, and Sven's legendary material is patently bookish. Most of his deviations from Skjǫldung matter in Icelandic sources can be accounted for by reference to the Lejre Chronicle or to the St Albans *Vitae duorum Offarum* (see p. 107, n. 16 below). The story of Thyrwi is his own embroidery of the Jelling epitaph, a fashionable model (p. 117, n. 62 below). His account of Sven Forkbeard's capture and ransom elaborates what he could read in the Roskilde Chronicle (SM, i 19) or extrapolate from the Jómsviking myth of the Icelanders. The appeal to oral testimony was another commonplace of twelfth-century historians' rhetoric, and here it was an opaque disguise for artistic invention.

For Sven exploited the remote past as a theatre in which to re-enact current affairs. There he was free to recount anti-German, patriotic episodes, which ought to have taken place under Valdemar I and his son, reigning under the shadow of the Hohenstaufen, but were in fact uncharacteristic of Sven's modern Denmark. Most recorded Danish rulers since the conversion had done all they could to ingratiate themselves with German kings and kaisers, and when they failed, they had submitted to invasion and chastisement. Even the reigning king, who had rejected imperial overlordship soon after 1182, hoped until 1187 to hand over his sisters and his mother as pledges of alliance with the Hohenstaufen and the Ascanians. Knut VI was himself married to Henry the Lion's daughter, and when his relations with the emperor soured, his relations with other German princes remained cordial. In practice, maintaining the southern frontier, and after 1187 extending it, meant rewarding and pleasing and coaxing the Teuton, not insulting and cheating him, as Sven seems to recommend.

His scorn and mistrust of Germans could either be a reaction against the bombastic imperialism of Frederick Barbarossa, or against Danish courtiers with German leanings. Yet no German army had invaded the Danes since 1157; no influx of German place-hunters yet took an unfair share of patronage in church or government. Only as merchants and artisans were they numerous within the kingdom, and Sven takes no notice of such people. Some distaste for German fashions at court is evident in Saxo, and he may be following Sven in that; but it was a distaste more probably learnt in the fastidious schools of France than derived from the ancestral virtue these two were apt to preach. In any case, Sven's prejudice cannot have recommended him to the rulers of

Denmark, even after the Queen Mother came home in 1187, humiliated and ill used by her Thuringian landgrave. Such simple antipathies were unhelpful to a foreign policy that grew more and more expansive.

Sven honours his king, but he was not therefore promoting a particular régime or policy. His review of modern history is even-handed, if not exactly open-minded. He naturally accepts the death of the king's grandfather, Knut Lavard, as a martyrdom; but he comes nearer than any other Danish writer to presenting the death of Knut V at Roskilde in the same light. As for Knut's avenger, the brutal Erik II, he is simply an unworthy instrument: God inspired him to rebel, he broke God's law, God destroyed him. Not a comfortably royalist doctrine. Nor is the elective element in royal inaugurations ever condemned or criticized. The reign of the elected Erik III is noted as prosperous, and the rise of Valdemar is explained by his middle position between rivals rather than by his hereditary claim. Valdemar is lavishly praised, but he is also criticized, apparently for his cruelty (see pp. 137–8, n. 195, below); and the praise is nicely balanced by some tender words about the beauty of his wife. Sven ignores the royal unction of 1170, although he notes that Knut VI succeeded in 1182 'by hereditary right'.

The work concludes on a triumphant but slightly insecure note. Duke Bugislav of Pomerania submits to Knut VI, but at the same hour a thunderstorm almost drowns the new vassal-prince along with the heir to the Danish throne. It is a warning of the power of the 'old Prevaricator', which leads to a final prayer for God's help. Peace is the ultimate goal; the 'tranquillity of peace' is the most frequently used phrase in the book (cf. p. 112, n. 46, below). Yet the history of the dynasty is the history of violence, and the contribution of Sven's father and grandfather to that violence is proudly noted. Peace comes through victory, victory through hereditary valour, helped by God. God denies his help to those who break his law, even the brave and the royal: Magnus, son of King Nicolaus, Erik II, Sven III. 'Goodness,' Sven complains, 'is always suspect to kings.' Nothing is secure, in a degenerating world.

Certainly Sven was unsure of his own position as a historian. In his preface he refers anxiously to possible critics, who might accuse him of presumption and over-inventiveness. A *topos*, no doubt, but heartfelt all the same, because much of the 'lost' past was indeed his own invention. Later he announces that he will skip the central part of his 'ancient history' for fear of being disbelieved. When he reaches recorded times, he reveals that his colleague Saxo is covering the same ground 'at greater length'. With such misgivings, why did he write the book at all?

Early in the following century Arnold of Lübeck was to write on the new breed of educated Danes:

> They are no less profound in the study of letters, for the nobler ones of the land send their sons to Paris, not only to be advanced as clerks but also to be instructed in secular affairs. There, having been imbued with the literature and language of that country [he means Latin], they are deeply versed not only in arts but also in theology . . . [57]

'Deeply versed' is too strong for Sven, who may never have gone to Paris; but he had certainly 'drunk from the spring' of literature, and it is worth asking whether it could have been the well-wrought histories of the Western world that moved him to bring order to the chaos of his own country's past. The hagiographers had somewhat civilized or sanitized the post-conversion period. The author of the Lejre Chronicle had essayed a few anecdotes from the pagan past. If other tales from that darkness survived in Denmark (and the evidence for that is certainly not in Sven), they had no connection with the life of the *gens* or the ruling dynasty. The folklore of landscape, demoted gods, trolls and priapic supermen needed a Saxo to be harnessed to the service of the state. However, by 1185, writers living under the French and Angevin monarchies habitually drew on the far past to justify the ambitions of their kings and nobles. And it was not only the local past of Geoffrey's 'British History', *Draco Normannicus* and Hugh of Fleury, but also the classical past reinvigorated by Walter of Châtillon and Joseph of Exeter and the cosmic fantasy of Alan of Lille.

Here was an intellectual challenge of which Sven may have been aware (some possible echoes of contemporary Latin literature are suggested in the notes on Sven's text). However, the obvious analogue of the Short History is no Western work, but the *Historia de antiquitate regum Norwagiensium* completed by the monk Theodricus at some date between 1176 and 1188, and dedicated to Archbishop Eysteinn of Trondheim. There are no chronological objections to Sven's having read this book, and the presence of Norwegian exiles in Denmark in the 1180s strengthens the possibility.[58]

The similarities between the two works are less noticeable than the differences. Both authors apologized for their uncultivated style and claimed to be writing 'briefly'. Both claimed to be restoring to memory the famous deeds of old neglected through the shortcomings of native writers. Both respected the historians of other lands and mentioned the Icelanders as a source. Both cited Ovid, Statius, Vergil and Lucan, and both showed a general knowledge of ancient history and the Bible. All of this can be explained by the probability that both accepted the normal historiographical conventions of the time, rather than as imitation.[59]

Both lamented the jealousy and quarrelsomeness of kings: a shared Nordic experience as well as a commonplace. Both declined to set down the lineage of their kings, Theodricus at the beginning, Sven in the middle, but for slightly different reasons. Both begin with sole monarchs, who are followed by fratricide successors, and both celebrate modern kings by itemizing their public works and conquests.[60]

This does not amount to much. I have been unable to identify any direct references to the text of Theodricus in Sven, and most of their common ground is crowded with other twelfth-century authors.[61] In other ways they stand apart. Theodricus has a much wider range of learned reference and intellectual interest. His ecclesiastical bias is stronger. He is learned in chronology, cosmology, geography and philosophy, and his digressions are elaborate. His language is less strained, his critical sense more acute; his criterion of the good ruler is more positively moral. He makes conversion a central rather than a peripheral event. He avoids the warfare of his own time as an unedifying subject. He is no admirer of women, and no lawyer.

Where Norwegian and Danish history intersect, Theodricus and Sven are in sharp opposition. Thus in Theodricus, chs. 4–6, the evil Queen Gunnhildr appears as the widow of King Eiríkr, *fratrum interfector* and the bane of his successors, until Hákon *malus* persuades the king of Denmark to propose marriage to her: 'He claimed that Denmark would be fortunate to have such a queen.' Deceived by the proposal, with 'womanly folly, too credulous', Gunnhildr accepted, and was drowned in a bog by the deceitful suitor, which put an end to her 'malignity'. There is no mention of this in Sven; instead, in the same period, there is an elaborate celebration of 'womanly astuteness' and the 'cunning' of the great Queen Thyrwi, who deceived her wooer and so freed her country. It was the German emperor who told her, deceitfully, that 'she ought, for her beauty and wisdom, to be empress of the Romans.' That emperor was Otto, praised by Theodricus as *christianissimus imperator* and conqueror of the Danes, whom he converted to Christianity. To Sven he is a scheming seducer, foiled by superior female guile.

In Theodricus, ch. 16, St Olaf is the saintly and patriotic hero who records the laws of Norway in the vernacular, and loses his kingdom to the ungovernable ambition of the Danish king. Sven refers to him once, in parenthesis, as the begetter of King Magnús by a concubine; even the conquest of Norway is alluded to only in passing. In Theodricus, ch. 18,

Knut of England and Denmark is a rapacious land-grabber, whose machinations inspired the author to lament the 'unlucky and woeful cupidity of mortal men'. For Sven he is admirable both for his 'elegant' conquests and for his achievements as legislator and evangelist. He merely 'deputes' his son to rule Norway and sends missionaries there and, indeed, all over the North.

For Theodricus, Magnús the Good is a peaceful inheritor of the Danish throne, by arrangement with Harthaknut. He saves the Danes from the Slavs, but is attacked by the rebel Sven Estrithsen, and in the end he bequeathes Denmark to Sven in recognition of his hereditary claim. Sven Aggesen presents Magnús as an invader of Sven's peaceful realm. He says nothing of his great victory over the Wends and in his Short History omits Magnús's by-name, 'the Good', although he used it in LC. Magnús dies in mid-career of a fall from his horse; recalling passages in Theodricus (chs. 28, 30) on the ominous falls of Haraldr harðráði and Charlemagne.

These contrasts may be accidental. Gudrun Lange has recently argued that Theodricus and the Norwegian 'synoptics' used a variety of written Icelandic sources, and it may seem rash to conclude that Sven wrote against Theodricus's History itself rather than against any other version of the stories it contains. Nevertheless, Sven's persistent contradiction of Theodricus wherever the Norwegian deals with Dano-Norwegian relations is remarkable. If Sven needed an example and a spur for his Short History, this was it: an equally urbane and useful summary of Scandinavian history which placed the Danes in an unfavourable light and drew attention to the dignity and piety of their chief Northern rivals.[62]

Sven may also have been moved to write by contemporary events. That raises the question of when did he write?

The last event he mentions is the surrender of Prince Bugislav to the Danes in the spring or early summer of 1185. After that, he says, 'We rowed home with immense jubilation. May the Ruler of all things order this conclusion in His peace.' These are not the words of a man writing ten or fifteen years later, as some have suggested: they reflect anxiety about what is going to happen not long after the Pomeranian surrender. Danish-Pomeranian relations are now peaceful—but they might turn out otherwise: there is not yet any final settlement. And there was no firm settlement until 1189, owing to the death of Bugislav on 18 March 1187 and the succession of two young sons under the rival guardianship of their mother, a cousin, and the neighbouring prince of Rugia. There was every chance of war between the two Danish dependencies of Rugia and Pomerania until an expedition from Denmark went south in 1189 and imposed a joint guardianship on the boy-rulers, Kazymar II and Bugislav II, and a careful partition of their territories. Thereafter tension was reduced; which narrows the time of writing to 1185-9.[63]

The tales of Uffi and Thyrwi provide other dating clues, assuming they are topical. They seem to reflect the events of 1187, a crowded year in which Knut VI finally ended the prospect of a Hohenstaufen marriage alliance by refusing to pay the full dower for his sisters and the Queen Mother Sophia returned home, repudiated by her German husband.[64] It ended with the knighting of the king's brother, Valdemar, in preparation for his guarding the southern frontier as duke of Schleswig.[65] This, too, was the year in which the emperor, Frederick I, returned to Germany from Italy, still nursing a grudge against the Danes for refusing to accept client status under his protection.[66] Until the emperor left North Germany at the end of 1188, en route for the Holy Land, his proximity troubled both King Knut and his father-in-law, Henry the Lion.

Once he had gone, everything changed. First the Welfs and then the Danes were able to take the offensive against the emperor's friends in the North. Lands to the south of the River Eider were claimed by Bishop Valdemar of Schleswig, King Knut's cousin, and a variety of competing territorial claims began a train of events which were to bring about full-scale Danish intervention in both Holstein and Mecklenburg.[67] After 1188 the 'liberation' of Denmark, which is the theme of both Thyrwi's story and Uffi's, was no longer a live issue: the boot was on the other foot. The adjustment of these stories by Saxo to fit in with the new mood of Danish aggression is one indicator of the change.

For these reasons, it is possible to claim 1188 as the most likely year for the composition of Sven's Short History—always bearing in mind that it need not have been a topical work, and that the evidence is wholly circumstantial.

(v) *The Lost Genealogy*

At the end of the prologue to LC, Sven promised that *circa finem huius opusculi* he would 'unravel the pedigrees of the kings and the order in which they reigned'. The reference must be to HC, in which Sven does what Rodulfus Glaber refused to do: 'recite the genealogy in the historical fashion'.[68] However, in the course of HC Sven breaks off the narration (p. 55 below) and declines to trace in detail the royal succession in the 'centuries' during which it passed through *nepotes* rather than from father to son. So he reached the end of HC without having fulfilled his initial promise.

In Stephanius's edition a full pedigree appears after HC, introduced by a sentence in the first person purporting to be Sven's. Unfortunately, the pedigree is too full: it goes down to 1259, and is evidently based on the work of Saxo and his interpreters. Known as 'The Genealogy of the Kings of Denmark by an Unknown Author', it is printed in Gertz, 112–14 (and in SM, i 186–94), with any Svenonian phrases clearly marked: for the Unknown Author made some use of Sven's language, even while rejecting his reconstruction of the royal lineage. His work is an important document for Danish history after 1250 (it is discussed by Hoffmann, 1975, 188–92), but it has survived at the expense of the more original work which it superseded.

For the brief introduction in S is evidently based on a longer passage which is found after the conclusion of HC in A (Gertz, 111; SM, i 142), and runs thus:

> Although the deeds of our earliest princes and kings were immense and deserving of eternal commemoration,[69] they are . . .[70] being wrapped in the shadow of oblivion, because no one has devoted attention to their accurate transmission, and once out of fashion they will slide into the labyrinth of forgetfulness.[71] However, lest the established sequence of kings and their reigns should also perish without being handed down, I will endeavour to unravel no more than the names of each [Gertz adds: of the kings] and their successions to the kingdom, so that our successors may strive to proclaim from honeyed throats and golden mouths[72] whomsoever infamy made remarkable, just as they may . . . highly adorn the noble deeds of each.[73]

With this Sven could be announcing a king-list, rather than a pedigree, but he promised a genealogy, and a genealogy was supplied by the Unknown Author to replace what was there.

It is worth noting that in HC Sven produced two fourteen-generation sequences, one from Skiold to Olaf, and one from Sighwarth's father-in-law to Knut VI. In the first chapter of St Matthew there are three fourteen-generation pedigrees from Abraham to Jesus; it is quite possible that, in accordance with the new political fashion of *Imitatio Christi*,[74] Sven's middle section also consisted of fourteen generations. The details are irretrievably lost.

(vi) *Translations*

The overwhelming reputation of Saxo restrained would-be translators of Sven for 150 years after the first edition. Stephanius, the editor, warned his readers 'not to expect too anxiously any elegance or refinement of diction in this our author', who had composed his 'illiterate historical compendium . . . more modestly than effectively'. The complimentary verses by Vitus Bering praised the editor more highly than the author, whose style he compared to a 'tattered cloth' and an 'unworthy prison'. The text was published on inferior paper in undersized volumes, unfit to associate with the folios of Saxo and his Danish translation by Vedel. Langebek, the next editor, made a lightly annotated Danish version of HC and some of LC before he died in 1774, but it was never published. The manuscript survives in the Royal Library, Copenhagen (Ny kgl. saml. 872 4to), and has been consulted, to little advantage, for the present work.

Since that time Sven has usually appeared to his fellow-countrymen in moments of national distress. Thus Dr Odin Wolff (1760–1830), a tireless journalist, lexicographer and plagiary, was inspired by the growing patriotic fervour of the Napoleonic years to publish a translation of Sven, at first in the periodical *Iris* and then as an offprint, *Den förste Danske Historieskriver Svend Aagesens kortfattede Danmarks Historie*. The year was the year of disaster, 1807. Anxiety over the future of the country and the monarchy led others, notably Ove Malling, to look back into history for examples of Danish heroism, and Wolff used Sven for this purpose. He followed the conventional opinion that Sven 'certainly cannot be set beside . . . great Saxo,' but recommended him to the public for two reasons. First, because there were so few twelfth-century authors worth reading, other than Saxo, 'the literary wonder', and Abelard. Second, because Sven was a Dane and a patriot, and so deserved to be cherished by all patriotic Danes. Although his style was 'hard, stiff and laboured', it was 'concise and original', and Wolff aimed to present him literally, 'in his ancient dress, not in modernized costume'. He was naturally unaware that the text of the 1642 edition was itself a modernization, or at least a revision, of Sven's words; apart from that, he achieved his aim.

By 1842 the Wolff translation was a rarity. However, this was a year of intensified nationalist and Scandinavianist fervour: the year of Orla Lehman's 'Eider policy', and the launching of the journal *Almuevennen* to agitate the masses over the Schleswig question. In such circles it was felt that Danish history must be inculcated in schools to raise national consciousness. So the theological student, Rasmus Theodor Fenger (1816–89), came out with *Svend Aagesens Danmarks Krøniker, oversat og oplyst* as the first-fruits of a long harvest of church-historical, educational and controversial writing. He decided that Wolff's translation was 'no longer suitable for popular reading, since the language seems insufficiently entertaining and forceful for the common people'. Not as entertaining and forceful, he meant, as the language in which his master, Grundtvig, had presented Saxo in his *Danmarks Krønike* (1818–22). Fenger wanted Sven's History to become a national 'school-book', a first text for Danish history lessons, for 'there is nothing which concerns childhood and youth so much as . . . the description of the childhood and youth of the nation.' Sven's professed respect for oral tradition recommended him highly to a Romantic generation, and Saxo-criticism had somewhat raised his reputation as an independent and earlier source. Nevertheless, the schoolmasters appear not to have taken Fenger's hint.

Jørgen Olrik's translation, *Sven Aggesøn: Danernes Historie* (in KV, 1900–1), was a final attempt to give an accurate rendering of the style of the S text, in a series of source-translations partly commissioned by the Ministry of Church Affairs and Education. Introducing the series, A. D. Jørgensen (1879, [iv–v]) wrote that it was 'first necessary to awaken a taste for the history of the Fatherland, or of the world, by means of a lively and lucid narration'; then 'to exercise the critical sense' by presenting various versions of the same events. So the serious educational impetus of the post-1864 generation embraced Sven as one of a range of medieval sources, and Olrik's work included a rendering of LC. This had already appeared in Danish as an appendix to Holberg's *Dansk Rigslovgivning* (1889), and was by then accepted as a document of constitutional importance for the twelfth rather than for the eleventh century.

Meanwhile, the 'critical sense' was demoting the S text to second-best. Gertz accompanied his reconstituted version of 1915 with *Sven Aggesøns historiske Skrifter* in Danish (published 1916/17), which included the two main works and the introduction to the lost genealogy. As a scholarly rendering by the architect of the X text it cannot be bettered, and it would be misleading to link the appearance of this translation with the renewed threat of German aggression during the Great War. However, the threat existed, and with the recurrence of national misfortune came the need for a 'little more fluent' translation of Sven's History. At the beginning of 1944 the leading Venstre journalist Paul Læssøe Müller published his *Kortfattet Historie om Danmarks Konger* in response to the humiliations of the German occupation: an illustrated edition, limited to 50 copies, for members of the Bibliophile Club. In his epilogue Læssøe Müller stressed the importance of the work as 'an expression of the Nation's self-consciousness, a word taken in its full sense'—as a code-word, he meant, for Resistance. Whether this small and luxurious edition served its political purpose may be doubted, but it is remarkable that it was published at all.

English interest has been mainly confined to LC as a supposed reflection of the customs of King Knut's army, and to the story of Uffi in HC as an analogue to the Offa legend in England. The part of HC from Skiold to Uffi appears in G. N. Garmonsway and J. Simpson, *Beowulf and its Analogues* (1968), but translated from the S text rather than from X. Summaries of LC were given in John Kemble, *The Saxons in England* (1876), and in two books by L. M. Larson, *The King's Household in England before the Norman Conquest* (1904) and *Canute the Great* (1912), but I have been unable to find a full translation.

As noted earlier, the translation of Sven's works in the present volume is made from Gertz's reconstructed X text. A few technical terms and names, italicized in the translation, are retained, in the form they have in X or given a standard spelling based on that text; and some words are similarly treated in the translation of the Old Danish Vederlov. Rare passages printed in square brackets have their source indicated in the notes.

THE LAW OF THE RETAINERS
OR OF THE COURT

Preface

The men of ancient times left many things to their posterity, for us to study with diligence,[1] and they also took care to make provision for the unity and brotherhood of the court, lest undisciplined young warriors who were serving together[2] should enjoy too much freedom, and should be allowed to provoke each other with insults and escape punishment. To restrain the boldness of the unruly ones[3] they authorized and promulgated a law, which they called the *Witherlogh*[4] in their language. Although it is a less appropriate name, we can call it 'the law of the retainers and the knights' or 'the law of the court' in the Latin language.[5]

As time passed, this law went out of date and was forgotten, because from then onwards there were very few who remembered the achievements even of the glorious men of old. It was only Absalon, the illustrious metropolitan of the whole kingdom of the Danes,[6] with his usual desire for knowledge and after careful and far-sighted consultation with his pupil (that is, with King Knut,[7] son of the first Valdemar), who wrote it down in a document.[8] For what is held to be out of date and antiquated can often be brought to life with the help of writing.

So, as I had found this recorded very briefly in our own language, I approached my task without much confidence in my learning or ability, for I was always afraid that I should seem to have forestalled, with arrogant presumption, those with greater learning than mine. However, I will still attempt to the best of my ability to translate the matter into Latin, however inelegant the style, for the sake of those fine young men who are making a successful study of the rules of composition. And at the end of this little work I shall unravel the pedigrees of the kings and the order in which they reigned,[9] as far as I have been able to trace them from what has been reliably handed down by aged men.

First, therefore, I will explain about the makers of the laws of the court: who made them? why? and where?[10]

[1] Knut, the son of King Sven Forkbeard, came into his ancestral inheritance like a raging lion,[11] and by his undefeated endeavour he nobly enlarged the boundaries of his empire from farthest Thule to the empire of the Greeks, outdoing Geryon of Hesperus[12] by the force of his valour and almost equalling the great Alexander;[13] for he had annexed England, Norway, Slavia, and Finland[14] to his own kingdom, and so increased his might and power with ample splendour. And when he had subjected all the surrounding countries to the government of his own kingdom, warriors came flooding in on all sides, their number comparable to the garlands of Dodona,[15] on account of their reputation for courage and victory; and they impetuously vied with each other in doing him homage.

However, they came to him in so great a multitude that it became apparent that they were not all equally worthy, and in the end the king came to the following resolution. He decreed that, whereas his force of warriors had been thrown together, as it were, without any difference of rank, they were to be divided according to their merits and their proven virtue, and those of outstanding virtue were to be brought closer to himself. He wanted to be on more familiar terms with those who he knew were entitled to claim high descent and who rejoiced in plentiful wealth, so that those who came from the better lineages should try to excel in virtue; and they would not be embarrassed by lack of equipment for the wars inasmuch as they had been brought up in richer households.[16]

[2] Therefore he published an order and proclaimed by a herald that only those men who honoured the king and adorned

the force of warriors by shining resplendent with gilded axe-heads and sword-hilts[17] were to approach the clement king with the privilege of a closer association.[18] For it would do honour to the prince if a lordly throng should escort him, attended by a guard of brothers-in-arms.[19] And when this resolution had been published, those who were pressed by lack of private means decided that they would be out of place in the phalanx of the richer men.

And all at once, the cities echo with the sound of hammering from the smithies. For every ornament already made of shining gold is melted down to ingots by sweating smiths, so that the metal which the proud warriors formerly esteemed useless should be made to grace axe-heads and sword-hilts by the choice artistry of goldsmiths. So it happened that the human tendency[20] to ambition made them unwilling to spare any expense, and they attempted to outdo their companions in the more elegant workmanship of their weapons. For it is obvious that elegantly decorated weapons are appropriate for those who are brought up under more favourable auspices.

And when the numerous phalanx was gleaming with its new finery, it was decreed that the strength of this band should be fixed by a precise calculation of their number. The total was three thousand picked men. It was decided to name this body the *Tinglith* in their own language.[21]

[3] Now he had brought together men of such divergent national customs into the one household, his task was this: how, within the army of so great a king, gathered, as it were, from various peoples (that is, from all the kingdoms which had been subjected to his authority) and with a variety of usages that jarred against each other,[22] the warriors were to put their quarrels and differences to rest, forbear mutual wrangling, and serve together with equal devotion, as befits honest messmates[23] with the same lord. Untainted by division, malice and envy, they must rather be ready with one accord to obey the

commands of the king, like limbs subject to one head.[24] As faithful men, they must conceive no hostile mistrust one of another. However, it was no easy matter to pacify a crowd of so many quarrelsome men unless he checked them by punishment from falling into misconduct, so that the correction itself should be severe enough to restrain their bold delinquency.[25]

[4] Therefore, when the army was all assembled in England and the king was resting amid his warlike enterprises in the calm of peace,[26] he sent for the wiser men; and those he had previously discovered to be wisest of all were Øpi the Wise of Sjælland and his son, Eskil.[27] He had no fear of disclosing his own secret counsels to either of these men, because he had proof of their worldly wisdom[28] on account of his earlier choice of them as his privy councillors. With careful deliberation he inquired how to check the unruliness of the young men by a discipline that would restrain their high spirits in future and deter any man, whomsoever he be, from annoying any other with insults. And since human nature is inclined to fall into wrongdoing,[29] the task was to make careful provision so that appropriate remedies could be provided for every case of misconduct.[30] So they decided to deal very minutely with the deterrence of lesser as well as of greater offences.

In order that we may move on more expeditiously to the harsher remedies, we will first consider the small ones.[31] For in their wisdom the ancients tried to eliminate the smallest occasions of dispute, and they applied their best efforts to unite in the bond of brotherly love all those men whose spirits were seething with lust for combat.

[5] This then was the custom among the retainers of times gone by (they call them knights nowadays[32]): each man served the other alternately, and took turns in attendance without any squires or grooms. So they decided that, if a man should lead his comrade's horse to water with his own, he should ride the one horse going there and the other coming back. If it hap-

pened that he drove his own horse to water while riding another man's, whether it was work-horse, pony, hack or charger,[33] and he was led by dishonourable meanness to come back riding the same horse, and if he was charged three times with the same dishonest offence and convicted on the testimony of two fellow-warriors, it was decided that he should be seated one place downwards in the dining hall. For it was the custom that the warriors should sit in places assigned to them according to their claim to worth, whether by seniority in age or by the higher nobility of their descent, so that the elders and betters took the more honourable places.[34] Clearly, therefore, no man could be moved from his usual seat without shame and dishonour.

A similar sentence befell any man who fed his own horse with his comrade's palfrey and on three occasions should be convicted by the testimony of two men, as above, of having offered the ears of corn to his own steed. They also decreed that the same punishment should await any warrior who went upstream against the current while they were watering horses and disturbed the water so that the others could only drink muddy water—always provided that the same testimony established that this had been done three times. He incurred the same sentence, because the same punishment befalls a similar fault.[35]

Furthermore, if any man's persistent audacity should mark him as incorrigible after three offences, and he should refuse to come to his senses, they decreed that he should be seated last of all, and pelted with bones at any man's pleasure.[36] Moreover, no man will share either food or drink with him. He is to be content with his own dish and cup, all by himself.[37]

However, if his excellency the king should decide to protect[38] a man from prosecution, to the extent of placing him in the first seat and making him his own neighbour, they allowed him this as an act of clemency by the prince, but with this condition added: that he be entirely deprived of the support of his fellow-warriors and relieved of his former rights and duties under the law.[39]

[6] But while the law had to be made to cover many matters, it came into being primarily as a result of the respect in which the prince was held. Just as he laid down the pattern and rule of obedience for his men, so his own conduct should be gracious and familiar.[40] Therefore it was enacted that the king with an army in attendance,[41] or anyone else entitled to the same honour, should himself display the loyalty he demanded from them. He should present a cheerful countenance, and deny none of them a courteous reception.[42] He was also to give them the reward of their labour and pay his warriors their wages without delay or any kind of argument, whenever it was customary or when they were short of money. Once they had received their pay, the men would show the same goodness and generosity in return[43] towards their lords, and would be prepared to obey whatever commands they gave and not fail to carry out their orders. For the man who does not pay what he owes asks in vain for what he wants.[44]

[7] The men of old did not forget to prescribe a method by which any man would be able to transfer his homage to another lord, while leaving the majesty of the prince unimpaired and the honour of the warrior undiminished. They decided that on the eve of the Circumcision, which is when the New Year begins according to the superstitious assertion of the gentiles,[46] it was proper for the tried warrior seeking a change of lordship to depute two of his comrades to go to the lord from whose lordship and authority he wished to be free, and they were to resign to him that man's homage and service. Thus it was agreed that he should be able to resort to another homage without any shaming reproach or disrespect to the lord.[47]

[8] However, quarrels and insults stir up and encourage a general unruliness, and the men of old in their wisdom re-

solved to prevent the common bond of brotherly union from being disrupted by divisive anger and weakened by insults offered among the men. They therefore served up a magical antidote for cases of this kind,[48] in order to anticipate the discord at source and so eliminate it. As Ovid puts it,

> Stop! ere you start; med'cine's too late to stay
> Sickness encourag'd by a long delay.[49]

For those wounds, 'that by mere poultices will not be heal'd', must be lanced with the knife.[50] And so it was decreed that, if any man were to abuse or insult his comrade or start any sort of quarrel by offering a visible affront,[51] all his fellow-warriors were to be called together in the presence of the king, and the plea was to be heard in the meeting which is called *Huskarlastefna*.[52] Because if the plaintiff were able to prove with the witness of two of his fellow-warriors that his comrade was guilty of having insulted him as a *Witherlogh* man,[53] and the witnesses confirmed their testimony with an oath sworn on the sacraments, then it was ordained that the convicted man should be seated one place downwards in the dining hall.[54] And it was determined by a general ordinance[55] that all disputes arising between the warriors should not be ended or conducted anywhere except in that same assembly.

[9] It was also laid down by a general ordinance that all disputes arising between fellow-warriors over farms and fields,[56] or even over robbery from houses, which is called *Boran* in our language,[57] should be raised and settled within the assembly mentioned above. The man entitled by the judgment of his fellow-warriors to make good his claim to property[58] is obliged to prove that he has been in continuous occupation of the land with the help of six men drawn by lot from his company, that is from his *Fjarthing*,[59] or that his prescriptive title is protected by the appropriate law.[60]

Now it was decided to settle lesser disputes with the testimony of two fellow-warriors, and by the old arrangement it was with the testimony of the two who in the dining hall sat on either side of the man concerned.[61] However, the men of today decide that the rigour of the law ought to be softened in many respects, so that even in the matter dealt with in the present clause they bring the case to judgment with the help of two fellow-soldiers got from anywhere in the hall.

[10] The law had not been established for long when the one who lies in ambush for the blood of mankind, the hater of prosperity, the perverter of justice,[62] made an attack on the high standing of the prince. He tried to persuade the king to evade the law, so that once the head had been infected with aconite, the corrupting poison would spread through the rest of the limbs.[63] For while he was still in England, enjoying peace and tranquillity, the maker of the law, King Knut himself, fell into a passion[64] and drew his sword and killed one of his own warriors. At this, the whole phalanx was convulsed with rage; the legions came pouring in on all sides and ran to arms without delay. But when they discovered that the hand of the king had committed this killing, they gathered into a body and made careful inquiry into what they were to do.

For their opinions were divided, and their verdict was doubtful and uncertain: whether to punish the king with death on account of the novelty of the crime, or was he entitled to pardon?[65] For if the king were to undergo the prescribed sentence, they would be driven out of this foreign country as leaderless fugitives; but if they were swayed by their reverence for the king, the example of their corrupt indulgence would enable others to commit the same offence.

In the end this sentence was passed by the whole cohort, and no wrong conclusion[66] was to be drawn from it thereafter. The throne was to be placed in the middle of the assembly, and his grace the king was to prostrate himself before it and there await a decision either for pardon or for severity. When that had been done and the king's grace had made atonement and all further consequences of the crime had been eliminated, they raised him up and pardoned him, and all together shouted their unanimous confirmation.[67]

However, any man who committed this kind of misdeed in future was to be disqualified from any dispensation, nor was he to make compensation for the crime. He was to expiate the gravity of the offence by submitting to an inexorable sentence of death, or at least, were the law to be relaxed, he was to depart from the whole association of warriors as an exile and a fugitive and an utter outcast, named by the shameful word of *Nithingsorth*.[68]

[11] After the great king had expiated the crime of which he was guilty in the manner recorded above, the code was loyally maintained and remained continuously unbroken through the reigns of eight kings. That is to say, during the time of old Knut, who was also the maker of the law, and of his son Knut, surnamed 'the harsh' or 'the hard'—although he never succeeded to the kingdom of his forerunner, he was a sort of helper during the time his father had command of the helm of state, as we shall explain more clearly afterwards.[69] And then during the reigns of Magnus the Good and Sven Estrithsen and Harald Whetstone; and of Knut, who was crowned with martyrdom in the church at Odense, and of Olaf, his brother, and of Erik the Good; and it was not violated until the reign of the ninth king, that is of Nicolaus.[70] Then Kristiarn Svensen[71] drew his sword and wounded Thuri Doki,[72] and he was the first offender to break the law of the retainers and the knights after the king had made his amends.

After that, the king was faced by a difficult decision. For he thought it would be harmful to the authority of his government and would undermine its security, if Kristiarn were to be expelled from the court with the shameful name of *Nithingsorth*. It would also offend all the man's kinsmen, who were the most powerful men in the realm, and all the more so because two of his brothers were greatly renowned bishops at the time. Asser, the elder, was the first archbishop of the see of Lund,[73] and the second was Sven, bishop of Viborg.[74] The other two brothers, Eskil[75] and Aggi, and their revered father Sven, son of Thrugot, were also respected in their day as foremost among the leaders of the kingdom.[76]

These men were more concerned to preserve their honour than their wealth, and they decided that, however heavy the award, it was better to pay compensation for the crime that had been committed than to put their good name in jeopardy. So they made a careful investigation, and in their penetrating enquiries they consulted Bo Hithinsen from Vendel, both because he was very old and because he had been a famous warrior of old Knut, who is held to have made and published those laws.[77] They also brought in the older men of the day, those who were used to committing the doings of past times to memory, and asked them whether any of them could remember any similar offence which had been made good by compensation alone. And when they had made diligent inquiry and were unable to remember any similar breach of the law, that same Bo of Vendel replied with this advice: 'It has not been precisely settled by any man's estimate[78] hitherto. It is worth our trouble[79] to prescribe to our posterity a fixed method of compensation now. Therefore let a penalty be laid down so severe that it will deter all our successors from daring to break the law.'

And so, with the consent of the whole court and with the king's agreement, he promulgated a new ordinance, that 'hereafter whosoever shall dare to violate by his rash and presumptuous audacity the ordinance of the present law—that is, the *Witherlogh*—by inflicting a wound on his fellow-warrior shall make satisfaction to the king of forty marks, and shall appease the man he injured with another forty, adding as proof of his shame at his own misconduct two marks weight of gold—called *Gyrsum*[80] in our common speech—and he shall also hand over a third forty marks to all his fellow-warriors bound by the terms of the same law.'[81]

However, the human condition is always prone to evil,[82] and some time after this Aggi Thver[83] followed the corrupting example and wounded Esger Ebbesen, who had been the bailiff at Varde,[84] while Esger was under the wing of King Nicolaus, in the house of Withi the Staller at Borg.[85] When that happened, the king was enraged, and he ordered Aggi's arrest at the wish of nearly all his fellow-warriors, but Withi objected and spoke against it. Now he offered the same sort of compensation and made the same amends as we recalled above that Kristiarn had made. And this is said to have happened in Lime[86] at Bo Ketilsen's house. After this, time passed and, with evil deeds growing more frequent,[87] corruption gradually crept in and such payments became rather numerous, following the example of the first payment in reparation for the above-mentioned crime.

[12] However, the inflexible rule of the old law was that, if any man should happen to strike his fellow-warrior in anger with a fist or with any weapon whatsoever, and the fact should be substantiated with the testimony of only two fellow-warriors, then no compensation was to be payable thereafter.[88] It is the moderation of the men of today which has brought about the softening of this rule under a new law. Thus, if the fact is well established by evidence or testimony and the accused is unable to defend himself by any sort of denial, it is settled that he must kneel[89] at the feet of the man to whom he has given offence by his insult, so that the most abject shame may be duly expunged by the most humiliating form of reparation. However, if the plaintiff fails to convict the accused with witnesses, it is a general ordinance that this man who brought the charge may remove the infamy with the oaths of six of his fellow-warriors.[90]

[13] Provocations to violence are as diverse as the suggestions of the Old Serpent. For it often happens that a man inflicts a wound on another man, either wittingly or in ignorance:[91] sometimes he wounds his own comrade, whom he recognizes, but sometimes he thinks that his comrade is not his comrade. If any man ignorantly and unknowingly wounds his fellow-warrior while trying to wound another, or hurts him by accident, and is sued for it, he may vouch with two fellow-warriors[92] that he inflicted the harm in ignorance and unwillingly. But if he fails at the oath-taking, he shall make satisfaction by the procedure mentioned above.[93]

But when a man wounds his fellow-warrior knowingly and deliberately but unaware that he is bound to that man by the law cited above, it was enacted that this kind of ignorance did not exonerate him from liability for the offence.[94] For by the same law it was provided that[95] . . . all disputes involving a legal hearing[96] are to be settled either with a group of six fellow-warriors, for the more serious, or, for those that are moderately grave, with two or three, as we have explained above.

[14] Now that we have run through the laws by which lesser disputes are to be settled, it remains for us to pass on to greater matters.

Seeing therefore that by his continual watchfulness the wily foe knows how to circumvent us, he leads us up the ladder of undutifulness to the last step of damnation.[97] For while by his baleful suggestions he finds work for his followers in small matters, he is always urging them on to attempt greater infamy. Indeed, he who has been already trained to quarrel with his fellow-warriors at the risk of bloodshed proceeds at the last boldly to contrive the death or betrayal of his lord and prince.[98] So if any man should incur this abominable disgrace, and should be stained with the curse of Judas the traitor[99] and commit a crime like his and be sentenced and condemned for making plans to betray his own lord, that man, they decreed, was to lose his life and all his property.[100]

To this end they ordained that, if the king were to [accuse] any man of treason or of the crime[101] ... the wind should fill the sail and remove it out of sight of the onlookers; and if the West Wind's favour[102] was not granted, then he had to row across the sea until the oars were seen no longer, while they had to wait on the shore. So, while he was hidden far out to sea, they yelled three times as if giving a signal for battle, and it was decreed that the rights he enjoyed as a former confederate should be annulled.[103]

Furthermore, if he should dishonour himself by the aforesaid crime while in his native land[104] and should be convicted of it, as above, the whole band of warriors was obliged to escort him to a dense wood and wait on the edge of the wood while he withdrew from them and pursued his course into some dark wilderness where he was unable to hear the din of their shouting.[105] Then all his fellow-warriors are called together in a body, and with all their might they give their yell three times in unison. And after that they are held bound by this law: that whichever one of them meets that man thereafter and has the advantage of him by one man or one weapon at the least and does not attack him, then he shall incur the same penalty of ignominious discharge.[106]

So far I have unravelled the law of the knights, albeit in a disjointed style, as far as I have been able to discover it by careful inquiry among old writers and old men. It remains for our posterity, whom one authority considers to be dwarves on the shoulders of giants,[107] to beautify this treatise with rhetorical figures and high-flown language[108] and to supply what is missing by bringing it to a conclusion in a style more elegant.

SUPPLEMENT TO LEX CASTRENSIS
The Old Danish *Vederlov*

The *Witherlax ræt* (see pp. 5–6 above) is here translated, with occasional light paraphrase, from the version in the Uppsala manuscript, De la Gardie 44, fol. 159r, written in the first half of the fifteenth century. The edition followed is that by Erik Kroman in DR, 1–5. It begins: *Incipit statutum Kanuti regis filii Waldemari regis et archiepiscopi Absalonis quod dicitur witherlax ræt*. The page-numbers in brackets refer to the comparable passages in the LC translation above.

[pp. 31–2, 34] This is the Law of the *Witherlag* which King Knut, son of Valdemar, and Archbishop Absalon caused to be written down just as it was in Old Knut's days. Old Knut was king in Denmark and England and Norway and Samland and had a large *hird* gathered from the lands he was king over, and he was unable to keep them united and at peace unless there were strict justice for those who offended others. And for that reason he, and with him Øpi Snialli of Sjælland and Eskil Øpi's son, made in England the *Witherlag*[1] severe and strict so that no man should dare to offend another.

[p. 36] And he ordained first that the king, and other honourable men who might have a *hird*, should stand by their men and be kindly towards them and be prompt in giving them their pay.[2] Men should show loyalty and service towards their lords, and be ready to obey all their commands.

[pp. 42–3] If any man should become a bold and miscreant traitor and contrive Judas-work with evil plotting against his lord, then he has forfeited his own life and all that he owns.

[pp. 36–8] If the king wishes to dismiss a man from the *Witherlag*, then in his household he should first get two men of the *Witherlag* to summon him, in his company and in his 'quarter'[3], to appear at a *huskarlastefna*, and announce to him the place and the day. If he does not come to the meeting, then

the king shall have them go home to his house and summon him a second time, and tell him the place and the day. Should he not heed the summons, then he shall have him summoned a third time, at home at his house, and tell him when and where he shall attend. If he does not attend the meeting, then let him be condemned and flee the country and let the king take all that he owned. If he comes to the meeting, and the king, with the witness of two men of the *Witherlag* and with a sacred oath, can prove him guilty of the charge that he willed an attack either on his life or on his country, then he has lost his place in the *Witherlag* and forfeited his life. If men of the *Witherlag* do not dare to bear witness to that and to swear a sacred oath, then he shall be either lost or saved by God's verdict, that is by the ordeal of hot iron, according to the laws that Old Knut made.
[p. 36] If any man should want to leave his lord's service, then he should get two men of the *Witherlag* to renounce his service on the eighth eve of Christmas.[4] Then he may serve another lord thereafter.
[p. 42] If a man infringes the *Witherlag* by giving a blow or a wound, then he shall be driven from the king's household with the name of *Nithing*, and flee from all the lands that Knut was king over. And after that, any man of the *Witherlag* who meets him should attack him if he be one shield stronger than him, or else he shall be called *Nithing* without having offended by giving a blow or a wound.
[p. 37] If anyone complains that a man[5] of the *Witherlag* had done him wrong, then that should be prosecuted at the *huskarlastefna*. If he can prove it by the witness of two men of the *Witherlag* and with a sacred oath, then the other should sit one place farther out than he sat before. And all the disputes that arise between them shall be prosecuted at the *huskarlastefna* and nowhere else.
[p. 37] If there are disputes concerning property or seizure of household goods,[6] then the one who is judged by the house-

carles to have the law more on his side shall bring as proof the oath of six men chosen by lot from his 'quarter'. Lesser cases shall all be settled by the oath of two men of the *Witherlag*, one who sits in from him and one who sits out from him.

[pp. 39–41] The *Witherlag* was faithfully accepted between lords and their men and stood thus unblemished through the days of eight kings—Old Knut, Harthaknut, Magnus the Good, Sven Estrithsen, Harald Whetstone, St Knut at Odense, his brother Olaf, and Erik the Ever-good—and it was not infringed before the days of the ninth king—that was Nicolaus. Then Kristiarn Svensen made an assault and used a weapon on Thuri Doki,[7] and that was the first infringement of the *Witherlag*. Then both the king and Kristiarn's kinsmen thought it a bad thing to drive him away from the king's household with the name of *Nithing*, for two of his brothers were bishops, Archbishop Asser and Bishop Sven of Viborg, and two other brothers of his, Eskil and Aggi, and their father, Sven Thrugun's son, were chief men in Denmark, and these would rather let the case be settled by compensation. Then they inquired of Bo Hithinsen of Vendel, who had been a man of Old Knut's, and of others who were the oldest men in Denmark, if there were any instances when the *Witherlag* had previously been infringed and compensation paid afterwards; and they could find no precedents. Then Bo Hithinsen said: 'Since there is no precedent for such a thing before our days, then let us set a precedent to stand after our days: that is, that the man who infringes the *Witherlag* by giving a blow or a wound shall atone to the king with forty marks, and to all the men of the *Witherlag* with another forty marks, and to the man who was injured with forty marks, and give two marks of gold as *gørsom*.[8]

After that, Aggi Thver used a weapon on Esger Ebbesen, the bailiff of Varde, at Withi the Staller's house at Borg, under the arm of King Nicolaus.[9] Then the king and all the king's men wanted to seize Aggi, but Withi would not let him be taken, but stood in their way and offered compensation and guarantees in accordance with the precedent of the payment Kristiarn had made. And the compensation was paid at Bo Ketilsen's in Lime, and since then many compensations have been paid in accordance with the precedent of Kristiarn's payment.

A SHORT HISTORY OF THE KINGS OF DENMARK

Preface

Often, as I was studying the books of the ancients[1] and discovering numerous deeds of early times recorded in the most elegant language, I sighed continually at the perpetual silence to which the mightiest achievements of our own kings and chiefs have been consigned. They were no less great in their merit and in their proven virtue, but their distinction has not been proclaimed aloud to the same extent.

However, as this world grows old and evils gather apace, a man can strive to commemorate the things that ought to be remembered with all the care and industry he can muster, and he will still be wholly unable to deflect the shafts of defamation.[2] And so for a long time I was in two minds: should I accept the charge of presumption and write down a short record of the pedigrees and successive reigns of our kings in my own style, unpolished as it is, or should I let them all pass away into silence? However, I thought it better not to avoid displaying my arrogance, and to penetrate the thickets of the neglected past, thus clearing the way for our successors, who will be armed with a sharp and lively intelligence and a fertile store of elegant learning, rather than that I should let the achievements of our famous princes be clouded over by the gloom of oblivion.

However, Martianus tells us that 'the statement of the unknown must not appear to be mixed with falsehood,'[3] and lest I should seem to be narrating fable as history, I shall give an abbreviated account of what I have been able to ascertain by questioning aged men and ancient authorities.[4] Not all kings have been equally celebrated for their victories, nor have all triumphed alike, and they certainly differed from each other in their claims to the kingdom. Therefore I shall attempt to commemorate those whose famous deeds I found to be known with more certainty. To the deeds of those whom fleeting fame has passed by I shall attend less urgently.

Peasants and princes share the common nature of all men, whereby reputation instigates this man to do well, while love of sloth tarnishes that one.[5] This man endeavours to perpetuate his claims to nobility; little cares the other if glorious renown be dimmed. And so our tale will now restore to life the man whom our remotest forebears[6] first commended to eternal remembrance.

[1] I have learned that Skiold was the first man to rule over the Danes, and if we may make a pun on his name, he was called this because he used to protect most nobly all the boundaries of the realm with the shielding power of his kingship.[7] He was the first after whom kings were called *Skioldunger* in the poetry of the Icelanders.[8]

He left heirs to the kingdom called Frothi and Halfdan.[9] These brothers fought each other for the kingdom, and eventually Halfdan killed his brother and obtained the sole kingly authority.[10] He begot a son called Helghi to inherit the kingdom, and Helghi was so exceedingly valiant that he became a pirate chief, and occupied himself with constant pirate raids. And since he had laid waste the shores of all the surrounding kingdoms and subjected them to his command with his pirate fleet, he was known as king of the sea.[11]

His successor as king was his son, Rolf Kraki,[12] who became powerful through his inherited valour, and was killed at Lejre. This was then the king's most famous residence, but now, near the city of Roskilde, it lies scarcely inhabited among quite the meanest of villages.[13]

His son Rokil ruled after him, and he was known by the surname of Slagenback.[14]

His son succeeded him as king and won a surname by his speed and vigour: in our common tongue people used to call him Frothi the Bold.[15]

[2] His son and the inheritor of his kingdom was Wermund, and he so excelled in the virtue of prudence that he acquired a name for that. He is called Wermund the Wise.[16]

He had a son called Uffi, who repressed his power of speech until the thirtieth year of his age. This was because of a dreadful disgrace which befell the Danes at that time. Two Danes had set out for Sweden to avenge their father, and together had killed his slayer.[17] For at that time it was a shameful disgrace if two men put an end to one, especially as the superstitious heathens of those days[18] tried to devote their energy solely to acts of valour. So Wermund, mentioned above, held the government of his kingdom until his old age, and at last he was so worn out with age that his eyes were dimmed with senility.[19]

When the news of his infirmity was spread abroad in the lands beyond the Elbe, the proud Teutons pompously puffed themselves up, for they were never content with their own boundaries. Their emperor sharpened his furious rage against the Danes, with a view to conquering the kingdom and acquiring a new sceptre.[20] Emissaries[21] were therefore sent to carry the commands of the proud prince to the king of the Danes—to Wermund, that is—and they laid before him a choice of two courses, neither of which was fit to choose. For he ordered him either to resign his kingdom to the Roman empire and pay tribute, or to find a man sufficiently skilled in battle to settle the matter by taking on the emperor's champion in single combat.

When the king heard this, he was dismayed. He called together all the chiefs of the kingdom in a body and questioned them carefully about what was to be done. For the king declared that he was unable to come to a decision. It was his duty to fight, and he was bound to protect the kingdom; but blindness had darkened his sight, and the heir to the kingdom was speechless and had grown slack with inactivity, so that it was commonly held that there was no hope of salvation to be expected from him. For Uffi, whom we mentioned above, had been sunk in gluttony from childhood, and had diligently applied himself to the kitchen and the cellar in the manner of the Epicureans.[22] In such matters he had served with diligence rather than with sloth; for in his youth he had decided to preserve the strength of his body unspent. And so the king revealed the ambition of the Germans to the assembled chiefs and to a gathering of the whole kingdom, and the old man made repeated inquiries into how he was to make a choice which was scarcely a choice at all.

And while the whole crowd was sunk in perplexity and plunged into silence, Uffi was the only one who rose to his feet in the middle of the assembly. When all the people caught sight of him, they were astonished beyond words, for a speechless man was taking up an attitude as if to make a speech.[23] As every rarity is held to be worth looking at,[24] he held the attention of all of them.

Thus risen, from on high his speech he thus began.[25]

'Let us not be troubled by the threats of these challengers. That habit of Teutonic turgidity is something they are born with: to brag with bombastic words and to dismay the weak and cowardly by threatening them with flatulent menaces.[26] Nature brought me forth to be the sole and true heir of the kingdom: surely you must know that it rests on me alone boldly to meet the test of single combat, and to fall for the sake of the realm. Let us therefore knock the wind out of their threats, and tell them to carry back this message to the emperor: that his son and the heir to his empire, along with his most outstanding champion, must dare to meet me on my own.'

He spake, and thus pronounced these words with haughty voice.[27]

When he had finished the speech, the old man asked those sitting beside him whose oration it was. And when he heard from the bystanders that it was his own son who had uttered these words, who until then had been as if he were dumb, he ordered him to draw near and let him feel him. He touched him all over his shoulders and chest, his buttocks, calves and shins, and the other limbs of his body, and then he said: 'I call to mind that such a one was I, in the flower of my youth.'[28]

What then? The date and place of the combat were fixed, and the envoys went back to their own country with the answer they had received.

[3] All that remains is to gather arms indisputably worthy of the warrior. The king had the best swords in the kingdom sought out and brought together, and Uffi wielded each one of them with his right hand and smashed them into the smallest fragments. 'Are these the weapons,' he asked, 'with which I am to defend my life and the honour of my kingdom?'

And when his father discovered how very outstanding was his skill at arms, he said, 'There is only one refuge left both for our kingdom and for our life.'

He ordered that he be led to a burial mound where he had once hidden a most well-tested sword,[29] and, instructed by marks among the characters on the stones,[30] he told them to dig up this supreme blade. He seized it at once in his right hand and declared, 'Here it is, my boy. Many a time have I triumphed with it, and it always protected me without fail.' So saying, he handed the sword to his son.

It was not long before the time appointed for the conflict was near at hand. Uncountable masses came together from all directions, and the place of battle was fixed on an island in the River Eider[31] so that the combatants should be separated from the crowds on either side and remain unassisted by any of their supporters. So the Germans sat down together across the river in Holstein, and the Danes were drawn up on this side of the stream. The king chose to sit in the middle of the bridge,[32] so that if his only son should fall, he might throw himself into the depths of the river rather than survive the loss of both his son and his kingdom 'to carry his white hairs in sorrow' to the other world.[33]

The combatants were let loose on either side and came together on the island in midstream. And when our noble warrior caught sight of the two men who were hastening to meet him as arranged, he roared from his mighty breast like a lion[34] and with a steady heart rushed boldly and without delay towards the two picked men, wearing at his side the blade which his father had kept hidden, as told above, and holding another drawn sword in his right hand.

As soon as he met them, he addressed them both in turn. We seldom read of such an occurrence, but our most rare of champions,[35] whose 'remembrance will never be effaced,'[36] encouraged his own adversaries to fight:[37] 'If longing for our kingdom fires your ambition, and you want to gain possession of our wealth and power and plenty, you ought by rights to go ahead of your retainer. Then you may both extend the boundaries of your kingdom and win a reputation for valour in front of your watching warriors. However, let us set to![38] Take a lesson in skill from your opponent, and feel the stroke of the smiter.'

But he addressed the champion like this: 'Here is the place to broadcast the proof of your valour. Take the lead now, and make known to the Danes without more ado the prowess you have already exhibited to the Germans.[39] Now you will be able to add to your reputation for skill in battle. If you go before your lord and protect him with your defending shield, you will be enriched with a gift of outstanding generosity. I implore you: let the experienced and valiant Germans do their best to instruct the Danes in the finer points of the art of combat,[40] so that you may win the longed-for victory at last, and go back to your native land rejoicing in triumph.'

When he had finished his words of encouragement, he struck the champion's helmet with all his might, and the sword he struck with was 'distributed in two'.[41] It made a noise that echoed throughout the whole gathering of warriors.[42] The German cohort shouted aloud with delight, and the Danish phalanx on the opposite side were stricken with sorrowful despair and groaned in their grief. As soon as the king heard that his son's blade was shattered, he ordered that they should place him on the edge of the bridge.

And suddenly Uffi drew the sword he was wearing, dyed it in gore from that champion's hip, and with no further delay sliced off his head as well.

Thus 'playful Fortune, variable as the moon',[43] now mocked what had happened before, and looked with the unfriendly gaze of a stepmother[44] on those she had just now favoured to their boundless jubilation. When the old man heard of this, he regained his confidence and had himself returned to his former seat.

The victory was not in doubt for long, for now Uffi drove the heir of the empire to the bank of the island and there had no difficulty in slaying him with the sword. Thus he defeated two men on his own, and by his glorious courage he erased with splendour enough the shame which the Danes had incurred long before. The Germans went home ashamed of their dishonour, and their threats and their outrageous verbosity[45] were brought to nothing. After that, far-famed[46] Uffi ruled his kingdom in peace and tranquillity.

[4] He begot a son to whom he gave the name of Dan; Dan also bore the surname of the High-minded or the Proud.[47] He was succeeded as king by his son Frothi, who was also called the Old.

After him his son Frithlefer undertook the government of the realm. His son was Frothi *Frithgothæ*, who was also called the Magnificent because he embraced liberality above all other virtues: gold and silver he 'counted as clay'.[48] His son Ingiald succeeded him.[49]

After his time no son succeeded his father to the throne for a space of many centuries. It passed to grandsons, or nephews, who, to be sure, were sprung from the royal stock on the one side.[50]

The one who succeeded next, Olaf, vigorously subdued all the surrounding countries, even as far as across the River Danube, where he marched in triumph for seven days.[51] However, in case I should be accused of making up stories and telling untruths, by stringing together the reigns of kings whom I have learned to be quite widely separated by intervals of time,[52] and since I may have passed over many illustrious men, owing not to my idleness but to the unfruitfulness of my research, so I leave the inquiry to my diligent successor,[53] that by his careful investigation he may supply what I have left out through memory's eclipse.[54]

After this Sighwarth, the son of Regner *Lothbrogh*, invaded the kingdom of Denmark; having joined battle with the king, he killed the king and gained the kingdom. And while he was in possession of the conquered kingdom he took to his bed the daughter of the slain king.[55] When he had had knowledge of her as a wife, the king's daughter asked him what he should call their offspring. The king answered and told her that after she had given birth, the mother would remember her girdle. And when the time of her giving birth had passed, she called the boy Knut, alluding to the word for knot,[56] and he was the first who had that name in Denmark. And he was the only one sprung from the royal line after the Frothi whom we mentioned above.[57]

While he was still a boy, a landowner from Sjælland called Ennignup[58] was made guardian of the kingdom; but as soon as Knut came to manhood, he took control of the kingdom. Time passed, and he had a son whom he chose to call Snio.⁵⁹ He had a son whom he called Klak-Harald.⁶⁰

He was followed by his son and heir, Gorm *Løghæ*, a sluggard who merely indulged in sensuality and regal drinking-bouts.⁶¹ His wife was that most glorious queen called Thyrwi, who was surnamed the Ornament of the Realm.⁶² And I cannot refrain from speaking of her laudable renown. For it is customary to relate the deeds of those whose reputation stands high above the rest.

[5] Now this Thyrwi whom we have mentioned was a woman conspicuous for every virtue. Nature strove to bless her with uncountable gifts. For she was fair of face, and the rose and the lily had been wedded to paint the pinkness⁶³ of her cheeks; and she was chaste, modest and cheerful, overflowing with an abundance⁶⁴ of all manner of courtesy. Furthermore, the kindness of Providence had enlightened her mind with such radiance that she was believed to have drunk from one spring the prudence of Nestor, the cunning of Ulysses, and the wisdom of Solomon. If only she had been cleansed by the spring of baptism, she might indeed be accepted as a queen of Sheba, who came to learn wisdom of Solomon: if only that lady had been orthodox.⁶⁵

In those days the emperor, Otto, had made Denmark tributary.⁶⁶ I think it was because of the inactivity of the king, who was given over to the pleasures of gluttony, as we recorded above. When Otto learned of this, he arrogantly conceived a fierce longing to try and inflict a mark of shame⁶⁷ on the kingdom. He even made a thorough attempt to ensnare the modesty of the above-mentioned queen with his wiles. He therefore sent envoys to meet the queen in private under the pretext of collecting the tribute, and they were also given instructions to suggest to her that a queen of her surpassing beauty and prudence ought rather to be an empress, and rule over the Roman empire, than remain the queen of a tributary or no more than middling kingdom. 'So take the wiser course,' say they. 'Do not carelessly refuse the powers that are offered you. Cherish the renown of so famous a prince in your inward affection with a lasting and unshakeable return of his love, and just as his love's embrace enfolds you, so let your reciprocal emotion succumb to his friendly vigour.'[68]

When she heard those words, she asked for time to deliberate, so that she might reply to such a choice greeting with a kindly and appropriate answer in the same terms. And since they delayed but a short while, the urgency of the matter drove her to collect her thoughts more pressingly. Thus, when they asked her what answer they should take back to their lord, that far-famed and commendably virtuous lady, who alone deserved to be called queen, had devised a stratagem in her cunning mind, and she began to coax them with the most honeyed words[69]—as the saying goes, 'You bear honey in your mouth, but gall lies hidden in your heart.'[70]

These were the words she poured forth, as if in prophecy: 'May my tongue cleave to my jaws if I remember thee not.'[71] To her questioners she indicated that she consented and was ready to carry out the vow. However, she made it clear that, if she were to scorn the bed of her own husband and fly to the embraces of another man as an adulteress, she would be embarking on a momentous undertaking. Much money would therefore be needed to atone for and indemnify so great an undertaking and so infamous a wrong: money to be paid out to the inhabitants of the kingdom, both male and female, to stop the mouths of slanderers. Indeed, she contrived with womanly blandishments that, if they wished to accomplish their purpose, they must concede the tribute to herself for three years in order to atone for that same misdeed.

And so they immediately set out for the emperor at great speed to bring back to him her reply and the condition attached to it. This he accepted with the utmost readiness and joyfully promised what she asked for, provided only that she gave security for their pact with hostages. The envoys hasten back to Denmark and convey the emperor's wishes to the queen, demanding hostages to confirm the agreement. Twelve of the most noble sons of her chief men are selected as hostages without delay, to go to Saxony with the envoys.

[6] Meanwhile the queen sent a decree throughout the kingdom that the entire population of the whole realm[72] should be called together and assemble near Schleswig,[73] and all those who had their abode within the kingdom were to set to work with their own hands to build a strong fortification with all speed. However, she helped those who were pressed by lack of worldly goods by supporting them with the tribute: this was how she spent the tribute which she had obtained by deceit. She gave none the privilege of exemption: the young, the old, and all adults who were neither impeded by their infancy nor prevented by the weakness of old age, were obliged to labour at that fortification.[74] They all had to obey her, because everyone, rich and poor alike, tilled her fields like tenant farmers. For in those days our kings exercised lordship over all land in the kingdom by right, just as they possessed the power to rule.[75] And so it was she, first of all, who built that marvellous work which thereafter always presented the surest defence of the Danes against the fury of the Germans, as if they were fenced in by a hedge.[76]

When she had devoted two years' labour to this, news of this enormous construction came to the emperor's ears. Once again he sent envoys to Denmark, and they shrewdly inquired why the queen was applying herself to this kind of work, unless she was trying to break their agreement. The queen always had a ready answer, and this is how she replied to them: 'I cannot adequately express my astonishment that a prince of such outstanding prudence, who by the grace of the Lord has borne aloft his throne almost to the stars[77] and by his penetrating counsel has subjected so many ferocious peoples to his empire, should deign to inquire the meaning of her plans from an incapable woman. For I think what even your intelligence must have deduced cannot have been hidden from his: that there is no way through for the passage of infantry or cavalry in your direction except over a smallish stretch of level ground where I have now erected this enormous obstacle of a wall. Whereas previously the kingdom was patently open to all, now the road is closely blocked by the obtruding wall, and a very narrow gateway will keep in those who wish to leave. Of course, as the faithful servant of my lord I shall carry out his design, and when I have gathered in the entire wealth of the kingdom, I shall surrender myself to your will, and our infuriated people will be held back by the retaining wall. The entrance which will allow us an unhindered passage will remove the possibility of pursuit by the national army.'

When the envoys heard this, they greatly commended the cunning of the woman and went joyfully back to their own country, reassured that she would keep her promise. Meanwhile the queen pushed on all the more earnestly with the work she had begun; and thus the cunning of a woman deceived the inflated vanity of the Germans. And when three years had passed and the building of this ingenious work was brought to a conclusion, and it was properly adorned with bastions, they gave this most magnificent construction the name of Danevirke,[78] because it had been accomplished and completed by the sweat of the Danes. As for the queen by whose peerless ingenuity freedom has been won for the Danes to remember for evermore, they gave her the not unworthy name she fully deserved: Thyrwi, the Ornament of Denmark.[79]

[7] The emperor immediately orders picked knights of the empire to set out for Denmark with immense parade to meet the queen. A crew of minstrels, making music with viols[80] and harps and 'timbrels and dances'[81], escort them with noisy

rhythm. They sent on a few of the more important men into Denmark to sound the mind and wishes of the queen, and pitched their tents by the Eider to await her arrival.

And when she learned of their arrival, she summoned to her the wiser men of her kingdom, and in the hearing of them all she gave the following reply: 'What the emperor demands, I deny. What he desires, I refuse. What he seeks, I avoid.[82] I will not play the adultress, and at once disgrace the kingdom, defame my sex, and dishonour the king. You reproach me with the king's inactivity. You may be certain that this suits me very well. The whole kingdom obeys my wishes, and there is not a lawsuit or prosecution which is settled otherwise than at our pleasure. Thus, as you know, I am fully respected both as king and as queen. And you may rest assured that the king is highly distinguished in the nobility of his birth, for he is the offspring of kings on either side. Therefore, even if he cannot match[83] the size of the emperor's power, he is in no way inferior in his royal lineage. And to conclude my short speech: I shall forthwith liberate the Danes from the yoke of servile tribute, and they will owe you no further submission or respect whatever.'[84]

The legates were immediately stunned to silence by the dreadful disrespect[85] of this unlooked-for reply, and they hastened in disarray back to the tents of the nobles mentioned above. A crowd of these nobles converged on them in troops, asking what it could be that sped their return at so urgent a pace. Without hesitation the envoys reported directly to all of them that they had been foiled in their intentions and outwitted by the cunning of a woman.

When the emperor discovered this, he ordered that the hostages should undergo sentence of death on the spot. For that most illustrious queen knew a long time in advance that this would be the outcome of the matter, as if she were gifted with knowledge of things to come.[86] However, she decided that it was better to redeem the whole kingdom from servitude by the death of a few rather than to serve foreigners to the very end.[87]

Then was the ambition of the Germans confounded and their joy turned to grief. Back they went, grieving and lamenting. And when that famous queen and the king her husband had completed their span of years, leaving a son, Harald Bluetooth,[88] who was also the heir to the kingdom, Harald had both his parents buried according to heathen rites in almost identical mounds of equal size by the king's residence at Jelling, to serve as glorious mausoleums.[89]

[8] This Harald held sway over the kingdom with his royal sceptre for a long time afterwards. This was the first king to reject the filth of idolatry and worship the cross of Christ.[90] However, he sent the army to haul the immense rock which he intended to have raised over his mother's mound in memory of her achievements, and disorder began to seethe among the people. It was caused both by the new religious observances and by the unbearable servile yoke.[91] Then the commons broke out in rebellion against the king, and all together they drove him from the kingdom. He fled with speed, for 'fear added wings to his feet,'[92] and arrived in Slavia as a refugee. There he is said to have had a peaceful reception and to have founded the city which is now called Jomsborg; whose walls I, Sven, saw levelled to the ground by Archbishop Absalon.[93]

During his exile his son Sven was raised to the throne; he was surnamed Forkbeard.[94] And he adopted as a true worshipper of God the faith which his fugitive father had in the end renounced.[95] Reborn in the holy waters of baptism and made orthodox in the faith, he ordered the seeds of God's word to be sown throughout the land.

In the course of time envoys arrived to repair the discord which had arisen between the fugitive father and the son who occupied the royal throne. The king therefore decided that his father and the Slavs should meet him in the straits of Grønsund[96] to make peace. The king arrived there first with the Danish fleet at the time appointed, and waited a long time for his father. The fugitive Harald meanwhile accepted the suggestion of one of his counsellors—that is, of Palna-Toki, a man with two names[97]—and constructed for himself a rapid vessel best suited for rowing. This he manned with the most experienced sailors and put the above-mentioned Palna-Toki in charge, who set off with all speed to meet the king.

When he reached the Danish fleet, he ranged his oarsmen on deck and, with treachery in mind, gave orders that his ship should make for the king's. With his crew in position, at the first light of dawn he quietly roused the king in his resting-place.[98] When the king woke, he asked who it was. 'It is us,' he said, 'the envoys of your father. We have been sent over to you to discuss peace-terms.' When he gathered this, the king wanted to inquire more closely into how his father was, and he put his head a little way over the gunwale of the ship.[99] Then Palna-Toki grabbed him by the ears and the hair, gave a more powerful heave against his unavailing resistance, and dragged him willy-nilly out of his own ship. Although he yelled and shouted, just a little, they made their escape with furious oar-strokes while everyone else slumbered in ignorance. Nor did they heave to until they reached the city of Jomsborg.[100]

When the Slavs caught sight of him, the people rose up and condemned the prisoner to various forms of death and refined torture. However, the better sort of their leaders prevailed with wiser counsel. They decided that, rather than put an end to him by killing him forthwith, they would be better advised to have him ransomed for a large tribute; in that way the Danes would be impoverished and Slavia would perpetually rejoice in her wealth. It would yield but little profit to the community if they were to condemn their prisoner to death.

So they charge their envoys to announce to the kingdom that they may buy back their king with three times his weight in gold and silver; and they did so without much delay.[101] The Danes collected a levy from almost the entire kingdom, and when the Slavs arrived at Vindinge[102] with the captive monarch, they were eager to redeem their king. But the levy proved insufficient to release him, and in order to ransom him the married women agreed to make up the shortfall in coin with their own jewellery. They topped up the king's levy by adding rings, bracelets, ear-rings, necklaces and all their chains. And when it was complete, the Danes obtained from the king their first common rights over woods and groves.[103] Moreover, in recognition of the goodwill and generosity of the married women, he was also the first to concede that in future a sister should share with her brother a half portion of the division of the family inheritance;[104] for women had previously been wholly excluded from any share in what was inherited from the father. For he considered it was agreeable to all reason that a display of whole-hearted love and a giving of gifts ought to be rewarded in equal measure, as if to say, 'the same measure with which you have measured shall be measured unto you.'[105]

[9] When Sven died, his son Knut succeeded to the kingdom, and they also surnamed him the Old. He widened the boundaries of his kingdom by the amazing force of his valour. By his manifold prowess he added to his own empire the neighbouring kingdoms from farthest Thule almost to the empire of the Greeks. Yes indeed, with not inconsiderable gallantry he subjugated Ireland, England, France, Italy, Lombardy, Germany, Norway, Slavia, and Samland too.[106] And while he enjoyed the calm of peace in England, he was the first to make laws for his retainers, which I have outlined above according to the small measure of my slight abilities.[107]

He also had a daughter called Gunhild, a famous woman whom the Emperor Henry, son of the Emperor Conrad, took in marriage.[108] And when the Romans drove Henry from the royal throne by seditious riot, he went to his father-in-law and begged for his assistance. Seizing the opportunity thus afforded him, the noble and renowned Knut raised his own army and first invaded and ravaged Gaul; and so, marching on, he laid waste Lombardy and Italy, and afterwards forced the Romans to yield their city by his manifold valour. Thus he restored the emperor his son-in-law to the throne.[109] After that, he travelled with much rejoicing as far as France, and masterfully carried away with him from Tours to Rouen the relics of the blessed Martin. For Knut loved her more than others, with a special affection.[110]

The above-mentioned Knut also begot two sons. He called one of them by his own name, and he was given the surname Hard: it was a name he got not because he was harsh or inhuman, but because there was a province of the same name from which he came originally by birth.[111] His father put this son in charge of the kingdom of Denmark. He called the other son Sven and delegated the government of Norway to him. Knut himself ruled England [as king for nearly five quinquennia, and during that time the sons to whom he had committed those kingdoms[112]] paid the debt of Adam and left their father as survivor.

When the king heard that the kingdom of his fathers was bereft of a ruler, he speedily returned to Denmark. Because the church was newly planted in Denmark[113] he brought with him many priests and bishops; some he kept by him and others he sent out to preach. Scattered abroad throughout Sweden, Götaland and Norway, and sent over to Iceland as well, they sowed the seed of God's word and gained many souls for Christ—as it is written, 'Their sound has gone out to all lands, and their words to the ends of the earth.' Among them were the bishops Gerbrand and Rodulf, and one of them—that is, Gerbrand—he appointed as the first to rule the church of Roskilde, while to the governance of Rodulf he entrusted the church of Schleswig.[114]

Now, as he was unable to attend to several kingdoms on his own, he invested his nephew (Sven, that is), despite his youth, with royal rank and entrusted him with the government of Denmark. His father was Ulf, who was known by the surname Sprakaleg,[115] and his mother was the king's sister Estrith.

[10] When King Knut was dead, his nephew, this same Sven who had been placed on the throne by his uncle, undertook the government of the realm. Not long did he rule it in peace and quiet,[116] for the Norwegian king, Magnus, son of the blessed King Olaf by a concubine,[117] invaded Denmark with his fleet in pursuit of conquest. King Sven met him near Helgenæs and fought a sea-battle with him, in which Magnus triumphed and won Jutland, Fyn and Slavia.[118] But while the victor was trying to chase Sven into Scania, he met an unexpected accident in Sjælland: he was thrown from his falling mount,[119] hit a tree and died. After that, Sven was restored to the kingdom and held the government of the realm in peace.

The rustics called him 'the father of kings' because he was a most prolific begetter of numerous sons,[120] five of whom wore the shining diadem of kingship in succession. I have deemed it superfluous to recount their deeds in full, lest they should be repeated too often and weary my readers, for the noble Archbishop Absalon informed me that my colleague Saxo was working to describe at greater length the deeds of them all in a more elegant style.[121]

However, it ought not to be overlooked in passing that it was the primeval custom of our forefathers that, when kings were raised to the throne, all the Danes came together in a body at Isøre, so that royal inaugurations should be enhanced by the consent of all.[122] And so, when King Sven died, his son Harald, whom they called the Whetstone because of his complaisant softness, was raised to the throne.[123] He was the first to give laws to the Danes in the place where kings were enthroned, which we have mentioned.[124]

[11] When he died, his brother Knut succeeded to the kingdom, and the church of Odense boasts of him as their crowned martyr: killed not, as some consider, on account of his excessive harshness or because of the unbearable yoke which he would have imposed on the plebs as a result of his harshness.[125] For the reason why he was persecuted was the following.

At the time when he enjoyed the 'plenitude of power', he grieved that he had not inherited the sovereign sway of his father's uncle. So he summoned an army and a fleet for the invasion and conquest of England, and went to Humlum, which in those days was a harbour connected to the sea; there he ordered the army to assemble.[126] He was waiting for a following east wind with the assembled fleet when a sudden rumour reached the king's ears that treachery against the realm had arisen at Schleswig. He hastened there with all speed to put an end to that conspiracy[127] at the outset, and when he arrived there, he arrested and bound the originators of the crime and took them into his own keeping. He then hastened back with extreme rapidity to the fleet he had unexpectedly abandoned, and thought to find his men in the same place where he had unfortunately left them.

However, when he came to the appointed place, he discovered that the whole lot of them had mutinously and disobediently rowed back to their homes. Blazing with over-much fury, he anxiously asks himself how to inflict the signal retribution[128] which so great a misdeed deserved. For the unhappy king was in two minds,[129] considering that he ought to be less severe because it would involve the undoing of so many men, nor would he be able to punish so great a communal crime with as much strictness as was needed to deter the misdeed of a private person. Therefore each steersman was made liable to pay a composition of forty marks, just as the rigour of the king had ordained, and the compensation also required of each sailor was three marks, because they had ruined the king's army by their dispersal.[130]

While visiting each province he would exact payment with the full rigour of the law;[131] and he began to levy the fine among the Vendel-dwellers first of all.[132] This was a brutal and uncivilized people, who were thirsting for innocent blood with ferocious cruelty, and instead of their tax they presented their innate fury. Moreover, such a mass of people had come together that not a single householder had the privilege of staying at home. When the king learned of their outrageousness, he took instruction from the words of truth, 'If you are persecuted in one city, flee to another';[133] and he tried to escape their rage and deprive them of the opportunity of doing evil. But the enemy were infected by the suggestions of the Old Prevaricator;[134] their frenzy mounts, to threaten the king's head; profane plebeians devise the prince's death.[135] Whispering rumour spread, urgently resounding, and with repeated slanders roused the whole body of the realm against the king's harshness.

> Good news flies slow, by envy stayed,
> Bad news on feather'd wings doth spread.[136]

Nor did the frenzy of the infuriated rabble cease[137] before he had been driven out across the Little Belt[138] and pursued to Odense. And there he was crowned with martyrdom, and commended his soul to Paradise.[139]

[12] Once he was dead, his brother Olaf was made king, and in his time there was a famine so terrible that the common people called him the Famished; but it lasted no longer than seven years.[140] On his death his brother Erik the Good takes his place.[141] And at the end of his reign he followed Christ and took the cross upon his shoulders.[142] For he set out for Jerusalem and committed his soul to Christ on the way; having removed himself from the prison of this life, he rests in the island of

Cyprus. During his reign he was the proud begetter of children from a noble stock, although from various successive hymeneal unions.[143] For he begat Knut of Ringsted, father of King Valdemar, [and also Erik, the father of King Sven, and Harald Kesia, the father of Biorn Ironside[144] and his eleven brothers. After] Erik his brother Nicolaus succeeded, and the rabble named him the Old because he governed the kingdom for seven quinquennia.[145] He had a son by lawful marriage who was called Magnus, great in name and great in height. For, like King Saul, 'from the shoulder and upwards he stood above'[146] all the warriors of the kingdom and his contemporaries.

[13] During the time of that same king, Knut of Ringsted,[147] a man who was wise, discriminating, courteous, energetic and strong in the virtue of honesty, became famous as the duke of Schleswig. He cowed the wild fury of the Slavs by his wonderful vigour and prudence[148] and brought them under his jurisdiction by his extraordinary virtue. Envy meditated on his virtues... and began to grow sick, for her head is apt to hang low at the prosperity of others.[149]

With timorous ambition, Magnus began to plot his death, so that he would not be deprived of the transient kingdom[150] even if he failed to win the everlasting crown. For goodness is always suspect to kings:

> ... all power will be
> Impatient of a consort....[151]

and thus:

> Right, law and goodness perish,
> And all respect for life and death.[152]

For they put aside the ties of kinship and joined together with the same Duke Knut's kinsman—that is, with Henrik the Lame[153]—and took counsel [for the killing of Knut[154]] in covert conclave, as if it were a high matter of state.

So they appointed a place in the wood at Haraldsted[155] to confer with him. And the fearless champion of Christ,[156] conscious of his own good faith alone, did not hesitate to meet them. Marked out only by the banner of the Holy Cross, protected neither by shield nor by helmet and escorted by no more than two guards, the lamb stood there ready for the furious wolves. The criminals arrive later, wolves in sheep's clothing,[157] with hoods and cloaks concealing coats of mail and helmets. Without delay the enemies of peace make haste to slaughter the 'Israelite indeed',[158] their own cousin, and occupy themselves in sending to Heaven the soul that had previously been held captive within the prison of the flesh. Followers of Christ afterwards bear his lifeless body to Ringsted for burial,[159] where by the divine power of the Lord many miracles were worked by Christ before numerous witnesses.

[14] And so this monstrous crime subsequently stirred up a fierce rebellion in the kingdom. Erik is moved by the finger of the Lord[160] to avenge his brother, while his uncle Nicolaus, mentioned above, is still ruling, and he is stirred up to try the issue in battle. Erik was raised to the throne with the title of king and afflicted his uncle with manifold persecutions. They fought each other often but the most famous fields of battle were these.

First they fought at Rønbjerg[161], where Nicolaus won the day, and he captured my grandfather Kristiarn and sent him, bound with iron shackles, to be held in custody at the fort which overlooks the town of Schleswig.

After a while there was another meeting between the contestants at the bridge at Onsild,[162] and although the fighting was even fiercer, Nicolaus's party prevailed again. Erik's army turned tail, and he would have been captured on the spot had not the Biorn mentioned above, who was nicknamed Ironside on account of his famous strength, in company with my father Aggi, fought back manfully in the middle of the bridge. They resisted a shower of missiles with such courage that they were thought to be immovable pillars.[163] While defending the way across the bridge, they beat back the enraged attackers with such wonderful valour that they might have crossed the bed of the stream dry-shod on the corpses of the slain. Although hampered by numerous wounds, they did not cease to guard the bridge until the king had embarked on his ships and was ready to escape. They followed him at once and accompanied him in his flight to Scania.

King Nicolaus had now triumphed in two encounters.[164] Therefore he tries to drive his hostile nephew out of the kingdom altogether. He gathered a fleet and pursued him to Scania, where he made a rapid landing at a place which is commonly known as Fotavik[165] and belongs to Lund. The commons of Scania, who are always mightily upright,[166] had called together the entire manpower of the land. This was a well-equipped force, and they had no hesitation in meeting him. Battle was joined, and they hacked and haled to Hades the king's son Magnus, the perpetrator of the crime previously spoken of, along with two prelates.[167]

And so King Nicolaus was beaten, and bereft of his son and heir at the same time, and he sailed to Schleswig, and the burghers of that city received him within their enclosing walls and treacherously slew him.[168]

[15] Having gained a glorious victory, the above-mentioned Erik, who is known as Ever-memorable,[169] held the kingdom after him in peace, and freed the aforesaid Kristiarn from his chains. So he gained the kingdom but, having risen to power, he forgot the reason for the vengeance he had wrought, and began to rage against his own kinsmen more cruelly than the tiger. For with anger in his heart he had his brother, Harald Kesia, summoned to a meeting in the silence of the dead of night[170], while he was staying at his manor of Skibing [?].[171] Bidden from his bed, boding naught baleful, once roused he hastened to the king his brother, weaponless. And in that very place commissioners caught him and cut off his head.[172]

Not long after that he meted out a dire retribution to repay his own nephew, the Biorn mentioned above. He seized him, tied him to a millstone, and sank him in the depths of a bottomless pit.[173] He ordered Biorn's brothers to be put to death by the sword as well. They numbered ten adults, some flourishing youths and some children.[174] In this he bore little resemblance to his father.[175]

And since he was the author of so great a crime and had wholly exterminated these budding kinglets,[176] the righteous judgment of God's authority went against the exalted power of the king, and the avenger of innocence quickly destroyed the author of the crime 'in the breath of his mouth'.[177] For Plogh the Black ran him through with a spear at the Urne-thing, while he was surrounded by a circle of warriors.[178]

[16] And so the king was killed, and another Erik was placed on the throne. They called him the Lamb on account of his sweet and gentle nature, and in his days there was a plenteous abundance of everything.[179]

And when he was dead, Knut, the son of that Magnus who had been killed in Scania (as we have recorded above), was made king at the Viborg assembly, and Sven, the son of the above-mentioned cruel Erik, was put on the throne by the Scanians. And while they were engaged in numerous battles, Valdemar, the scion of holy blood, the son of Knut of Ringsted, gained possession of his father's fief[180] and gave assistance to both in turn, as if he stood between them.

However, after a long time, a council was held in Lolland[181], and the rulers decided to divide the kingdom into equal thirds and to confirm the treaty by an oath. But the treaty did not remain firm for long, as the outcome of the arrangement showed. For after the council had been held, the three we have mentioned came together that autumn in the city of Roskilde for a feast, and they dined first with King Sven.[182] The peace and trust between them had been broken, and he had prepared a trap: he plans to kill Knut and Valdemar that evening after vespers by means of commissioners previously instructed.[183] When the lights had been snuffed,[184] they slew Knut and crowned him with martyrdom;[185] but while they were trying to run Valdemar through with a naked sword, he was seriously wounded in the thigh,[186] but God's grace preserved him[187] and he escaped. However, as soon as he had recovered somewhat from the pain of his wound, he set out for Jutland and gathered together an army.

[17] Sven, who was king of Scania, hastened after Valdemar, king of Jutland, and they joined battle at Grathe.[188] Nor was the victory long in doubt, for Sven was beaten, and killed by the hand of a peasant. And so the glorious victor, King Valdemar, gained possession of the kingdom.

After that he governed the realm for five quinquennia and two years.[189] This man secured[190] the boundaries of the kingdom with such glorious valour that, whereas previously the wild Slavs were encouraged by our internal divisions and laid waste all our sea-coasts and our islands as well, he tamed the seaways, brought them under his jurisdiction, and subjugated the Slavs, making them pay tribute to himself.

[18] He accomplished many things worth remembering, but his memory shines with a starry radiance from three of them alone.[191]

In the first place, under his rod of iron and outstretched arm,[192] he compelled the Rugians to be regenerated in the waters of holy baptism.

And the second remarkable feat was that he was the first to build a tower of fired bricks, on the island of Sprogø.[193]

And the third was that he first repaired the rampart of the Danevirke with a brick wall, but he was prevented by his death from completing it.[194]

For while he lived he was a man found acceptable in all things: fair of face, courteous, discriminating, wise, most penetrating in counsel, vigorous, an outstanding warrior, an accomplished wit, victorious, popular, always successful; only more cruel towards his own people than was just.[195]

[19] This Valdemar took to himself in marriage as his queen Sophia,[196] sister of Knut, the king at Roskilde. Nature strove immoderately to enhance the utter loveliness of her appearance. For all the skill of the ancients would fail to describe her.[197] However, I borrow no solicited opinions for the 'blazoning of her beauty',[198] for many a time I used to see the much admired masterpiece of Nature with my own eyes.

And in the end, God's grace increased the reputation of the illustrious King Valdemar so widely that surrounding kings and princes strove to pay him honours as if they were his due.[199]

[20] And when he had paid the debt of Adam, his son Knut followed by hereditary right and succeeded to his father's kingdom without degenerating from his father's virtue. Indeed, he repressed the wild Slavs with such manful courage that he laid waste the whole territory of the Slavs and the Pomeranians with his fleet[200] and forced their duke, Bugislav, to pay him tribute and homage. This was done aboard the king's ship, glittering with gilding on stem and stern,[201] not far from the city which was founded by the fugitive Harald, as we recalled above;[202] and I saw it done. And I have decided that it is worth recounting the heavenly sign of that submission.

For after they had concluded the treaty, such a thunderclap rang out that they thought the elements were collapsing. Indeed, we considered that this was done with God's permission by the Old Prevaricator[203] and the Enemy of Peace. For the same violent whirlwind and storm almost swamped and sank the smaller boats, which were carrying the bishop of Kamien[204] and the above-mentioned Bugislav, along with the king's brother Valdemar,[205] a young man of the most brilliant natural abilities. When that was concluded, we rowed homeward with immense jubilation. May the Ruler of all things order this conclusion in His peace![206]

NOTES TO THE INTRODUCTION

1. Saxo's debt to Sven has often been demonstrated, e.g. by Curt Weibull 1918. But there are no tributes to the precursor in Saxo's work. Instead, Saxo implies that he had none (GD, 3; PF, 4), or at least very poor ones (GD, 100; PF, 109). At the beginnning of book seven he seems to dissent from one of Sven's genealogical guesses (GD, 181; PF, 201), and later (GD, 265; PF, 294) he slights the historians who dealt with the regent Ennignup: they included Sven. He spoils, or underplays, Sven's best stories.
2. GD, 410 (EC, 414) for the 'temerity' of Aggi. He advised King Sven to attack rather than wear out Valdemar's army, despite Valdemar's superiority in numbers.
3. *De Eskillo archiepiscopo et duobus Eskilii patruis narratio*, from the *Exordium Magnum*, composed c.1200; SM, ii 428–42.
4. According to Saxo (an unsympathetic witness), Eskil first sold his loyalty to Knut V and Valdemar, and then abandoned Sven III on a pretext by which Sven was not deceived (GD, 398; EC, 396).
5. Gertz, 158, 196, followed by Arup, i 253, and others. On Danes in Paris see now Munk Olsen.
6. Gertz, 197, n. 26; Skyum-Nielsen, 205, 214. Most of Skyum-Nielsen's precursors assumed that Sven was a *hirdman*, even if Saxo may not have been. Fenger 1989, 205–8, refers more cautiously to Sven's 'connection with the *hird* of Valdemar and Knut VI'.
7. DD, i:3, no. 96 (c.1180-3) and no. 225 (1197-1201).
8. NL, 122, for Archdeacon Sven. Another Sven is the fourteenth in the list of deacons. On Asser Svensen see Weeke, 141, 225.
9. For the synod of 1187 see Hamsfort in SRD, i 282, and Skyum-Nielsen, 224–5; for the archidiaconate, Eskil's 1145 charter, DD, i:2, no. 88.
10. Provost Asser's bequests are recorded in the *Liber daticus* of Lund and of Sorø (an ultimate beneficiary, thanks to Absalon). He died on 25 March in some year between 1185, when he was still in exile, witnessing Magdeburg charters (DD, i:3, no. 127), and 21 Oct. 1194, when his successor Salomon was in office. He left a house in Lund, an assart near Venestad in Scania, and land at Bjæverskov in Sjælland. See Weeke, 70, and SRD, iv 360, 470.
11. Lagerbring, i 218ff., ii 99; SRD, i 42ff.; Velschow, xviii–xxiv.
12. The older historians found what they wanted in the void which is Sven's biography. Steenstrup 1896, 707, praised 'the heartiness that

distinguishes this enthusiastic, almost fantastic, nobleman', and J. Olrik (KV, 26, 32) was sure that 'he certainly did not belong to the clerical order, but ... was a member of the ... *Tinglid'* with a 'naive love of life'; 'no churchman,' wrote Arup (i 253), 'but solely a royal *hirdman'*. Skyum-Nielsen, 205, insisted on the social divisiveness of the *Vederlov* as it appeared in LC: 'aristocratic in the worst sense of the word'. Fenger 1989, 207, n. 8, describe's Sven's treatise as 'ideological propaganda for a growing royal power', and Birgit Sawyer 1985a, 51–2, argues for the unofficial standpoint of Saxo but maintains that Sven was 'making propaganda for royal power by the grace of God', claiming that 'there is no doubt that Sven Aggesen wrote in support of royal policy.' See however her interesting argument (1985b, 688–91) that 'Sven Aggesen's and Saxo's works may ... be seen as representing ... two families, each claiming to be official history but in fact offering partisan views.' Perhaps; but neither makes such a claim openly, and I doubt whether the concept of 'official history' existed in Denmark before the sixteenth century. Nanna Damsholt 1985, 157–60, elaborates on the partisanship of Sven. My own views, as expressed in EC, esp. 156 and 228, are tainted by an uncritical acceptance of Sven as a political propagandist, and have since been revised.

13. Cf. Saxo's formal acknowledgment of his debt to Absalon and his dedication to Archbishop Anders Sunesen (GD, 3; PF, 4), and Theodricus's dedication to Archbishop Eysteinn (MHN, 3–4). A true political propagandist like Otto of Freising left his readers in no doubt of his commission by expounding it in an epistle to the emperor and two prologues.
14. The conventional courtliness of Sven's eulogy of the Queen Mother was insisted on by Karsten Christensen and Niels Skyum-Nielsen in SS, 130, 138; cf. p. 73 above, and p. 138, nn. 197–8, below.
15. DD, i:4, no. 24, with bibliography, and DGL, i:2, 774: a decree which applied only to Scania and was not strictly speaking a national law.
16. Harald Whetstone's laws are mentioned by Ælnoth and specified by Saxo; see J. Olrik 1899–1900. *Frithkøp* occurs in the Lund charter of 1085 as a royal perquisite. The situation was memorably summed up by Axel E. Christensen as 'law without power'; see Axel E. Christensen 1978, 11–29, where gild regulations are used as examples of consensual rather than public law.
17. As suggested by Brøndum-Nielsen.
18. Recorded in the Rüde Annals (*c*.1250), and from them in the fourteenth-century Ribe Annals; DMA, 166, 258.

19. DD, i:2, no. 143: 'We concede moreover to ailing *fideles* at the end of their lives that in obedience to the law of the Danes they may give half of all their possessions clearly and freely to the . . . brothers . . .'
20. As in the preamble to the Sjælland and Scanian church law, DGL, i:2, 821.
21. The best edition is in DGL, ii. This law never became valid for the whole kingdom, but Kroman 1973 argued that 'it was originally intended to apply to the whole country.'
22. In 1898 Erslev deduced an annual income of 33,000 marks and upwards from the sources listed in KVJ (Skyum-Nielsen, 305). Carpenter calculates revenues for the young Henry III well below this in 1225, when he got only £16,500 (21,994 marks). The comparison is unfortunately almost meaningless because the estimate of Henry's revenues depends on recorded receipts, which do not exist for Valdemar II's Denmark. Valdemar's ransom, finally agreed in 1225, included a cash payment of 45,000 marks. Richard I's ransom of 150,000 marks may be a more realistic indicator of their relative wealth.
23. The text of *Hirðskrá* is in NGL, ii 387–450. See also KL, vi 580–2 (Seip), and the discussion of the *hird* in Foote and Wilson, 100–5.
24. Danish historians agree that the composition and function of the *hird* changed significantly in the period 1086–1186, but not when or how. The question of whether it developed into a brotherhood of administrators, as Arup argued, or, as in Bolin's view, that it became a new knightly élite of nobles enjoying privileged status by their membership of the royal household, was not resolved by Aksel E. Christensen 1945, and now appears to have been an opposition between two rather hypothetical positions. More recent historians tend to be less sure of the twelfth-century *hird*: see Skyum-Nielsen, 174–8, Riis, 227–35, Hørby, 192–4, Fenger 1989, 44–5. For a brief summary see KL, vi 577–9 (H. Nielsen). I doubt whether the *hird* actually existed as an institution before Sven. It was just a name given to any great man's following. Cf. Lindow, 64–7, who argues that the term *hird* was not used in Denmark either before or after Knut's time, and that the author of WR employed it 'only in a strictly historical context'. He thinks WR is earlier than Sven's LC. If he had concluded that it was later, as it certainly seems to be, his case is stronger.
25. GD, 298 (EC, 44). Saxo's narrative of twelfth-century events includes several which are hard to square with Sven's LC. In 1131 Magnus, son of King Nicolaus, was prosecuted at a popular 'thing' for murder and exiled but recalled by his father's royal will (GD, 357–8;

EC, 130–2). In 1137 Erik II fined Eskil, then bishop of Roskilde, twenty gold marks (160 of silver), for opposing his wishes. That was the equivalent of the highest *bot* laid down in the *Vederlov*; the fine was levied after an appeal for clemency by Kristiarn Svensen rather than after a trial by the men of the *Witherlag* (GD, 370; EC, 354). Sven III (1146–57) introduced judicial combat as a way of settling cases at law (GD, 388; EC, 382); and Valdemar I threatened his cousin and retainer, Magnus Eriksen, with the ordeal by hot iron as the Danish mode of defence against treason charges (GD, 508; EC, 557)—a mode absent in LC in both Sven's and Saxo's version but present in WR.

26. ... *amaris cum conviciis insequuntur* ... *etiam contumeliae damnationem iunxerunt* (GD, 398; EC, 397). The best study of the light shed on the *hird* by Saxo is by Skyum-Nielsen in SS, 180–91.

27. For the best texts see DR, nos. 7–10. I am unconvinced by Riis, 48–54, who attempts to redate the Treason Law to 1139–40, and adhere to the fundamental work of Holberg. To these documents must be added the brother-list appended to KVJ. It contains 215 male names organized into 62 brotherhoods (of 3–8 men) under headings corresponding to the main administrative areas west of Scania: Jutland's fourteen *syssler*, Fyn and Sjælland. The identifiable names belong to nobles, officials and bishops in the period *c.*1190–1202, a few from before and after. Tage E. Christiansen doubted whether this was primarily a list of royal retainers and suggested an analogy with the English *jurati ad pacem*; others have argued for a monastic fraternity associated with Sorø. Hørby, 159, prefers the older view that this was 'an exploitation of the old *hirdman* ideology', binding all the chief men to the new hereditary kingship as 'brothers'; and most commentators agree with Aksel E. Christensen 1945, 47–8, that the list 'can scarcely be explained except in connexion with the royal *hird.*' If so, the extension of the household to include 'country members' as well as 'boarders' in one association coincides with the composition of LC by Sven to define the terms of the association.

28. See *Jómsvíkinga saga* (1962), ch. 16; (1969), ch. 14, for the ten or dozen laws of the Jómsborg Vikings. In the first of the three chapters, of uncertain date, appended to the Flateyjarbók recension of *Jómsvíkinga saga*, it is reported that Sven Forkbeard established *þingamannalið* garrisons at London and 'Slessvik' and that the troops made laws (*Þingamenn settu þau lög at* ...), though the rubric of the chapter reads *Lagasetning Sveins konungs*; see *Flat.*, i 203, and a normalised text from there in EE, 92–3. Cf. EE, 89, where it is concluded that it is

'obvious' that the author of the Flateyjarbók chapters took the laws of the *þingamenn* from *Jómsvíkinga saga* itself. Individually these laws are not strictly comparable with LC, neither are the laws of *hólmganga* in *Kormáks saga* or the rules of the Hálfsrekkar in *Hálfs saga*. And see now Abels, 161–3, for an apt dismissal of the Jómsborg connection.

29. Snorri ascribed a household law to Óláfr in his *Óláfs saga helga* of c.1230 (ch. 43 in *Den store Saga*; ch. 57 in *Heimskringla*); there is no earlier reference. For St Olaf's other reputed laws see Authén Blom, 61–75.
30. See Liebermann, i 620–6. He dated the *Constitutiones de Foresta* to the later years of Henry II, following the Woodstock decrees of 1184, which imposed a real forest code. The *Constitutiones* are comparable to LC not because of any textual relationship but because both documents justify innovations by invoking the same highly respected legislator of the past. The genuine codes of Knut kept his reputation alive in England: apart from Anglo-Saxon copies, at least ten twelfth-century manuscripts of the Latin versions survive (Liebermann, iii 330, 334), and at St Albans these versions were regarded as Knut's own work (see Roger of Wendover, s.a. 1022).
31. The gild theory goes back to Lappenberg and Kemble, was adopted by Steenstrup, *Normannerne*, iv, ch. 6, and expounded by Larson 1904, 160ff. Stenton followed suit: 'It is clear from later Danish evidence that the members of this body formed a highly organized military guild' (Stenton 1950, 406; cf. Stenton 1932, 119–21). Ditto Hollister, 11–12; ditto even the vigilant Abels, 165, who concludes 'that Cnut would have organized his household in this manner is far from implausible, since guilds seem to abound in tenth and eleventh century England.' Far from implausible, perhaps: but, as Hooper, esp. 167–70, has demonstrated, there is no contemporary evidence that this particular gild, which would have been the most important in the country, ever existed.
32. The loan-word *husting* was applied to the London *gemot*, never to gild-meetings; see Nightingale.
33. In st. 4 of Gísl Illugason's *erfikvæði* on King Magnús Bareleg (d. 1103) *húsþing* refers to a council-of-war held by the king on a punitive expedition to Trøndelag against the party of Steigar-Þórir, probably in 1094. The conjecture made by Hofmann, 203, that the word is a contracted form of *húskarlaþing* is groundless, since the latter term is never found. A *húsþing* was in effect a private meeting (sometimes indoors) as opposed to a public meeting. Cf. also Steenstrup, *Normannerne*, iv 175–80.

34. Þingalið occurs on a Swedish rune-stone at Kalsta (Häggeby parish, Uppland). The compound þing(a)mannalið is found in saga texts. Not long before Haraldr harðráði's invasion of England in 1066 the king's stallari, Úlfr Óspaksson, could refer to a picked man of the English army as a þingamaðr: ef... hrøkkva... skulu tveir fyr einum... undan ... þingamanni (Skj. A, i 403, B, i 372; Morkinskinna is the oldest source for the strophe).
35. Kinch argued for thegn, but Steenstrup, Normannerne, iv 133–4, for þegning. Hofmann, 75, gives Bugge and Steenstrup as authorities for this loan but has doubts; Alexander Jóhannesson, 1228, had none. Peter Sawyer, 303, refers to 'Knuds thegnlith', and Abels, 170, repeats Larson: 'thingmenn, an Anglo-Saxon loan-word derived from thegnung, 'service', and related etymologically to thegn'. The word þegn evidently had several meanings in Scandinavia: see Moltke, 284–91, for a concise discussion of this vexed problem.
36. There are 20 examples in Lexicon Poeticum, and Foote discusses the poetic references. The verb þinga may be a more helpful source of explanation than the chief recorded sense of the noun, and a plausible analogue for þingamaðr found in the term málamaðr, a man who receives máli, pay by contract, esp. for military service—for a good collection of references see Cleasby–Vigfússon, s.v. máli.
37. E.g. the horse-tending rules, applied before the knights employed grooms; the bootlessness of all crimes of violence under the old law; the old restriction on the choice of oath-helpers, and on the right of counter-oath; the process of outlawry by sea, which only applied to warriors stationed abroad.
38. Saxo: Adeo quondam castrensis notae dedecora iudiciali repellebantur umbone (GD, 296; EC, 42). Nunc vero, solutis hebetatisque pristinis militiae nervis ... priscae consuetudinis forma convellitur (GD, 298; EC, 44). Contrast Sven's triumphant announcement that the old customs have been revived and recorded.
39. The brief and scattered allusions to ius militare in Justinian's Code won the concept some recognition in Gratian and the glosses of the canonists; see Decretum, pt 1, dist. 2, 3, c. x. Isidore offered a working definition in Etym., V, vii.
40. Edited as 'Den Gamle Gaardsret' in KR, v 23–46. On these texts see Maurer, Jørgensen, 61–2, and KL, v 645–6 (Liedgren).
41. Clause 5 of the Proem to the Institutes refers to law desuetudine inumbratum imperiali remedio illuminatum.

42. Sven has: *controversiae* (chs. 3 and 9) for disputes at law; *calumnia* (chs. 5 and 8) and *contumelia* (ch. 8), both varieties of *iniuria* in Roman law; *generalis constitutio* (chs. 8 and 9), distinguished in the *Institutes* from *constitutio personalis*; *querela* (ch. 9) for accusation; the two civil claims of *vendicatio* and *praescriptio* (ch. 9). But all these words are used by canonists. *Delictum* is unforensically modified by *transgressionis* in ch. 11, and in ch. 4 and elsewhere *praevaricatio* is used for simple 'transgression' rather than for 'sham accusation or defence; collusion'. On the whole, Cicero seems a likelier source of the civil law vocabulary than the Code; but not for the *herciscunda* or the *catholiciani* of HC; cf. pp. 124, 134, nn. 104, 172, below.
43. For a full etymology see Azo, lib. I, tit. xvii, *De Vetere Iure Enucleando*.
44. For law-texts in use under Archbishop Anders Sunesen see Haastrup, in Ebbesen, esp. 107–11, and on the archbishop's jurisprudence, Frosell, in Ebbesen, 243–53. See also N. K. Andersen.
45. As Bernard of Pavia, 3, put it at the beginning of his *Summa Decretalium* from 1187–91: 'The reason for making a *constitutio* is for the restraining of malice, and for the definition of a new point of law.' See p. 86, n. 3, below for Gratian's view of law, and note the references to sin and penance in Sven's text.
46. The excommunicated monk seeking absolution 'throws himself on the ground before the community' in RB, ch. xliv; cf. also Saxo's story of Sven II's self-abasement before the bishop of Roskilde (GD, 311–15; EC, 62–6). The affinity of the *Vederlag* with the monastic rule was noted by the Cistercian author of AR (DMA, 162; cf. DMA, 256, and SRD, ii 170). He says that Knut (he calls him 'Hartheknut') *quasi religiosis leges et statuta prescribebat honestatis*.
47. See MGH, *Epp.* iv: *Epp. Karolini Aevi*, ii 24, for the shortened text. An English translation of most of the full text is in EHD, 773. Pope John VIII drew the same comparison for the bishops conspiring against Charles the Bald in 876; see MGH, *Epp.* vii: *Epp. Karolini Aevi*, v 319. From the seventh century Judas appears in the anathema section of charters as the prototype of treachery; not of treason. It is the clergy who most delight in flinging the epithet Judas at each other.
48. As in the preface to HC, p. 49 above: 'Peasants and princes share the common nature of all men, whereby reputation instigates this man to do well, while love of sloth tarnishes that one.'
49. See Skyum-Nielsen, 251–3, on *Hævn og Hærværk*.

50. Or, as Holberg, 37, argued, man-to-man relations within the *Witherlag* were regulated less harshly, but man-to-king relations more so.
51. See pp. 26–7 above. The combination *Leges—Reges—Genealogia* reverses the sequence of King Rothari's 'Edict' of 643, in which the kings and lineages come first, before the Lombard laws, but follows the practice of scribes and binders who gathered similar elements in the same order as Sven from the early eleventh century onwards, as e.g. in Codex Skoklosterianus, which has the law of the Visigoths followed by a chronicle of the kings (MGH, *Leg.*, i 457–61).
52. On *Annales Colbazenses* see Anne K. G. Kristensen 1969, 25–7, and for the text DMA, 1–11.
53. See Anne K. G. Kristensen 1968–9, a remarkable 'detective story'. Ralph Niger's two chronicles were edited by Anstruther in 1851; cf. Flahiff, and Gransden, 222.
54. For the theory that the pedigree from Skjǫldr was made by Sæmundr fróði see Bjarni Guðnason, 150–80: it seems that he provided his son Loptr with an ancestry to match his bride's, a daughter of King Magnús Bareleg of Norway. Whatever its origin, a version of this pedigree came to Sven's notice shortly before or about the same time as another version was used in *Skjǫldunga saga* (*c.*1180–1200). For collections of the various renderings and fragments of this lost saga see *Danakonunga sǫgur* and *Skjoldungernes Saga*.
55. The two versions of the text were edited by Gertz in SM, i 176–85, 152–5. It has been argued that Sven's genealogy could be later than Abbot William's; see Lukman and others *contra* in SS, 138–9.
56. For example: Knut's first cousin, Knut of Lolland, still alive in 1188, and his cousin once removed, Sverker Karlsson, who survived to 1208; Bishop Valdemar and Nicolaus, grandsons of King Nicolaus; King Knut of Sweden, son of Biorn Ironside's daughter; Benedikt, Birger Jarl and Magnus, the surviving great-grandsons of St Knut of Odense through his daughters; Poppo, future bishop of Bamberg, born before 1188, the grandson of Sven III.
57. *Chronica Slavorum*, iii 5; see now Munk Olsen, in Ebbesen, 75–94, and T. Riis 1982.
58. Before 1177 Bishop Absalon had 'many Norwegians' in his retinue: DD, i:2, no. 132 (witness-list). After 1180 Denmark was a refuge for Sverrir's enemies. While Archbishop Eysteinn went to England, King Magnús Erlingsson fled to Denmark in 1180/1 and 1183/4, and from 1185 the Kuflungs were maintained by a Danish magnate named Sven.

59. In the following Theodricus is cited before the dash, Sven after it:

> Rudi licet stylo ... perstrinxi — Stilo ... licet illepido
> breviter annotare — sub compendio memorie commendarem
> scriptorum inops — pari preconio non extiterunt
> Hugo ... canonicus Sancti Victoris ... Sigibertus quoque Gyemblacensis — veterum in codicibus contemplatione
> investigatum ab illis, quos nos ... Islendingos vocamus — modis Hislandensibus

For Theodricus's citations see Jens S. Th. Hansen; Tenney Frank, 82–3; A. O. Johnsen, 29–37. He cited Lucan eight times, Vergil once, Statius once (under Lucan's name), Ovid once.

60. Theodricus, chs. 3 and 6, for lineages. *Solus obtinuit regnum totius Noruagie* (ch. 1); *Ericus fratris interfector* (ch. 2); and King Eysteinn compared with Augustus (ch. 32).
61. Gertrud Simon offers the best survey of prefatory *topoi*.
62. I discount the possibility that Sven also knew the anonymous *Historia Norwegiae* (MHN, 70–124) because the arguments for a later date for the composition of it appear stronger; see Gudrun Lange, 141–63, for the most recent discussion of the problem. The prologues of the two works employ similar *topoi*, but this cannot prove interdependence. In the following the passages from *Historia Norwegiae* precede the dash, those from Sven Aggesen follow it:

> hucusque latino eloquio intentatum — in Latinum sermonem transferre conabor
> quam sit onerosum, et ob invidos quam sit periculosum ... illorum edacem livorem postponendo mea scripta — detractionibus tamen neuticam declinabit dispendium
> non rhetorico lepore polita — stilo, licet illepido
> in omnibus seniorem assertiones secutus — quantum ab annosis et veteribus certa valui inquisitione percunctam
> quoniam multorum magnificentias ... ob scriptorum inopiam a memoria modernorum quotidie elabi perspexi — nostrum ... immanissima gesta eterno deputari silentio ... obsoleta in negligentie illabuntur laberintum

63. On these events see *Danmarks Historie*, i 357–8, and Skyum-Nielsen, 213–16. The main sources are Arnold of Lübeck's *Chronica Slavorum*, composed *c*.1210–13, and the Danish *Annales Valdemarii* (DMA, 76–9), composed probably in the 1220s using a lost Lundensian source.
64. It has been suggested (e.g. by Lukman in SS, 138) that the tone and tense in which Sven wrote of Queen Sophia, *numerosius ... oculata fide perspicabar*, imply that she was dead at the time of writing, which would therefore be after 1198. However, the passage refers to the reign

of Valdemar I and to Sophia's prime; both were over by 1185 when she was in her mid-forties and absent from Denmark as the wife of the landgrave of Thuringia. An imperfect tense would be appropriate.

65. See p. 117, n. 62, below; *Annales Valdemarii*, s.a. 1187 (DMA, 76): *Dux Valdemarus II miles factus est 7. Kalendas Ianuarii*; and *Annales 1095–1194* (DMA, 308): . . . *cum magna solemnitate Roskildiæ*.

66. See *Chronica Slavorum*, iii, ch. 21: *Kanutus . . . manifestas ex illa die inimicitias contra imperatorem exercere cepit, ita ut omnem terram . . . usque ad Albiam sui iuris esse diceret . . . iustam se causam contra Teutonicos habere arbitratus est.* 1187 was the turning-point.

67. In 1190 Duke Valdemar and his cousin, Bishop Valdemar, invaded Holstein in the absence of Count Adolf (so according to a lost source used in the seventeenth-century *Annales Bartholiniani*, SRD, i 342); the Ditmarsk vassals of the archbishop of Bremen had already transferred their allegiance to Bishop Valdemar (*Chronica Slavorum*, iii, ch. 22). In 1194 King Knut conquered Holstein and levied tribute from Count Adolf. Thereafter Danish kings pursued aggressive policies along the Baltic littoral for nearly thirty years.

68. *Sed quia horum gesta non disposuimus, seu genealogiam historiali more narrare* . . . (Glaber, 10).

69. *iugique digna memoria*: the same phrase as is used of King Erik Emune in HC, p. 70 above.

70. Lacuna in A; *sensim*, 'slowly', supplied by Gertz.

71. *in negligentiæ illabuntur laberintum* A: as Gertz suggested, this spelling of the last word may have encouraged an etymology of 'labes-intus', a 'falling-within', as if a labyrinth were a pitfall; hence *illabuntur* (HS, 89). Cf. *Laborintus quasi labor intus* (Jones and Jones, *Commentary*, 37).

72. *melliti gutturis orisque aurei*: 'mellifluous mouth' is used by Boethius of Homer, and occurs in the epistle prefacing *Historia de Profectione Danorum*, SM, ii 457. Gertz detected *aurata vox* in Martianus Capella, v 429.

73. The conclusion of this sentence was rather boldly reconstructed by Gertz. I have not followed him. A reads:

> quali quisq: claruerit turpitudo q: singulorum gesta subperornent elegam.

Gertz in X:

> quali quisque claruerit triumpho, et singulorum gesta stili perornent elegantia.

And emended further in SM, i 142:

> quali quisque claruerit triumpho, nudaque singulorum gesta stili peroment elegantia.

Here *turpitudo* is clearly antithetical to *gesta (elegantia)*; the *q:* following it seems more likely to represent *quippe* than *-que*; and the *sub* prefixed to *peroment* is an unlikely misreading of *stili*: an abbreviated *subter* fits better, since Sven's invitation is for a continuation of what he has begun. X's *elegantia* may then be read for A's *elegam* but as an adj. qualifying *gesta* rather than as a noun.

74. See the superb clarification by Riis, 151–94. Riis provides the best analysis of the political and cultural milieu of twelfth- and thirteenth-century Denmark which has yet appeared in a language other than Scandinavian.

NOTES ON THE LAW OF THE RETAINERS

1. *reperta* is here interpolated by Gertz to help the sense: 'to be discovered by our diligent study'.
2. *contubernii iuventus militaris*: here used in the classical sense of soldiers sharing a tent or billet, rather than as in Mark 6: 39. In HC, p. 65 above, Sven refers to Saxo as his *contubernalis*, but the meaning in this case is uncertain; cf. Introduction, pp. 2–3.
3. *ut improborum refrenaret audaciam*: echoes Gratian, *Decretum*, pt 1, dist. 4, i: *Causa vero institutionis legum est ut humanam cohercere audaciam et nocendi facultatem refrenare*.
4. ODan. *witherlogh* has several meanings: punishment, retaliation, payment, or exchange (it is used for *commutatio* in Matthew 16: 26); see Kalkar, s.v. Here it seems to mean 'penalty, penalties' (the only sense of *viðrlǫg* in WN laws); and the WR title, *Witherlax ræt*, is correspondingly 'penal code'. As Sven says, it is not the same as his title, *Lex castrensis sive curie*. In the ordinances of King Kristofer from the 1250s (DR, 50–1) the *withærlogh* is the body of men subject to the household law. See A. D. Jørgensen 1876, 56–60.
5. *legem castrensem . . . militarem . . . curiae*: the usual meaning would be 'of the camp, military'. However, it appears from ch. 5 that by *milites* Sven means knights, and from the rest of the text that this is not a 'law of the camp'. Tertullian, *De Corona*, xii, used *castrenses* for palace attendants: 'There is also another kind of *militia* in the royal household, they are called *castrenses*.' Ducange, s.v. *castrum* (ad fin.), accepted that this was Sven's usage, and he has been followed here.
6. Absalon, son of Asser the Rich, was bishop of Roskilde 1158–92 and metropolitan archbishop of Lund 1178–1201.
7. Knut VI was born in 1162. He was crowned as his father's heir on 25 June 1170, and ruled as sole king 1182–1202. He is *primi Valdemari filius* because Valdemar II, Knut's brother, was already eminent as duke before he succeeded him in 1202. Saxo attests that Knut made his first raid overseas in 1179 under Absalon's protection (GD, 521; EC, 576). There is no other evidence that Absalon fostered him in any formal sense. The word *nutricius* used by Sven meant 'nurse, fosterer' in classical Latin but acquired the sense of 'pupil' in Carolingian times. Theodricus (MHN, 9) uses it to correspond to ON *fóstri*: Hocon *nutricius* Halstani for Hákon Aðalsteinsfóstri.
8. *in matriculam conscripsit*: *matricula* is 'muster-roll' in Vegetius, but it could mean any sort of list or scroll. Such rules came to be known

as *skrár* after the material on which they were written. Sven's phrase is like ON *setja á skrá, skrásetja*, 'record in writing, enter in a list'. His next sentence recalls Alan of Lille's prologue to AC: *Scribendi novitate vetus iuvenescere carta | Gaudet* ...
9. The reference is either to Sven's lost genealogy or to HC itself. A sentence which could be Sven's was detected by Gertz, 112–14, 195, at the beginning of the late thirteenth-century *Incerti Auctoris Genealogia*, a work which owes something to HC. See Introduction, p. 27.
10. *qui, quare et ubi*: the interrogative mode of the law-schools, cf. e.g. Azo, 871. The same approach had also become a recognised part of rhetorical *inventio*; cf. e.g. Arbusow, 94, Lausberg, §§ 40–2.
11. *tanquam leo frendens auitis potitus successibus*: I have translated the last word as *successionibus*. The lion is from Isaiah 5: 25, and Proverbs 20: 2: 'The fear of a king is as the roaring of a lion: whoso provoketh him to anger sinneth against his own soul.' In 1 Peter 5: 8 the raging lion is the Devil, but Knut VI and his successors used the shield of lions and hearts. King Sven is also called *Tygeskeg*, 'fork-beard', in CR, c.1140, and Abbot William's Genealogy, c.1193 (SM, i 19, 178); *tjúguskegg* in the Norwegian *Ágrip* of about the same date as the Genealogy.
12. *Gerionem praecellens Hesperium*: Aeneid, vii 662 and viii 202; Silius Italicus, i 277; Justin, xliv 4. The three-bodied monster slain by Hercules was usually celebrated for his monstrosity, not his valour. Peter of Blois (*Ep.* cxvii) used him as a type of the Devil, but others followed the note by Servius on *Aeneid*, vii 662, making him the amphibious ruler of the Balearic Isles. The *Commentary on the First Six Books of the Aeneid*, composed 1125–50 and attributed to Bernard Silvestris, says: 'We read that Geryon was a three-bodied monster, whom historians understand as having been a king who ruled three kingdoms' (Jones and Jones, *Commentary*, 75). In John of Genoa's *Catholicon*, a dictionary completed by 1286, he appears, s.n. *Gereones*, simply as 'a king of Spain'. Knut ruled five kingdoms, says Sven, which was more than Geryon. Gertz, HS, 4, n. 1, makes the unlikely suggestion that Sven merely confused Geryon with his slayer, Hercules.
13. *par Alexandro*: Gertz considered that Sven would have known of Alexander from one of the romances based on Pseudo-Callisthenes (on which see Cary, 24–61), but both Quintus Curtius and Walter of Châtillon were known to Saxo.
14. *Finlandiam* (A and S): rejected by Gertz, 154, as a misread *semlandiam* and as inherently improbable since Knut the Great had nothing

to do with Finland. However, when Sven refers to Samland (the Königsberg peninsula in East Prussia) in HC, he calls it *Samia*. 'Old' Knut may have had nothing to do with Finland, but young Knut VI sent raids there in 1191 and 1202. No expedition to Samland is known before Valdemar II's raid of 1210, which falls somewhat outside the terminus ante of Sven's work (see Szacherska 1988). Finland should stand.

15. Oak-leaves, garlanded to reward heroes: see Ovid, *Tristia*, iv 8, 23; Lucan, *Pharsalia*, vi 427; Jones and Jones, *Commentary*, 123.
16. *stemmatis titulis florere* . . . : cf. Sedulius Scottus, *Carmina*, ii 7, 55; LHL, 262: *florenti stemmate fulget*. Sven's distinction is not only by birth, but it implies that birth and wealth go together. Saxo fully accepts the coincidence of birth and valour in his *Bjarkamál* verses (*clarissima Martem | Stemmata conficiunt*), but he says nothing about this preliminary sifting, which has been seen as inspired by the nobiliary pretensions of the retainers of Sven's day. In the 1150s Sven III had advanced low-born men in his household, 'so that those he enriched might attribute their good fortune to the king's generosity rather than to their own birth' (GD, 388; EC, 381).
17. Gilded, or rather chased and inlaid, axe-heads of the Viking period survive, usually with silver or copper as the applied metal; the examples from Mammen and Bustorf are well known. See Graham-Campbell, 46, 49, 63–5, 244, 245. Plain axes were cheaper than swords; decoration made them acceptable as a status symbol, as borne by Godwin's shipmen in Florence of Worcester, s.a. 1040: *gladium deauratis capulis renibus accinctum, Danicam securim auro argentoque redimitam* . . . Even Alexander the Great was served by men with the *dacha bipennis* in *Alexandreis*, i 237.
18. A word *famulariter*, unknown to the dictionaries, was here substituted by Gertz for *familiariter* in A, perhaps to avoid the repetition of *familiaritas* . . . *familiariter* within the same clause. But Sven loves repetition.
19. *si cetus eum* . . . *comitetur herilis*: echoes *Aeneid*, viii 462, *gressumque canes comitantur herilem*.
20. *humana proclivis ambitioni conditio*: see also n. 29 for another use of the phrase 'human condition', drawn from the Fathers, e.g. Jerome's *Commentary on Jeremiah*, i 1, 16, *vitiis subiacet humana condicio*.
21. *subputeretur* could also mean just 'calculated'. The figure of three thousand is conventional for a picked force: Riis, 230, n. 22, cites 1 Kings 13: 2; 24: 3; 26: 2; 1 Maccabees 9: 5. Gideon's was only three

hundred, but that was after two selections. For *Tinglith* see Introduction, p. 12.
22. *quorum ritus dissona . . . varietate discrepabant*: echoes Martianus Capella, ii 102, *dissonans discrepantia nationum nec diversi gentium ritus*.
23. *contectales*: 'people living under the same roof', but usually 'married couple' (Niermeyer, s.v., and in Thietmar of Merseburg). Sven's contemporary, Jocelyn of Brakelond, has it for 'house-mate'. The preamble to *Consiliatio Cnuti* (SE English, *c*.1110–30) also presented Knut as a unifier of dissonant customs: 'He decreed, after rational reflection, that as the realm of England was ruled by one king, so it should have one common law' (Liebermann, i 618).
24. Sven's fondness for the 'organological' model of society (see also n. 63 below) recalls John of Salisbury.
25. *nisi pene . . . praecipitium temperaret excessus* (A): Gertz supplies *enormitate*, inspired by *immanitate* in S. Both seem too strong for the context.
26. *quietis tranquillitate*: variation of *pacis*; see p. 112, n. 46, below.
27. Øpi is a name compounded to form three Sjælland Øverups and Øverød near Copenhagen. Eskil is a name that recurs in Sven's own family; see the Appendix, p. 141. Neither occurs in any English record of Knut's reign, and Saxo drops Eskil.
28. *experientiae providentiam* in A becomes *experientiae propter evidentiam* in Gertz's reconstruction. Knut selected Øpi and Eskil as his *secretarii*. That could mean as scribes, secretaries, notaries, porters, ushers, or confidants, but Sven seems not to have a written code in mind—he means they were close to the king.
29. *ad transgressionis praecipitium humana sit proclivis conditio*: cf. n. 25 above; Augustine, *Enarratio in psalm. 145* (PL 37, 1897), *Ubi finitur via peccatorum, praecipitium est*.
30. *singulis praevaricationis casibus accurata . . . remedia*: the commonplace 'law as medicine' is also in Knut VI's homicide ordinance: *huic morbo providere curavimus medicinam*.
31. A is very corrupt here, and X most imaginative. Following S, Gertz reads the meaningless *Tuscani negotia* as a misinterpretation of abbreviated *transeamus negotia*.
32. *priscorum curialium qui et nunc militari censetur nomine*: now they were called *riddare*, once they were called *huskarlar* or *hirdmenn*. The literary evidence suggests that the knightly skills were found in Denmark

from the early twelfth century, but the earliest royal charter to be attested by *milites* is dated 1177 (DD, iii:1, no. 62). Whatever the term *huskarlar* had meant in the early eleventh century, by the late twelfth it chiefly meant 'servants', though in Norway, then and later, it was also used of the sworn retainers of kings and great men (cf. *Edda Snorra*, 162, where the author is describing the early thirteenth-century present, not the past). They are never mentioned in Danish sources except in the compound *huskarlastefna*; cf. n. 52 below. On housecarls in England see Hooper.

33. *alieno caballo, runcino, palefrido, dextrario subvectus*: four types of horse in ascending value, according to twelfth-century terminology. The *caballus* was the plain work-horse, for ploughing or transport. The *Vita* of St William of Æbelholt has a story about an old *roncinus*, which began to amble with spirit when ridden by the abbot: evidently a quiet sort of horse for an elderly clergyman (VSD, 333). But Abbot William also sent a magnificent 'golden-hued' Danish horse to Stephen of Tournai in 1179–85: the letters they exchanged suggest that Danish breeders knew the French market and would have labelled that horse *palefridus*. The army laws of Frederick Barbarossa draw a useful distinction: 'If a foreign knight shall come to the camp in peace, sitting on a palfrey without shield and arms, whoever harms him shall be judged a peace-breaker. If however he comes to the camp sitting on a destrier with his shield round his neck, his lance in his hand, whoever shall harm him has not broken the peace' (Rahewin, *Gesta Friderici*, iii, ch. 28). On Danish horses in German romance see Ohley. For the cooperative grooming Saxo offered a historical explanation: 'Whenever the king undertook a cavalry operation, the warriors who had no horses remained on duty to take turns in grooming them' (GD, 294; EC, 38). The author of WR ignored the whole matter. Sven may have had religious disciplines in mind, e.g. 'Let the brethren wait on one another in turn,' RB, ch. xxxv. Saxo also reminds his readers at this point that Knut waged war by sea oftener than by land, and an attempt has been made to relate the *Vederlov* to a naval rather than a knightly organization; see Hjärne, esp. 92–110. Sven seems unaware of this possibility.

34. *ut pro porcione pociores et priores loca capesserent digniora*: Gertz's amendment of *vtppote* [sic] *posiores et priores* ... in A, which seems unnecessary. A fixed seating order for *hirðmenn* is insisted on in *Konungs skuggsjá*, ch. 37 (tr. Larson 1917, 210), but the principle of allocation is not mentioned. Saxo simplifies it to date of enlistment

(*militiae vetustas*), and adds that not even lateness could disqualify a man from his proper seat. The notion that Knut the Great sat down to dinner with 3000 men is absurd, but Saxo has Valdemar I dining in public with the *regia clientela, c.*1177, a force which he was able to assemble within his bed-chamber (GD, 506; EC, 554).

35. *similem . . . culpam par pena condempnat*: a maxim which echoes Isidore's *Sententiae*: *Neque enim erit impar supplicio cuius error quisque par est ac vitio* (PL 83, 723), also cited *c.*1090 by Bonizo in *Liber de vita Christiana*, 80. The earliest reference by a civilian appears to be in Godefroy's gloss on *Novella*, 127, ch. 4: *Paribus delictis par imponenda est poena*. Anders Sunesen, Hex., 6019, has *maior poena maiori debita culpae*.

36. Archbishop Ælfheah was pelted with bones, and finally dispatched with an axe, by Thorkel's men in 1012, according to the *Anglo-Saxon Chronicle* (C, D, E, F). What Sven describes here is horseplay, not capital punishment. For other examples in Saxo and *Hrólfs saga kraka* see SG, ii 74, and Kock, 179–81.

37. *communicabit*: the change to the future indicative suggests that this is current custom, or about to become so. Again, it was old monastic practice: 'Let that brother who is found guilty of a more grievous offence be excluded from the table . . . let none of the brothers consort with him . . . separated from the companionship of all, let him eat alone, his portion of wine being taken from him' (RB, chs. xxv, xliii). The Lund *Consuetudines* (*c.*1123) laid down that brothers who harm each other by word or deed should be separated from the common table, and be 'last of all in all places' (*Cons. Lund.*, 149). For degradation after three offences cf. RB, ch. xxiii.

38. *calumnie patronisare* (A): *calumnia* is defined by some canonists as 'a plea or refutation which is definitely known to be unjust' (Bernard of Pavia, 30; but cf. n. 90 below). The verb *patronisare* is apparently not found elsewhere before 1382, and then in the sense of captaining a ship; see Ducange, s.v. The *patrocinari* of S is better: cf. OFr. *patrociner*, 'to plead at law'.

39. This provision against favouritism is not found in other versions of the *Vederlov*, but Saxo inveighs against current indiscipline in similar terms: *qui culpae punitor esse debuerat, patronus existat* (GD, 298; EC, 44). His target must be Valdemar II.

40. A difficult sentence in A, not clarified by Gertz's emendations or by the paraphrase in S: 'But as the law had to be settled on many matters, King Knut instigated it, and it originated from his princely authority.

them the pattern and the need for obedience.'

Moreover, he wanted so to suit himself to the wishes of the warriors by his merciful and gentle disposition that he himself might prescribe for

41. *Placuit igitur exercitatus* (A): reconstructed by Gertz as *placuit igitur (regem) exerci(tu comi)tatum*.
42. This injunction is put near the beginning of WR, and Saxo puts something similar in the mouth of King Athelstan of England (GD, 269; EC, 3–4). Sven's *vultus hylaritatem exhibere* reflects Proverbs 16: 15, *In hilaritate vultus regis vita*.
43. *recumpensantes*: rare, but found by Quicherat in Gregory the Great, Aldhelm and Bede.
44. *Frustra . . . exigit qui quod debet non impendit*: another canonist's maxim. *Frustra petit debitum qui quod debet non impendit* is no. 35 in the brocards of Damasus (completed 1215–30).
45. *principis maiestate illibata* could mean 'without committing treason'. The *crimen laesae maiestatis* is invoked as early as *c*.1140 in a charter-writ of King Erik III protecting the monks of Næstved (DD, i:2, no. 79), and in 1158–62 Valdemar I also threatened offenders against his *maiestas* in his charters for Esrum and Ringsted (DD, i:2, nos. 128, 131).
46. A reference both to the usual calendar and to the January festival of the pagan Romans. Isidore insisted that the church fasted on 1 Jan. *propter errorem gentilitatis* (*De ecclesiasticis officiis*, ch. 41; PL 83, 774), and the canonists anethematized those who celebrated the day *ritu paganorum* (*Decretum*, pt 2, causa xxvi, quaest. vii, cc. xv–xvi).
47. Saxo dates the discharge as the first of the Kalends of Jan., WR similarly as the eighth evening of Yule (i.e. after nones on 31 Dec.).
48. *causis hujusmodi incantationis antidotum*: 'enchantment' ('Dølgesang', HS, 13) fits here, but it may be that we should take it that the remedy was inspired by Ovid's song cited below, cf. n. 49, and Sven's phrase rendered 'antidote from the Song'. In Valdemar IV's privilege for Malmö (1360) *incantare* is used to mean 'warn, give notice' in the legal sense (DGK, 30), but a 'remedial summonsing' here in Sven would be too clumsy.
49. From Ovid, *Remedia Amoris*, 91–2: *Principiis obsta . . .* It is also cited at the beginning of the *Vita* (*c*.1230) of St William of Æbelholt (VSD, 302).
50. This next sentence is not from Ovid, who took the opposite view in *Ex Ponto*, ii 2, 59: *Vulnus id genus est . . .* Gertz detected a debt to John of Salisbury's *Policraticus*, iv 8 (ed. Webb, i 262), but the sentiment is

also in the prologue to the *Decreti* and *Panormia* (c.1096) of Ivo of Chartres: *et nunc ferro secat, cui fomento subvenire non poterat* (PL 161, 48); cf. Sven: *Ferro enim resecanda sunt vulnera, que fomentorum non senserunt medicinam* (SM, i 76).

51. *iniuriam viz. inferendo*: for a fuller definition of personal affronts and actionable insults see e.g. the Norwegian Gulathing Law, chs. 195–6 (NGL, i 69–70).

52. *Huskarlastefna*: 'muster of retainers', like the Norw. *hirðstefna*, the house-meeting of the king's followers. This has been seen as the embryo of the Danish parliament (*danehof*) by e.g. Riis, 256–60, and as the equivalent of the supposed 'thing' of the London *þingamenn*: for objections see p. 12 above. Saxo avoids giving the court a name and refers to it simply as *concio*, 'assembly'; but Sven means to insist on the exclusive jurisdiction of this court over members of the household.

53. *Witterlog mannæ* (A): Saxo deals with the procedure for the prosecution of lesser offences only in connexion with the plea of wrongful displacement at table. Thus the citation of the two *proxime circumsedentes* as oath-helpers to the plaintiff appears to relate to this kind of charge rather than to others (see n. 61 below). Cf. the Schleswig Law, ch. 15 (DGK, i 6), for a burgher's purgation with 'five neighbours chosen three from his right-hand side and two from his left'. The procedure agrees in principle with the provisions of the Gulathing Law, ch. 187 (NGL, i 68), 'On quarrelling in an ale-house', except that the accused's immediate table-mates (*sessar*) or his messmates (*mǫtunautar*) or his nearby table-mates (*násessar*) were cited in that order for the defence, or failing them men from among the drinkers in general; and if convicted he paid fifteen marks to the king and double compensation to the injured.

54. There is no provision for rebutting the charge. Saxo (GD, 295; EC, 40) made much of this omission, as proof of the inflexible veracity of the ancients.

55. *constitutione ... generali cautum est*: the civilians (and the canonists) distinguished between the general and the personal *constitutio*. In this context the distinction is not obviously useful, although the provisions for the treatment of the *nithing* might perhaps have qualified as personal.

56. *controversia de fundis et agris*: not in Saxo, but WR, ch. 8, begins *Of iortha dela ær*. Sven may have had ODan. *iorth oc akær* in mind.

57. According to Valdemar II's Jutland Law (ii, ch. 44; DGL, ii 219), *boran* is 'when a man enters another man's enclosure and takes away

any of his cattle or clothes or weapons or anything else to the value of half a mark in money.' It is one of several varieties of *ran*, or daylight robbery. In civil courts, conviction meant compensating the injured party and paying three marks to the king.

58. *ius venditionis* (A and S): emended by Gertz, following Kinch, 260, to *ius vendi(ca)tionis*, the Roman law action respecting title to property, as in *Digest*, 44, 7, 24, and Azo, 215, on *Institutes*, iv, tit. vi, c. 15, defining *vindicatio* and *condictio*.

59. *in suo cetu, id est fjarthing*: this fourth part of the *hird* must therefore have consisted of more than seven men, but this makes the total size of the force in Sven's day no easier to calculate, *pace* Skyum-Nielsen, 205 and n. 13. WR, § 4, says that a man should be summoned in his *sveet* and in his *fiarthing*: no proof that *sveet* was a subdivision of the *fiarthing*. ON *sveit* is a common and early word for a band of men, later conventionally numbered at a dozen; cf. Hjärne, 85, 100, and Kinch, 275-6.

60. *prescriptionem . . . tueatur*: in Roman law a title based on 30 years' occupation, but Anders Sunesen used the word to express Dan. *hævd*, a claim to land made good by three years' possession, like the Roman *usucapio*; see Azo, 215 and 770, and for the canonist view of prescription, Bernard of Pavia, 53-6; for *de prescripcione* in Scanian law see DGL, i:2, 510. Saxo says nothing of these property cases.

61. These oath-helpers are the *sessar* of Norwegian law; see n. 53 above. The *vetus constitutio* must be the rules prior to Absalon's codification, rather than an imaginary reconstruction of the precepts of Øpi the Wise.

62. *humani sanguinis insidiator, prosperitatis emulus, iusticie calumniator*: Satan is called *insidiator* by Anders Sunesen, Hex., 6219, one among many including Gregory the Great. Anders Sunesen was also to blame 'the enemy of the human race' for the homicidal tendencies of the Danes in his Scanian laws, ch. 43 (DGL, i:2, 552).

63. The 'organological' model again; see n. 24 above. Aconite, or wolf's bane, was best known from Ovid, *Metamorphoses*, vii 416-19, where Medea attempts to poison Theseus with this herb.

64. *iracundie accensus furore*: another parallel with Alexander the Great who, according to Seneca, *Ep*. 113, 'though victor over so many kings and peoples, fell victim to anger.' In Saxo's version of the story Knut was drunk.

65. *ambigua sententia . . . indulgentia*: the *quaestio* is an interesting one, bearing in mind the maxim that 'the rank of the offender aggravates the

offence' (Damasus, rule no. 62) and the Roman law presumption in favour of the prince's immunity. In his note on Saxo's book ten Stephanius noted how many ancient legislators were supposed to have broken their own laws: Lycurgus, Pericles, Solon, Zaleucus of Locris, Charondas the Thurian, Tennes of Sidon. Peter of Blois reminded Henry II that 'even Alexander the Great was fearlessly prosecuted by his fellow-soldiers before a military tribunal and condemned' (*Ep.* 95; PL 207, 302). However, Sven may be arguing for the accountability of kings, or he may be inventing a precedent for the indulgence shown to his own grandfather later on in ch. 12. He may be building on the well-known story that Knut had ordered the killing of his own follower, Ulf Jarl; but that tale involves payment of compensation, to Ulf's widow, Knut's sister, who afterwards apportioned it 'as a tithe' to Trinity church in Roskilde (so in Saxo, GD, 293, EC, 36; straight to the church in which Ulf was killed in Snorri's *Óláfs saga helga*, ch. 145 in *Den store Saga*, ch. 153 in *Heimskringla*). Cf. n. 67 below.

66. *ne in posterum traheretur inconsequentiam* (A): Gertz emended the last word to *inde consequentiam*, in which case it would mean 'so that no consequence was to be drawn from it in future', i.e., that it was not to serve as a precedent. However, *inconsequentia* occurs in Quintilian, and the prospect of men drawing the 'wrong' conclusion from the king's self-abasement needed to be averted.

67. In Saxo's version the homicide is expiated by a royal submission to the court, followed by a verdict that the king should punish himself. Knut paid a huge fine of 360 marks of silver plus nine marks of gold, to be divided equally among the king, the warriors and the kinsmen of the victim. The king assigned his share to the church. This is a brash distortion of the story Sven tells about his own grandfather in ch. 12, which Saxo omits.

68. *nithingsorth*: ON *níðingsorð* or *níðingsnafn*, the name of utter vileness incurred on conviction of quite a large category of crimes in Norway; see the Gulathing Law, ch. 178 (NGL, i 66). The name of *nithing* occurs less frequently in Danish codes, but the outlaw status that went with it was the ordinary penalty for varieties of aggravated homicide, rape and arson specified in the ordinances of Knut VI and Valdemar II and in Anders Sunesen's Scanian laws, ch. 61 (DGL, i:2, 552, 721, 732). The name also went with expulsion from the Odense gild.

69. *in sequentibus clarius edocebimus*: the reference is to HC, see p. 64, where Sven claims that Harthaknut was not in fact harsh or cruel but

was named after the province where he was born. Knut is called 'old' Knut in three sets of annals; see DMA, 83, 161, 268.
70. Nicolaus reigned from 1103/4 to 1134. According to Saxo (GD, 342; EC, 108), he reduced his ordinary guard to a detail of six or seven warriors; according to *Knýtlinga saga*, ch. 94, he maintained a larger following later.
71. *Christiernus Suenonis filius*: Kristiarn was apparently a magnate in Jutland, an open enemy of King Nicolaus in the civil war of 1131–4, and a king-maker in 1137 (GD, 360–1, 367, 371; EC, 134–6, 350, 356). In HC, ch. 14, Sven relates that, after losing the battle of Rønbjerg in 1132, Kristiarn was captured by Nicolaus and imprisoned at Schleswig. He was held in irons, the deepest insult of all. After 1134, according to Saxo, he advised Erik II to murder his nephews, for reasons of security.
72. *Turidokæ* (A), *Thukonem Dokæ* (S), *Thura Doka* (WR): Thuri cannot be identified. *Tilnavne*, s.n., identifies his by-name as either the Frisian personal name *Doke* or as ON *doki*, 'strip', but the latter is a non-existent word, see Fritzner IV, s.v. Thuri's addition might be the same as ON *dokka*, 'windlass; doll', found as a by-name in Norway; see *Personbinamn*, 62. Was this the first wounding between the king's men, or the first mitigation of the penalty of outlawry?
73. Asser was archbishop and metropolitan from 1104 to his death in 1137. All contemporary sources confirm Sven's view of his importance.
74. Sven was bishop of Viborg 1133–53. He cannot have been bishop at the time of this incident, which must predate the civil war of 1131–4.
75. The Cistercian author of the *Exordium Magnum* records that Eskil and his brothers *inter . . . proceres post regem videbantur sublimiores*, and that Eskil fought for King Erik Emune and died on pilgrimage about 1153–4 (SM, ii 437–9).
76. *Sueno filius* (A), *Sveno filius Trugoti* (S), *Swen Thrundason* (WR): see the Appendix on Sven Aggesen's family, p. 141.
77. *Wandalum* (A), *af Wænla* (WR): i.e. from Vendel or Vendsyssel, the northern extremity of Jutland. Freeman called him 'Boethius the Wend'.
78. *taxatio humana*: not here in the civil law sense of a 'delimiting clause', but as in Anders Sunesen, Hex., 2866–9: 'certain things cannot by right be bought or sold, since there is no *taxatio justa* of their value . . .' Thus, 'scale, tariff' (of compensations).
79. *opere precium*: a cliché of medieval latinists, including Theodricus (MHN, 3) and Abbot William of Æbelholt (SM, i 176).

80. *gyrsum*: ON *gersemi*, *gørsemi*, 'jewel, costly and precious thing'. The term is not used in WN or Swedish laws but is explained in Valdemar II's Jutland Law as a payment added to *bot* to placate the more powerful kinsmen of the injured party (DGL, ii 190, 395–6). Stephanius, 186, noted the proverb, 'Awe makes most *gørsum*'. In the Scanian Law it is called *iwirbøther* (cf. WN *yfirbœtr*) and came to 26$^{2}/_{3}$ silver marks over the 30 mark *mantzboodth* (DGL, i:2, 755). In the 1284 Schleswig Law *gørsum* of one gold mark was payable in addition to the *bot* for homicide (DGK, i 4). King Erik's Sjælland Law refers to the stranded whales and sturgeon that belonged to the king's household as *gørsums fisk* (DGL, v 354). The tripling of the normal *bot* of 40 marks for homicide is also found in the ordinances of King Abel and King Kristofer (apparently issued 1251–9) which laid down that 'if a *hirdman* (*decurion*) kills another *hirdman*, he shall be obliged to pay compensation for homicide three times over, and three sums of forty marks, so that he hands over the first to the heirs of the slain man, the second to the king, and the third to the community of the court' (DR, 44). The same applied to wounding. Here, however, Sven says nothing of the nature of the sums paid by Kristiarn: they are *pena, satisfactio* and *emendatio*, without distinction. It may be that he takes the payment of ordinary compensation for wounding for granted. If this really was the law in the royal household before 1200, it served as a model for the aggravation of penalties for homicide found in the royal ordinances after that date and introduced to the provincial laws. Anders Sunesen complained that in the older law of Scania the payment for homicide never exceeded fifteen marks (DGL, i:2, 522); but in the new law, aggravated homicides incurred additional payments of 80 marks (DGL, i:2, 550). Saxo applies the compensation-story to the account of Knut the law-breaker, and raises the sum to 360 marks plus nine gold marks (GD, 297–8; EC, 43). Thus he sees the payment as *sui generis*, not as a precedent: a sign of royal magnanimity rather than of royal weakness, as in Sven.

81. The allocation of the third payment to the rest of the warriors anticipates the ordinances of King Abel and King Kristofer (see n. 80 above) and is paralleled by the rules of the gild of St Knut at Flensburg, chs. 4 and 30; see Nyrop, 8, 12.

82. Cf. p. 88, n. 20, above.

83. *Aggi thuer* (A), *Aggo Thuer* (S), *Aggi Thwer* (WR): presumably ODan. *thuær*, 'cross, contrary', perhaps in the sense 'gaaende paa tværs, skæv'; cf. *Tilnavne*, s.n. *Thwer*.

84. *Esgi Ebbonis filium in Warwath functum villicatione* (A), *Æsgi Ebbesun Bryte aff Wartwik* (WR): i.e., he was bailiff or reeve in charge of Varde, a royal manor and administrative centre 25 miles NW of Ribe in West Jutland. *Ebbe villicus* witnessed King Nicolaus's grant of a share in the Lønborg fishery to the Odense churches (DD, i:2, no. 34): Esger's father? Esger's membership of the household is evidence that it included administrative officials, or that members of the household were appointed to act as such; see N. C.Hansen, 89–90. Esger was *sub regis ascella* (A); for the sense of 'wing, protection' for *ascella*, 'armpit', see Blaise, 99.

85. *in Burgh, in Guidonis ede stabularii* (A), *at Withe Staller i Byrgh* (WR): 'Wido' the staller, with the stallers 'Johannes' and 'Wolff', witnessed King Nicolaus's privilege for St Knut's at Odense (1104–17; DD, i:2, no. 32). Borg is too common a place-name element for identification, but there is a strong argument for believing it was the hall at Nonnebakken in Odense; see N. C. Hansen, 84–9.

86. *in Lymum* (A), *in Lynum* (S), *i Limum* (v.l. *Lund*)(WR): identified as Lime or Lihme, which lies off Venø Bugt at the west end of the Limfjord in North Jutland, in Rødding herred in Salling. That must be the place, for in the 1170s another Bo Ketilsen was living at Lime; see N. C. Hansen, 84.

87. Saxo emphasizes the indiscipline and degeneracy of modern warriors about the court, and blames 'the princes of our time', i.e. Knut VI and Valdemar II, for their tolerance and partiality. Here, Sven seems to be alluding to tensions within the household resulting from the civil wars of 1131–57.

88. Blows with the fist or a stick were highly actionable in Danish civil law, classed as *Stangehug*. Both the Scanian laws and Valdemar's Sjælland Law made all violence against the person without weapons liable to a three-mark fine, and the charge could only be rebutted by a twelve-man oath. If an attack with a stick had been sworn to by two men, it could only be denied by going to the ordeal; otherwise the *bot* was of six marks. According to Anders Sunesen, 'more shame accompanies the beaten man from the rod than the wounded man from the wound' (DGL, i:2, 560). Saxo states that blows finally became subject to compensation payment, but not blows with a stick 'because this was how dogs were driven off, and our proud ancestors attached deep disgrace to a shameful blow' (GD, 297; EC, 42).

89. *eius pedibus geniculari*: *geniculor* in the sense of 'kneel' is post-

classical; S prefers the more classical *pedibus advolveretur*. Saxo says nothing of this.

90. *cum sex commilitionibus suam aboleat infamiam* (A): Saxo agrees; WR mentions the *siax manna eth* only in connexion with charges of *boran* or property claims. *Is qui calumniatur*: 'he who has brought a claim' rather than a 'false claim'; see Holberg, 271, and Eskil's Villingerød charter of 1176–4 (DD, i:2, no. 184) for a lawful *calumpnia* by a canon of Lund.

91. *aut sciens aut ignarus* (A): Saxo has less to say about this class of offence, but Anders Sunesen discusses it in his Scanian laws, ch. 67: 'If anyone wounds another by chance . . . the injured party shall not receive less than the whole compensation on that account, because it cannot lessen the injury that it was inflicted by chance rather than by design . . . but nothing is owed for this to the king or the bishop.' If challenged by the king's or bishop's officer, the accused can establish his innocence by a twelve-man oath including himself and the injured party (DGL, i:2, 662). The Old Serpent who is blamed for this problem by Sven was tracked by Gertz to Revelations 12: 9 and 20: 2. Among many other contexts, he occurs in prayers for the reconsecration of violated churches and cemeteries in the Lund Pontifical (Strömberg, 106, 151).

92. According to Saxo, six oath-helpers were needed to establish inadvertent injury.

93. *iuxta formam pretaxatam* (X): i.e. by kneeling before the injured party.

94. *ignorantia a transgressionis (peccato) non excusare* (X): Gertz inserted *peccato* but *reatu* (S) seems better: this is a question of liability, not of sin. The maxim is common to many legal systems; *Leges Henrici Primi*, ch. 90, 11a, claims that 'it is a rule of law that a person who unwittingly commits a crime shall wittingly make amends,' and cites an OE saw to the same effect.

95. Here Gertz inserted a passage, which may be translated: 'that all the warriors serving together in the household must know each other. For that is dealt with in the general ordinance by which it is ordered that . . .' The second sentence he took from S. The preceding passage appears to be his own invention but, as he admits, it is an improbable rule (Gertz, 152). The whole in S reads: 'For by the same laws it was forbidden that any man should smirch the flower of military renown with the soot of ignorance. For it is fitting to live honourably, and men of noble blood should not blacken titles of honour with slothful

ignorance. Therefore it was determined by a general ordinance that
...' This is awkward too, but may be just as close to the original as X.
96. *omnes controversias quae legum discisione sunt divisae* (A): *discissio*
makes little sense here, but Gertz keeps it; S reads *decisio*. I suggest a
misread *legum discussione*, in the common ecclesiastical sense of
'trial'; see Niermeyer, s.v.
97. The last word of the sentence is missing in A. Gertz proposed *gradum*
or *culmen* to agree with *ultimum*; Kroman preferred *cumulum*. The
ladder of sin is in A, and may be traced from Pseudo-Augustine, for
example, although in quite a different sense from Sven's: 'We make a
ladder of our vices, if we tread down the vices themselves' (Sermon
176, 4; PL 38, 2082). All other authors, including St Bernard, see the
steps of sin as leading downwards; this may be one of Sven's misunderstandings (cf. n. 107).
98. *principis sui perditionem vel mortem ... aggreditur machinari*: Sven
does not name the *crimen laesae maiestatis* here, *pace* Fenger 1989, 51;
the words occur in the chapter-title in S and in the passage supplied by
Gertz to make good the following gap in A and S (see n. 101).
99. WR has *iudas wærk at winna meth ilt rath gen herra sinum*; Saxo *si
maiestati insidias struxisset*. Inspired by WR, Gertz reconstructed *quod
inde proditoris* in A as *quod Jude proditoris*. This makes good sense.
It does not follow that 'Judas's work' was a common phrase for
treachery (it occurs nowhere else), but it seems rather that the Danish
author of the WR was translating Sven as best he could. See p. 16
above for the significance of Judas, who appeared as the type of treason
and regicide in the *legenda* both of St Knut of Odense and of St Knut
of Ringsted (VSD, 114, 116, 151, 198, 214).
100. The old Scanian Law, ch. 90 (DGL, i:1, 69), states that the outlaw
loses all his goods to the king but not his lands. Anders Sunesen's
version, ch. 62 (DGL, i:2, 553), claims that 'in a certain case, the real
estate as well as the moveables are awarded to the king's majesty, that
is, when anyone dares to enter the kingdom with hostile intent to attack
the king.' This is probably a case of clarification rather than innovation. As Riis has pointed out, there are examples of the confiscation of
lands for treason going back, in his opinion, to the 1140s. I would
suggest further back still, to the 1120s, with the disinheriting and
degradation of Jarl Elef as related in Saxo (GD, 344–5; EC, 112).
101. A gap in both A and S at this point is filled by Gertz with a lengthy
text confected from Saxo and WR, see Gertz, 44. Saxo's version of the
outlawry procedure for graver crimes, including treason, involves three

summonses of the accused, an unanswerable attestation of guilt by only two accusers, and a verdict by the whole court. Then the condemned man could choose to depart by land or sea. If by sea, then he was given a boat, food, water, sail and oars. WR, § 4, implies that, on the contrary, the accused could clear himself by going to the ordeal. Whatever the procedure described by Sven, it probably differed little from Saxo's, and was omitted as giving the accused rights curtailed by the legislation of the 1250s, e.g. to an oral summons, superseded by *literae ammonitoriae* in DR, 45.

102. *Favonii favor non affuerit* (X), *Favonio non favente* (S), *favoni favor non faverit* (A): A is clumsy but should stand: the alliteration and repetition are typical. *Favonius* just means 'a light, unsteady wind' in *Thesaurus Novus*, 224.

103. *terno quasi classici clangore* (X), *classico clangore* (A and S). Sven evidently intended to liken the yell to the *classicum*, 'battle trumpet or signal', as in *Aeneid*, ii 313, vii 637. This rough music is like, but not the same as, the *vapnatak*, outlawry of a man 'by words, and the clashing and rattle of weapons', described in the Scanian laws (DGL i:1, 112, i:2, 592).

104. *si in solo natali extiterit* (X): this phrase suggests that the accused was not given the choice of exile as in Saxo (*terra profugere maluisset*), but made to float if overseas and take to the wilds if in Denmark.

105. King Erik's Sjælland Law gave the fugitive outlaw the rest of the day and all night to escape into the woods. After that he could be chased or killed (DGL, v 93).

106. Literally, 'shall incur the penalty of throwing out with the word of shameful naming'—*probose nuncupationis* in S. Saxo repeated this provision, which is in the spirit of his imaginary laws of King Frothi: 'He also ruled that any of the military who sought a name for proven courage must attack a single opponent, take on two, evade three by stepping back a short distance, and only be unashamed when he ran from four adversaries' (GD, 133; PF, 148). In his LC he added to the ceremonies of outlawry a solemn curse by the bishops of Knut's three kingdoms (DR, 39).

107. The image illustrates Priscian's *Quanto iuniores, tanto perspicatiores* (*Institutes*, prol.), and was ascribed to Bernard of Chartres (d. 1130) by John of Salisbury (*Metalogicon*, iii 4). It was used by Alan of Lille in the prologue to AC and by Peter of Blois (*Ep.*, 92; PL 207, 290), and Otto of Freising explained it at length in the preface to book five of the *Chronicle of Two Cities*. Sven sees himself as a

superannuated dwarf, unsupported by the gigantic learning of the Ancients, which will be at the disposal of his successors. Or perhaps, as Gertz imagined, he is saying to those successors: 'It is certainly possible that you can put the theme on which I have written into a finer and more decorative Latin style than I have achieved: but you owe the whole foundation to me' (HS, 29 n. 1, and Gertz, 158 n.). The passage is not in S.

108. *verborum scematibus oratione . . . falerata* (X): Gertz was reminded of Quintilian's *schemata orationis* (*Institutes*, ix 1, 1) and of the *phalerata dicta* of Terence's *Phormio*, i 500 (3, 12, 16). This is another commonplace: cf. Geoffrey of Monmouth's disclaimer, *tametsi infra alienos ortulos falerata verba non collegerim*, and *rhetoricis fucata schematibus* in the prologue of *De profectione Danorum* (SM, ii 459). Kinch made the unlikely deduction that Sven used the adj. *phaleratus*, lit. 'ornamented on breast and head', of his *oratio*, because he was a knight in armour rather than a cleric: demolished by Holberg, 268–9. Sven's own real or assumed modesty, and his insistence on harmony, decorum, and restraint among the knights, cast doubt on Jaeger's claim, 136–7, that 'the vocabulary and concepts of courtliness' are entirely Saxo's contribution to the *Vederlov* and that 'there is no trace of them in the text of Sven Aggesen.'

NOTES ON THE SUPPLEMENT TO THE LEX CASTRENSIS

1. Acc. pl. with suffixed article, *witherloghen*, may here mean simply 'the penalties'; cf. p. 86, n. 4. *Witherlag, -log* is used both of the law that bound the body of retainers and of that body itself; it is kept in the translation and is to be understood according to context.
2. *rætta . . . rætheligha male therra*: 'hand over readily their pay'. The verb *rætta* is not construed with a dat. object and *male* is best taken as the relic of an original *mala*, acc. sg. of *mali*, 'contracted pay, esp. for military service' (cf. p. 80, n. 36). (The form *male* was perhaps influenced by *at første male*, 'first', in the opening clause of the sentence.) This word does not seem to appear in dictionaries of older Danish but is common in early Swedish and WN sources. Cf. von Schwerin, 195 and n. 2 there for refs. The clause in WR then answers in all brevity to Sven's: *Opere precium etiam fuit adnectere, ut stipendia militibus suis, cum usus uel necessitas postulauisset, sine mora omnique contradictione remota ministraret . . .* (p. 36 above).
3. The numbers in, and even the distinction between, these 'company' and *fjarthing* divisions of the *Witherlag* are uncertain. Cf. p. 94, n. 59.
4. *skulde han . . . latæ after sigia thiæneste sin meth twa witherlaghæ mæn*: the same construction as in § 4 above: *skulde han* [the king] *. . . meth twa witherlagha men latæ hannum . . . stefna*. On the timing cf. p. 92, n. 47.
5. The text has pl. *men*.
6. On *boran* see p. 93, n. 57.
7. (Kristiarn, Aggi) 'used a weapon on': here and at the beginning of the next paragraph for the indeterminate *hio* of the text.
8. On *gørsom* see p. 97, n. 80.
9. *vnder Niclis kunungs arm*: this looks like a literal translation of Sven's *sub regis ascella Nicolai* (p. 41) but perhaps by someone who did not understand *ascella* in its postulated metaphorical sense (p. 98, n. 84). At least, there appears to be no record of an idiom 'under someone's arm' in the early Scandinavian languages meaning 'under someone's protection, wing' (*pace* Alboge, 309), though the phrase *undir hendi e–s* in that sense is well attested. On Borg see p. 98, n. 85.

NOTES ON THE SHORT HISTORY

1. *perspicabar* (A), *perspicerem* (S): passive for active voice, perhaps by analogy with dep. *sus-*, *con-* and *de-spicari* (Gertz, 174). Sven uses it to mean 'note' or 'perceive', and later, SM, i 140, *oculata fide perspicabar* is used for his admiring the Queen Mother. This is the sort of eccentricity the S text tends to smooth out. I cannot find an earlier example than in the late twelfth-century *Thesaurus Novus*, 524. The 'books of the ancients' is a frequent *topos* among historians of this period, and the demands of unrecorded virtue another; see Curtius, 85-9, and Simon, 71-83. The closest analogue seems to be Regino of Prüm's Preface to his *Chronicon*. Gertz changed *diutius . . . gemitibus* in A to *diurnis . . .* because A reads *diurne* for *divino* in the proem to LC. But S has *diutinis* here, and to sigh every day or all day over this matter seems excessive; cf. Gertz, 139.
2. *commendibilia . . . quis conatur commendare . . . detractionis . . . declinabat dispendium*: an attempt to reproduce Sven's frequent alliteration has been made in the translation. 'As the world grows old . . .' is another common theme, also in LC, p. 31, and in *De Profectione Danorum*, ch. 1: 'As the world draws to its close, and various evils grow more frequent . . .' (SM, ii 460). It can be traced back to St Gregory in his *Epistola ad Leandro* (*Moralia in Iob*, i 2), and was used in the prologue to Fredegar's *Chronicle*. In justifying his efforts, Sven employs the same *topos* as the Encomiast of Emma and Einhard in his prologue to the *Vita Karoli*: 'the dignity of the subject outweighs the author's failings.' See Simon, 85-7, 91-2.
3. Martianus Capella, viii 831, on the constellations visible from the antarctic circle, which he forbore to describe 'lest my unverified statement appear to smack of falsehood'. See Gertz, 51 and 111, nn., for two possible echoes of Martianus later on: the debt is very small. The appeal to the more learned and polished latinists of the future is also in *De Profectione Danorum* (SM, ii 459-60). On the *topos* of humility see Simon, 101-2, 108-19.
4. *ab annosis* (= living ancients) *et veteribus* (= dead authorities); but Gertz preferred 'hos aarrige og gamle Hjemmelsmænd' (HS, 35). The memory of Sven's father and of his uncle, Archbishop Eskil, will have extended back at least to the 1120s, but there is little sign that Sven used any personal recollections or old men's tales in HC. This is another historian's *topos*; see Simon, 91 and 89-90.
5. A generalization translated quite differently by J. Olrik ('The same

disposition is not to be found among all men, for as with peasants, so with princes . . .', KV, 36) and by Gertz ('For as for peasants, so also for princes and magnates, there is a natural condition to all, that . . .', HS, 35), but it comes to much the same thing: different forms of emulation affect man's nature whether he be of high or low birth. Sven is not simply endorsing the anti-rustic proverbs of the time (e.g. Walther, 27001, 27002, 27024a, 27026, 27028), nor the obsequiousness of William of Malmesbury in his epistle to Robert, earl of Gloucester, at the beginning of *De Gestis Regum*: 'The lower classes make the virtues of their superiors their own by venerating those great actions to the practice of which they cannot themselves aspire' (tr. Giles). Sven later praises the *plebs Scanensium* (p. 70).

6. *retexat oratio*: perhaps simply 'narrate', but *retexere* is used in the sense of 'restore to life' in Ovid, *Metamorphoses*, x 31 and xv 249. *priscorum annositas* is lit. 'the agedness of our earliest forbears'.

7. Note the resemblance to the opening lines of *Beowulf*; but the immediate source must be a version of the pedigree of the *Oddaverjar* confected by the Icelander Sæmundr Sigfússon before 1133, on which see Bjarni Guðnason, 175–7, Jakob Benediktsson, 60–1, and A. Olrik, 396–412. To the Icelanders Skjǫldr was little more than a name: a son of Óðinn in *Skjǫldunga saga* and the pedigrees in *Flat.*, i 26, 27; a son of Skelfir in *Flat.*, i 25; or of *Heremóð* in *Edda Snorra*, 4. The ruler as shielder of his land was a poetic commonplace; see Malmros 1985, 120, for a table of examples from the skalds. The derivation of kingship from the useful function of defence rather than from depredation (*latrocinium* in St Augustine) is found in Justin, i 1: 'The custom was to protect the boundaries of empire rather than to push them outwards; kingship was confined to the native land.'

8. *Modis Hislandensibus skiolding* (A), *Skioldunger* (S): see *Lexicon Poeticum* for many references. It seems likely that a personal name Skjǫldr was formed from *skjǫldungr*, 'shield-bearer', rather than vice versa. In *Hyndluljóð*, st. 16, *Skjǫldungar, Skilfingar, Qðlingar, Ynglingar* and *Ylfingar* all appear as descendants of Hálfdan, and Hálfdan himself was 'the highest of the *Skjǫldungar*'.

9. Frothi and Halfdan appeared as father and son in the Icelandic pedigrees seventeen generations below Skiold. Here Sven uses CL, which introduced Helgi and 'Haldanus' as sons of Ro, ruling the sea and the land respectively.

10. According to *Skjǫldunga saga* Hálfdan was killed by Ingjaldr (AJ, 22); but Sven needs a primeval fratricide on the model of Romulus. For

the ramifications of the story see A. Olrik, 294–301. Gertz interpreted the *super regni ambitione* of A and S as *semper* . . . ; but *super* makes sense. 'Sole authority' (*monarchia*) is in the exordium of the 1186 diploma, DD, i:3, no. 134.

11. In CL, ch. 7, and in *Skjǫldunga saga* Helgi was the Viking and his brother 'Roas' stayed at home and was killed by his nephews, Hrœrekr and Fróði, sons of Ingjaldr (AJ, 26). Sven avoids telling the story of Helgi's rape and incest found in CL (SM, i 47–8), but gives him the Ciceronian title of *archipirata*.

12. Rolf Kraki: not in A, supplied in S; cf. CL, ch. 7. The full story is in Saxo (GD, 48–62; PF, 51–64) and in *Hrólfs saga kraka*. Sven summarizes the account given in CL; on the Hrólfr of the sagas see Bjarni Guðnason, 162–73.

13. CL emphasizes the wealth and importance of Lejre in early times. It was not mentioned in KVJ of *c*.1230, and appears in the 1688 landregister as a churchless hamlet of six farms within the parish of Allerslev. The recent discovery there of post-holes indicating a large hall suggests that it was not insignificant as late as *c*.1000. The bishops of Roskilde owned land in Allerslev in the fourteenth century (SRD, vii 66, 120), and the contiguous manor of Kornerup was assigned to the chapter by the bishop before 1194 (DD, 1:3, no. 118). On the Lejre (*Hleiðra*) of the sagas see A. Olrik, 324–47, and H. Andersen. It was only of passing interest to Sven, as a *topos* of vanished greatness, like Walter of Châtillon's lines on Troy, *Alexandreis*, i 464–7.

14. *Rokill* . . . *Slagenback* (A), *Rokil* . . . *Slaghenback* (S): alias Hrœrekr hnǫggvan(d)baugi, Hrœrekr slǫngvan(d)baugi, two separate rulers in Icelandic sources, one the miser, the other the flinger of rings. This version of the by-name, like Saxo's *Roricus Slyngebond*, suggests blind copying of a written source (Bjarni Guðnason, 287). In *Skjǫldunga saga* he is the son of Hálfdan, not of Hrólfr. Sven appears to discard CL at this point because it gave Rolf no son. He returns to the Icelandic pedigree, but picks the wrong Hrœrekr, or gives the wrong by-name to the right one; see A. Olrik, 68–74, for the connexion with Hrethric son of Hrothgar in *Beowulf*.

15. *Frothi hin Frökni* (X): the same cognomen is given to Leifr Herleifsson (AJ, 8), but there Fróði is *magnus* and his brother Áli is *hinn fræckne* (AJ, 16–17). In *Ynglinga saga*, ch. 26, Fróði became *hinn frœkni*; by alliteration? CL made Frothi the grandson of Rolf by a daughter (SM, i 52). Saxo put Frothi 'the Active' (*vegetus*) in quite a different context (GD, 101; PF, 110). The pedigrees in *Flat.* made Fróði hinn frœkni son

of Friðleifr and father of Ingjaldr; they made Vermundr the son of an earlier Fróði.

16. *Vermundus... Prudens*: Vermundr hinn vitri in *Skjǫldunga saga*; the *Wærmund* of the Mercian genealogy (*Wermundus* in the Florence of Worcester appendix), and *Warmundus* in the St Albans *Vitæ duorum Offarum* (c.1200). Saxo offers an explanation of the nickname (GD, 94–5; PF, 103–4). The large literature on Vermund and Uffi/Offa is summarized in SG, ii 67–9. Did Sven get the story from England or Denmark or Iceland? The Icelanders knew the name of Vermundr, and Uffi appears to crop up as Óláfr hinn lítilláti (*Flat.*, i 27); the duel on the Eider escaped their notice. *Widsith* and *Beowulf* allude to the duel, which is relocated to the West Midlands in the St Albans *Vitæ*. Sven is the first Northern writer to use this material, and the arguments of Rickert and of Boberg in favour of his borrowing from England are strong, but not overwhelming. The Danish form of the name, Uffi, and the location of the duel on the Eider do not necessarily point to a Danish source. The poet of *Widsith* placed the fight on the Eider, and Sven was capable of naturalizing names. However, the view of Olrik and Chadwick that Sven and Saxo used an independent Danish tradition is still widely held; see Chadwick, ch. 6, and SG, i 93. As the St Albans *Vitæ* are conventionally dated after 1195 (on insecure grounds), Sven cannot have used the surviving text.

17. An allusion to the story of Keti and Vigi who killed Athisl of Sweden to avenge their father Frovin, told at length by Saxo (GD, 95–6; PF, 104–6) and in AR (DMA, 153). Saxo makes Uffi marry the sister of the avenging brothers but does not explain his speechlessness as a result of their deed—there is no necessary connexion here. Uffi's silence, or inertia, appears to have originated as a play on his English name Offa, which is the Latin for 'lump, shapeless mass, abortion': *aufer illam offam porcinam* in Plautus, *Miles gloriosus*, iii 1. Thus the Offa of the St Albans *Vitæ* was blind to the age of seven and dumb to the age of thirty (Chambers, 218–19). Saxo possibly employed this restraint of the *fandi possibilitas* (Martianus Capella, iv 335) as a reference to Knut VI's failure to 'speak out' against German influence until after his accession (cf. n. 20 below; Johannesson, 313).

18. Saxo qualified this statement by claiming that Vermund approved of the deed, although among foreigners it became proverbial as a breach of custom (GD, 97; PF, 106). It seems he interpreted Sven's *gentiles* in a purely ethnic sense rather than as 'the heathen', as in Judith 14: 6. As Kemp Malone pointed out, 'the interpretation of a two-against-one

fight as shameful or unfair has no place in the Heroic Age; such a point of view belongs rather to . . . the Age of Chivalry' (*Widsith*, 134; and see Ellis Davidson, 199–200, and *contra*, Stephanius, 21).

19. He is called *Wermundus Blinde* in AR (DMA, 153) and other Danish sources post 1200; Vermundr hinn vitri in *Skjǫldunga saga* (cf. Boberg, 140–1). In the St Albans *Vitæ* Offa is blind (until his seventh year), Warmundus is merely decrepit.

20. *Transalpinas partes* (A and S): *Transalbinas partes*, 'beyond the Elbe', so Gertz following Langebek; *turgiditate Teutonica intumit*: cf. n. 26 below. The German claim to Denmark, or to overlordship of the Danish king, had been asserted at various times since the 1130s, but according to Saxo was rejected by Knut VI at Absalon's prompting in 1182/3. There was a state of mistrust and covert hostility between Knut and Frederick Barbarossa thereafter, and some fear of Hohenstaufen reprisals for the subjugation of the Pomeranian duke in 1185; see pp. 25–6 above. Sven evidently read contemporary tensions back to the distant past. In *Widsith* Offa's opponents were called Myrgingas. In the St Albans *Vitæ* he fought an ambitious Mercian noble called Riganus or Aliel. But there was another English Offa legend, told by Walter Map, 86–7, in which the Roman emperor laid claim to his kingdom and was frustrated by the champion Gado.

21. *spiculatores* (A and S) occurs in Mark 6: 27 and the St Albans *Vitæ* (Chambers, 242) in the sense of 'executioners'; similarly in Theodricus (MHN, 51). In the Roman army however *speculatores* were special imperial runners or military messengers, which is what is meant here. Garmonsway and Simpson, 223, prefer the earlier sense of 'spearmen'.

22. *Epicureorum more*: cf. the several denunciations of Epicureans as 'followers of vain pleasure' in John of Salisbury's *Policraticus*. According to Salvian of Marseilles, they confused pleasure with virtue, and so God with *incuria* and *torpor* (*De Gubernatione Dei*, i 5); see also Glaber, iii 27.

23. *orationem gestus informaret*: Cicero uses *informare oratorem* in the same way in *Orator ad Brutum*, 9, 33. In the St Albans *Vitæ* Offa also begins to speak *ore facundo, sermone rhethorico* to the astonishment of his hearers (Chambers, 219).

24. Proverbial, although according to Walther, no. 40258, not found earlier than Gruter's *Enchiridion* (1625) in the form *Rebus admirationem raritate compares*.

25. *Sic tantus orsus cæpit ab alto* in A becomes *Sic fatum solio tunc orsus cepit ab alto* in X, which, as Gertz says, is a Leonine hexameter

reminiscent of *Æneid*, xi 301 or ii 2. But *Tandem sic orsus cœpit* in S suggests that the original was *Sic tandem orsus cepit ab alto*, and that the A copyist misread an abbreviated *tandem* as *tantus*; no need for a hexameter.

26. Uffi's scorn arms him with rare words: *turgiditas* is in *Thesaurus Novus*, 587, as an alternative to *turgor*. Alan of Lille uses *ampullositas* twice in *De Planctu Naturæ* (1179–82; PL 210, 467, 468; on arrogance and envy), probably referring to Horace's *proicit ampullas et sesquipedalia verba*. But *comminitatio* is Gertz's unwarranted substitute for *communicatione* (A) and *comminatione* (S): the latter will do, as in Saxo, *sub duelli comminatione* (GD, 186; PF, 206). Sven's formation of abstract nouns strongly recalls Alan of Lille who in the passages cited above also uses *pompositas* and *verbositas*. Gibes at Teutonic pomposity, guile and arrogance were common: e.g. John of Salisbury in the 1160s, *The Letters*, i 205–6, 207; ii 54, 592: *loquuntur grandia, minis tument*; and Suger, *Vita Ludovici Grossi*, 56, 60.

27. For 'haughty voice' Gertz recalls *voce superba*, *Æneid*, vii 544; cf. Statius, *Thebaid*, xi 360, and elsewhere: here there is a hexameter. The assertion of hereditary monarchy resembles the St Albans *Vitæ*, where Offa announces that he will not 'abandon the fatherland which hitherto the successive members of our family have held by hereditary right' (Chambers, 219). In Denmark Valdemar I had devoted many years to ensuring the succession of his son Knut, but Knut had to face opposition, both in Jutland on his accession and in the revolt of two pretenders from collateral branches, Harald Skrænk in 1183 and Bishop Valdemar of Schleswig in 1192.

28. In the St Albans *Vitæ* Offa I is introduced as 'tall of stature, whole of body, and most elegantly shaped' (Chambers, 218–19); Saxo emphasized his hugeness (GD, 98; PF, 107).

29. *mucronem expientissimum* (A), *mucronem experientissimum* (S): as in 2 Maccabees 8: 9, *in bellicis rebus experientissimo*, 'a captain who in matters of war had great experience'. That must be right, although Gertz preferred *mucronem exuperantissimum*, which is a superlative used only by Appuleius among the ancients, once in *De Platone* and twice in *De Mundo*, of the attributes of the supreme being (*Opuscules philosophiques*, 72, 146, 150). I doubt that Sven read these pieces or developed *exsuperans* (Ovid and Aulus Gellius) on his own initiative. Saxo names the sword *Skrep* and laboriously explains why it was hidden: when brought to light it seemed so brittle and corroded that Uffi durst not test it before battle.

30. *intersigniis* (X), 'among the characters', following S; *inter singulis* in A. *Intersignum* could mean 'brand' in twelfth-century France (Niermeyer, s.v.), and Alan of Lille used pl. *intersigna* (AC, iv 188); *intersignium* (Bailey's appendix to Forcellini). As elsewhere, Gertz's preference is open to doubt. Garmonsway and Simpson, 225, translate 'by means of tokens marked on the rocks'; Gertz, HS, 41, 'anbragt med Mellemrum ved Mærker paa Stenene', which is better. No doubt Sven had runes in mind. On Nordic swords in grave-mounds see SG, ii 69; but a closer analogue is the story of King Ægeus of Athens who left his son Theseus a sword under a rock, and who later cast himself into the sea in the belief that Theseus was dead (Hyginus, *Fables*, xliii: Ariadne). In the St Albans *Vitæ* the episode is reduced to 'the king ... girded his son with a sword in a solemn royal ceremony' (Chambers, 220). There may be an allusion by Sven to the events of 26 Dec. 1187, when the seventeen-year-old Duke Valdemar was knighted and put in charge of the southern frontier of Denmark at Schleswig (DMA, 76).
31. *mediamnia*: properly an eyot; defined as a freshwater island by Priscian and others (Ducange, s.v.). According to Saxo, a fort was built on the same site by Sven II's son, Biorn (GD, 334; EC, 96); he probably meant Rendsborg. According to AR, the place was still called *Kunengikamp* in the thirteenth century (DMA, 154), and this points to Kampen, a royal manor NW of Rendsborg. Others prefer to locate the site nearer the mouth of the river, by Tönning or Dingsbüll. There is no reason to suppose that Sven had a particular site in mind, whatever may have been the folklore of the debatable swamplands. The island merely suits the ON word for duel, *hólmganga*. The great King Knut was later supposed to have fought for the lordship of England on a similar eyot in the Severn. The settlement of property disputes by (illegal) duels survived in Norway until the nineteenth century; for an example see Bø, 140.
32. In the St Albans *Vitæ* Warmundus retires to 'a safer place' while his son joins in a full-scale battle against the usurpers (Chambers, 223); his enemy, Riganus/Aliel, is drowned in the Avon after the deaths of his sons. On King Ægeus of Athens see n. 30 above.
33. Genesis 42: 38.
34. *tanquam leo pectore robusto infremuit*: perhaps from Silius Italicus, xi 247. Like Walter of Châtillon's Alexander, Uffi 'carries a lion in his lofty heart' (*Alexandreis*, i 57; tr. R. Telfryn Pritchard), for 'the virtue of the lion lies in his breast' according to Hugh of St Victor (*De Bestiis*, ii 1; PL 177, 57). In the St Albans *Vitæ* Offa charges the foe 'after the

manner of the lion and the lioness when their whelps have been taken from them' (Chambers, 222). The seal of Knut VI already bore the Danish arms of three lions passant gardant on a field semée of hearts; see Riis, 192–4.

35. *athleta noster elegantissimus*: the *vir elegans*, choice and handsome but not dainty or luxurious, is a type of medieval knighthood rather than a classical figure. On p. 74 the future Valdemar II is described as *iuvenis indolis elegantissimæ*.

36. Exodus 17: 14: 'I will utterly put out the remembrance of Amalek,' and Psalm 9: 6. The memorability of Uffi is a commonplace of all the versions of the story, as in the St Albans *Vitæ*—possibly as a result of the importance of the Eider as a frontier. Sven's words also echo those of CL on Dania, *quod nomen in eternum non delebitur* (SM, 1 45).

37. *quod raro legitur accidisse*: heroes of the classical epics do not incite their foes except by taunting. Even Byrhtnoth was terse in encouraging his enemy Vikings (*Maldon*, 93–5), and Offa in the St Albans *Vitæ* was enraged by the 'insulting and shameful words of his opponents' (Chambers, 222).

38. *agedum* (X), rather than *agendum* (A); an imperative favoured by Statius in the *Thebaid*. The sentence is missing in S, mangled in A, and owes everything to Gertz: see Löfstedt, 171.

39. *Alamanni*: here and on pp. 51, 52, and 54 Sven uses this word for Germans, elsewhere *Teutonici*. Chadwick suggests it might be derived from the *Swæfe* of the Offa lines in *Widsith*, since the *Suabi* were also called *Alamanni* (Chadwick, 129, with reference to Paulus Diaconus, *Historia Langobardorum*, iii 18). But *Alamanni, Alemanni* is normal twelfth-century usage for Germans, especially in France and Italy. In Saxo the foe are Saxons, no doubt because of deteriorating relations with the Schaumburgs and Welfs after 1190. Sven may have had the Hohenstaufen in mind, who were Alamanni in the Suabian sense.

40. *vafritiis artis pugillatoriæ*: the adj. from Plautus, *Rudens*, iii 4, 16.

41. *distribueretur*: an extraordinary word for the breaking of a sword: perhaps a facetious echo from the schools. 'Distribution' was both a method of argument and a stage in the presentation of a case; it was divided into the two categories of enumeration and exposition; see *Ad Herennium*, i 10 and 17, iv 35.

42. *fragor per universum intonuit exercitum*: cf. *Æneid*, viii 527 and ii 629, *subitoque fragore intonuit lævum*. In the St Albans *Vitæ* Offa splits the skull of Brutus/Hildebrand after penetrating his helmet, and mortally wounds his brother, Sven (Chambers, 222).

43. Proverb no. 14070 in Walther: *Ludus fortunæ variatur in ordine lunæ,* | *Crescit, decrescit, in eodem sistere nescit.*
44. *novercali vultu*: cf. Henricus Septimellensis, *Elegia de Diversitate Fortunæ* (c.1192): *Numinis ambiguos vultus deprendo: novercam* | *Sentio fortunam, que modo mater erat* (PL 204, 844, lines 1–2; Walther, no. 19128). Alan of Lille referred to *fortuna novercans* (AC, vii 369); and see *Alexandreis*, ii 175–81, for Walter of Châtillon's address to Fortune, *quis te impulit illi* | *velle novercari.*
45. *cassatisque minarum ampullositatibus*: see n. 26 above.
46. *in pacis tranquillitate præcluis (Wffo)* . . . *regebat*: 'tranquillity of peace' (not the same as 'peace of tranquillity', for which see Alan of Lille, *Summa de Arte Prædicatoria*, ch. 22; PL 205, 156) is used twice in LC (see p. 89, n. 26, and pp. 124, 126, nn. 107, 116). It originates in the prayer, *Deus regnorum omnium, regumque dominator*, included in the Mass in Time of War in most rites from the Gelasian Sacramentary (c.750) onwards. It is in Alcuin's supplement to the Gregorian Sacramentary (CBP, 1563 and 143) and in the eleventh-century Canterbury Benedictional (prayer *Pro Rege*, CBP, 1389), and in the Roman Missal (Blaise, *Vocab.*, s.v. *Pax*, and Bruylants, ii 128). It is used by other historians (e.g. EE, 52, *Vita Ædwardi*, 30, 51), but according to CR it was a catch-phrase of Bishop Peter of Roskilde (1124–34): 'if anything can remain with Mary and James in the tranquillity of peace' (of church property, SM, i 26). The adj. *præcluis* is probably borrowed from Martianus Capella (i 3 and 24, ix 906), but also occurs in the office for St Kjeld (c.1200; VSD, 280). In Saxo's version of the story Uffi wins not only freedom for the Danes but empire over the Saxons as well (GD, 100; PF, 109): a change of emphasis on which see pp. 21, 26 above.
47. *Dan nomen indidit*: Dan was a learned eponym in William of Jumièges, writing c.1070 (6–8; a passage used by Roger of Wendover and John of Wallingford), perhaps borrowed by Sæmundr, and transplanted in CL to the Danish islands. He founded Lejre, defeated the Emperor Augustus at the Danevirke, and was elected king of Denmark; his wife was Dannia and his son Ro. Abbot William of Æbelholt and Saxo accepted him as a founding ruler, but the Icelanders grafted him into the pedigree of the Skjǫldungar further down the sequence, either as the husband of Ólǫf Vermundardóttir or as the son of Óláfr hinn lítilláti Vermundarson: see *Langfeðgatal, Alfræði*, iii 59, and AJ, 8–11. Sven puts him here in obedience to his Icelandic source. *Elatus vel Superbus* becomes *hin Storlatene* in AR (DMA, 154); the epithet in AJ is *hinn*

mikilláti, which forms a doublet with *hinn lítilláti*. In AR it is suggested that he was in fact Olaf, Uffi's son; this was after Saxo had invented three separate Dans.

48. The sequence Frothi—Frithlef—Frothi—Ingiald occurs both in CL and in the Icelandic pedigrees. The duplication of Fróðis and Friðleifs sems to have been originally inspired by the preference of the early twelfth-century chiefs in Oddi for a lineage of 29 or 30 generations, like Christ's from King David in Matthew 1. CL refers to Frothi *largus*, which Sven explains by using Wisdom 7: 9: 'All gold in respect of her is as a little sand, and silver shall be counted as clay before her.'

49. Alias Ingjaldr Starkaðarfóstri, whose story is elaborated in Saxo's book six but who seems to have played little part in *Skjǫldunga saga*; cf. SG, ii 102. He first appears as Ingeld, son of Froda, in *Widsith* and *Beowulf*, or as Alcuin's Hinieldus (Chambers, 20–5). After him Gertz inserted an Olaus and his son Frothi, because the next King Frothi to be mentioned cannot be the Frothi *Frithgothæ* named above. However, neither A nor S has a lacuna at this point, and I doubt whether Sven thought Olaus was a son of Ingiald, since he places him after the break. All the Icelandic pedigrees give Ingjaldr a son, Hrœrekr hnǫggvan(d)baugi; cf. p. 106, n. 14, above.

50. *nepotes, altera nempe parte regali stirpe editi* (A): Gertz qualified *nepotes* by *filiarum*, 'grandsons through daughters', which is unwarranted—Sven just means 'relations', as in *Æneid*, vi 864, *magna de stirpe nepotum*. The pedigree in *Flat.* carried on undaunted at this point, with Hrœrekr—(Fróði)—Hálfdan—Hrœrekr—Haraldr hilditǫnn and Ráðbarðr, and CL gave Olavus—Asa. This divergence seems to have troubled Sven.

51. In CL Olaf (Olavus) is the son and successor of Ingiald (SM, i 53); but Saxo commented that 'some offer the doubtful opinion that he was the child of Ingeld's sister' (GD, 181; PF, 201). 'Some' probably means Sven: if so, it would help explain the reference below to Frothi as the last direct transmitter of royalty for several generations. Saxo also states that 'posterity has received little accurate information of his doings,' and he ignores the Danubian triumphs suggested by Sven: it sems that he has already used them in the war of Frothi against the Huns, when the Danes and their allies triumphed after *proelio septem dies extracto* (GD, 132; PF, 147–8). Battles against the Huns were attributed to King Angantýr in the *Saga Heiðreks konungs* (using the fragmentary *Hlǫðskviða*); cf. *The Saga of King Heidrek*, xxi–xxix; SG, ii 82–4.

52. *temporum interstitio*: Martianus Capella, vi 601. Saxo also uses *interstitium* in a temporal sense.
53. *diligenti . . . successori*: perhaps a reference to Saxo, who filled the gap between Olaf and Sigwarth with some 27 kings. The *Series ac Brevior* (*c*.1230) made do with 25, and AR (*c*.1288) produced 35.
54. *ex ecclipsi memorie* (cf. Gertz's constructed *virtutibus eclipsatus*, n. 149 below): Alan of Lille wrote of an 'eclipse' of the sense of touch, of 'the stars of virtue', and of probity (AC, iv 166, 327; *De Planctu Naturæ*, PL 210, 478).
55. *Regneri . . . regnum . . . rege . . . regem . . . regnum . . . regno . . . regis*: humorous alliteration; cf. n. 72 below. Stories about the Viking hero or villain Ragnar Lothbrok were current all round the North Sea in the eleventh century, and Icelanders began to insert him in their pedigrees in the early twelfth. In these he is given a father called Sigurðr ormr-í-auga, who may have had a historical antecedent in the Sigefridus of the *Annals of St Bertin* (s.a. 882) and Adam of Bremen. Sven rejected this scheme. He may have read in CR that the sons of 'Lothpard' were Norwegian pirates who enlisted the help of unnamed Danish kings to devastate Britain and the continent (SM, i 16–17). He was probably aware that in France the ninth-century raiders were seen as ancestors of the Danish royal family. In 1188, the eloquent abbot, Stephen of Tournai, was trying to raise money from Knut VI and Bishop Valdemar of Schleswig on the grounds that the abbey of St Geneviève in Paris had been destroyed in 857 by Berno, chief of the Loire Northmen; see DD, i:3, nos. 154–6, 158–9. This was a somewhat tainted connexion. The grafting of the Ragnar strain on to the royal Danish stock through a son who was not involved in the more lurid deeds of the Gallic Vikings may have been a way of lessening the taint. (Sigefridus was remembered, if at all, for having stabled his horses in the emperor's palace at Aachen, cf. *Ann. Fuld.*, s.a. 881, and CR, SM, i 17, a feat after Sven's own heart, although he doesn't mention it.) It was left for Saxo to make Ragnar a full king of the Danes, with characteristic awkwardness, in his book nine; even there, the connexion is through marriage. Some Icelanders had no such misgivings and produced a perfect male descent from Ingjaldr to Ragnarr in six generations (so in *Flat.*, ii 26–7, seven in the Resen manuscript, on which see Faulkes).
56. At this point Gertz, 154, inserted the words, 'He had been begotten at the first untying of her maidenly girdle, which is called *knut* by our common people.' There is no gap in A or S here, although the word

utpote ought, if used correctly, to introduce an explanation. There is no reason to interpret this tale as Danish folklore; it is probably Sven's own rather jocular gloss. The Icelanders explained the name more cumbrously, from the knotted cloth found with the foundling Knut; but it was the classical poets (e.g. *Æneid*, i 324), not the Danish peasantry, who used *nodus* as a synecdoche for a woman's girdle. Saxo omits the story and makes Knut the grandson rather than the son of Sighwarth. For a summary of the large literature on the name Knut see Søndergaard, esp. 157–8.

57. *primus in Dacia functus hoc nomine . . . solus post Froti . . . regali extitit oriundus prosapia*: This first King Knut disturbs the numbering originally favoured by Sven's own monarch, Knut, son of Valdemar. In an Odense charter of 20 Nov. 1183 he is referred to as 'the fifth' (corrected to 'fourth' in DD, i:3, no. 116), and in the great Odense donation of 21 March 1183 he is definitely 'the fourth' (DD, i:3, no. 111). This would make Knut, son of Magnus, who ruled 1146–57, Knut III; St Knut (1080–6) Knut II; and Knut the Great Knut I— Harthaknut not being accepted as a sole king in the Lund king-list or in Sven (see p. 64). It seems that between March and November 1183 someone found another Knut, probably in an Icelandic pedigree—a *Knútr fundinn* rather than a *Hǫrðaknútr*—and Sven makes use of the discovery. Abbot William subsequently introduced one more, by restoring Harthaknut to his place in the king-list after Knut the Great (SM, i 178–9), and so Knut son of Valdemar was retrospectively promoted to Knut VI in e.g. Vedel's translation of Saxo. Sven insists that this Knut *primus* was a son of a Danish king, even if his father Sighwarth was not. Sighwarth's predecessors had been merely *nepotes* of kings, all the way back to Frothi; but the last Frothi to be mentioned had been succeeded by his son Ingiald. There is no need to assume with Gertz that a passage about a later Frothi has been dropped. This raises more problems than it solves, because Sven states clearly above (it is in both A and S) that no son succeeded his father directly after the days of Ingiald. Either he meant that after 'the time of' King Frothi, who was succeeded by his son, the direct line was broken, or that the last king before Sighwarth had been Frothi, Sighwarth's father-in-law, mentioned but not named above.

58. *Sealendensis bondo*, after a gap in A: S supplies the name *Ennignup* ('forehead-crag, beetle-brow'), which appears to refer to the historical King Chnob, known from Adam of Bremen. He was subjugated by Henry the Fowler in 934 and is named as the father of King Sigtryg on

Haddeby stones 2 and 4 (gen. *knubu*; Moltke, 194–6). Saxo also noted that Ennignup was Knut's guardian, and complained that 'some inexpert historians ascribe a moderately important (not 'central', *pace* PF, 294) place to him in their chronicles' (*medium in fastis locum tribuunt*; GD, 265; cf. SG, ii 162). According to Saxo, the guardian was chosen by lot. Sven calls him *bondo*, ODan. *bondi*, a usual word in Danish charters for 'landowner, freeholder'. By *Sealendensis* he presumably meant that he came from Sjælland; as adj. or substantive the term does not occur elsewhere in Sven's writings, but it is common in other twelfth- and thirteenth-century Latin texts in that sense. It is perhaps conceivable that the base of the word is pl. *sjólǫnd*, which is occasionally found in Icelandic with reference to the Danish islands (those south of Sjælland and Fyn, viz. Møn, Falster, Lolland, Langeland—the usual Icelandic term for Sjælland is sg. *Sjá-, Sjóland*). Adam of Bremen says that Chnob/Gnupa came from Sweden, and archaeology suggests that his dynasty was strong in the southern islands and Schleswig (cf. Lis Jacobsen; and P. Sawyer, 217–19). The story told by Sven may be an Icelander's way of reconciling an account (Adam's?) of Chnob's rule with the series of Gorm's kingly ancestors in the Oddaverjar pedigree.

59. Snio occurs in CL as a shepherd promoted by the Swedes to be tyrant of Denmark in the days before Rolf kraki (SM, i 49). He appears in the *Catalogus Regum Daniæ* (1170–82) as the fifth ancient pagan king of the Danes (SM, i 159), and as Snær son of Frosti in the tracts *Hversu Nóregr byggðisk* and *Fundinn Nóregr, Flat.* i 21–2, 219–20. Sven may have fitted him in here because he wanted a link between Klak-Harald and Knut, and he connected the first element in Klak-Harald's name with the root in ON *klaki*, 'frozen ground'. Instead of Snio S has another Frothi, but Snio survived in the chronicles and king-lists because Saxo restored him as an ancient king; see GD, 235–8; PF 258–62; cf. SG, ii 140. In AR he is associated with the year 687 (DMA, 157–8).

60. Klakk-Haraldr in WN texts (e.g. *Jómsvíkinga saga*, ch. 2), where he appears as a jarl in Holstein and the father of Þyri Danmarkarbót rather than of Gormr. Danes tended to identify him with the King Herioldus who was baptized at Mainz on 24 June 826 and played a well-recorded part in Franco-Danish relations from 812 to 827; cf. *Series ac Brevior* (1220–42; SM, i 162) and *Annales Lundenses* (c.1265; DMA, 37–8). The relative failure of Herioldus as a king, as described in AB, i 15, may possibly have earned him his nickname—if we knew precisely

what it meant. In *Tilnavne* it is equated either with early Dan. *klak*, 'Smuds, Plet', or with ON *klakkr*, 'stejl og spids Klippe' (both *Klakker* and *Klack* occur as by-names in early Swedish). It is certainly not clear who Sven thought he was. In his persona as the first baptized king of the Danes Harald is not given the by-name Klak in CR, nor in the list of kings in the Lund necrology: on the contrary, Klak-Harald in CR is Harald Bluetooth. Saxo has a third King Harald, but he is described as an exile and a tyrant, not affiliated to the royal family (GD, 253, 255; PF, 282, 284).

61. *Gorm Løghæ*: Bram *Løghæ* (A), Gorm *Lóghæ* (S). In the *Incerti Auctoris Genealogia* (SM, i 186) he appears as Gorm *Løkæ*, and from this form a hypothetical derivation is given from an ODan. adj. **løker*, 'træg', related to the Norw. substantive *løkje*, 'tung, dorsk Person' (*Tilnavne*, s.n.). The nickname has also been associated with MDan. *loj*, explained in a seventeenth-century Comenius translation as 'vanmectig og doven', but this loan-word from German cannot be credited in Sven's text. In Icelandic sources he is most often referred to as Gormr the 'Old', but in *Jómsvíkinga saga* as the 'Stupid' and the 'Mighty' as well. Saxo disposes of the inconsistency by providing three separate Gorms: an active one in book eight, and in book nine one unsuccessful one and another who is inactive, blind and old. See Lukman 1976, 32, 44, for speculations on the subject; Ousager; and SG, ii 162–4.

62. This is the *purui* of Jelling stone 1; what follows is Sven's attempt to explain the epithet *tanmarkar* : *but* in that same inscription (Moltke, 206). She is described in terms similar to those used of Queen Sophia at the end of HC (p. 73 above), and her story seems to be connected with Sophia's adventures in 1185–7, when she was married to the count of Thuringia, the emperor's nephew, and then repudiated, to the fury of her son, Knut VI. Her daughters were also rejected as consorts by the emperor's sons (*Chronica Slavorum*, iii 21). Sven offered solace for these rebuffs in his tale of Queen Thyrwi. He may have been inspired by the dominant queens of Justin's *Historiæ*: Semiramis who 'outdid not only men but women in courage' and fortified Babylon; Tomyris who defied King Cyrus and avenged her son's death by trapping and destroying the Persian army; and most of all, Dido (or Elissa) who practised deceit to liberate the Tyrians in order to obtain land on which they could settle and to avoid becoming the wife of a neighbouring king, 'who sued for marriage under threat of waging war' (Justin, i 2 and 8, xviii 5 and 6). On Thyrwi in Sven and Saxo, see

L. Weibull; Damsholt 1985, 158–62; and Strand, 156–63, with full refs.
63. *et rosa lilio maritata purpureum genis colorem inpinxerat*: both Horace and Ovid use 'purple' for rosy or pink, and there are many similar passages in Sven's contemporaries, e.g. Alan of Lille, AC, iii 153–4, and William of Blois, *Alda*, 130–1 (ed. Cohen, i 135).
64. These phrases are later repeated in the eulogy of Valdemar I, p. 73. Here Gertz prefers *perfecta* to *reserta redundabat* in A, *referta erat* in S.
65. Divergences in A and S have here been skilfully reconciled by Gertz. Sven seems to have been influenced by the myth of creation in Bernard Sylvestris and his disciples. In this, Nature (rather than God) 'compounds bodies, the dwelling places of souls, out of the qualities and materials of the elements,' and Noys, or Providence, assists her in the creative act; thus *Cosmographia*, ch. 2 (tr. Wetherbee, 67–75). Alan of Lille believed that the qualities of the great ones of the past were immanent in the cosmos, at the disposal of the creator: hence Thyrwi's imaginary drinking-companions. The fount they shared was either the 'fount of wisdom' of Proverbs 18: 4, or the founts of wisdom and philosophy referred to by Cicero in *Tusculan Disputations*, i 3, 6; but it should also be noted that John of Hauteville, *Architrenius*, ii 291, believed that ordinary wine 'introduces Nestor to our hearts, Ulysses to our tongues.' Sven's comparison with the Queen of Sheba is engagingly maladroit. His wish that Thyrwi had been baptized into the orthodox faith came true in Saxo, who made her an English princess who, some said, 'declined the caresses of the nuptial couch so that by her abstinence she could win her bridegroom over to Christianity' (GD, 266; PF, 295). Osbert of Clare (*Vita Ædwardi*, 74) was able to compare the Confessor and Queen Edith to Solomon and Sheba unreservedly. See Damsholt 1985, 155–7, and on the influence of Alan of Lille and John of Hauteville on Anders Sunesen see Boje Mortensen, in Ebbesen, 209–19.
66. All Northern sources follow Adam of Bremen's mistake, AB, ii 3, where Otto I invades and conquers Denmark. He maintained some kind of hegemony there, but it was his father, Henry the Fowler, who subjugated the Danes in 934 (AB, i 7), and his son, Otto II, who invaded Denmark in 974.
67. *infamiæ discrimen*: the second word is translated as *crimen*, 'reproach, shame'; otherwise it would mean 'trial, test, danger', as in *famæ suæ discrimen* (SM, i 82). Gertz, HS, 48, has 'et Forsøg paa at sætte Riget i Fare for at plettes af Vanære'.
68. *virtutique commode mutuus succedat affectus*: I have not followed

Gertz in preferring *occedo*, 'go towards' (Plautus) to *succedo* in A, *non prosequi* in S. Otto wanted more than a meeting of emotions. We must note that the emperor 'is not in the least interested in Thyra herself, but only in using her as a means of disgracing Denmark. She is an object' (Damsholt 1985, 159 and cf. 162). Feminists make heavy weather of this story.

69. *dulcibus alloquiis*: Horace, *Epodes*, 13, 18. Damsholt feels that Thyrwi's stratagem reflects Danish policy towards the Germans: 'we deceived them whenever we could.' I suspect it was the Germans who deceived the Danes, at least in 1152, 1162 and 1181, and Sven felt it was time for a change.

70. LM suspected a Northern proverb here, but Gertz pointed out the resemblance to Plautus, *Truculentus*, 176: *in melle sunt linguæ sitæ vostræ atque orationes lacteque; corda in felle sunt sita atque acerbo aceto*; and there are several medieval Latin analogues; see Walther, nos. 14574, 14577, 38168e. Alan of Lille gave Logic a flower and a scorpion to hold: *Mel sapit ista manus, fellis gerit illa saporem* (AC, iii 27).

71. Psalm 136: 3. The ensuing passage repeats, ironically, the conclusion of the Kristiarn Svensen episode in LC, p. 40: honour has a price. But see Damsholt 1985, 159.

72. *regina . . . regnum . . . regni . . . regno*: cf. p. 114, n. 55 above, and e.g. Aldhelm, *Quam rex extorrem Romæ qui regna regebat* (LHL, iv 495), and *Rex ruit et regnum rapiens rex alter habebit* (MGH, *Script.*, xxiv 240).

73. *prope Slesuik*: not in A and added by Gertz from S, *prope Slesvicum*. For a summary of the archaeological dating of the Danevirke fortifications see *Danevirke*, i 79–84. A beginning was made on Danevirke III *c*.968, west of Hedeby, but there were no other great works in the tenth century. Sven's story reflects Valdemar I's rebuilding and extension of the old walls from 1163 onwards (DMA, 166), and the connexion of Semiramis with Babylon's walls, cf. p. 117, n. 62 above, and Orosius, ii 6, 8–11.

74. *operi* (S) *præfato insudarent*: Gertz supplied *munimini* to fill a gap in A. Valdemar II exacted dues in silver from contiguous districts to maintain the wall (KVJ, i:2, 9–11), but how his father found the labour to build it is unclear.

75. The theory that all land-rights had once been vested in the ruler was advanced by the twelfth-century Italian jurist Martinus (see Gierke, 79 and 178). Cf. however Snorri's account of Haraldr hárfagri's seizure of

Norwegian lands in his saga, ch. 6, in *Heimskringla*, and the pervasive folklore of ultimate or primeval royal land-ownership; see Hoebel, 226, and Diamond, 286. 'What no man owns, the king owns' is a statement in the 1241 Jutland Law (DGL, iii 61).

76. *tanquam inclusos indagine*: Sven means a hedge (as translated by Gertz, HS, 52) rather than a net; see Diefenbach, 293; Ducange, s.v.; *Synonyma*, line 536.

77. Cf. Vergil, *Eclogues*, ix 27: 'singing swans shall bear aloft to the stars.' For 'obstacle of a wall', *muri obicem*, at the end of the next sentence, cf. Orosius, iii 19, *muri obice*.

78. The name was used *c*.1170 in CL (*Danæwirchi*). In that source a wooden stockade had already stood there before the kingdom was founded; it was where Dan defeated Augustus Caesar before he became king (SM, i 44–5). Saxo insisted that Thyrwi built the earthworks after her husband's death (GD, 272; EC, 6); he evidently found Sven's tale too frivolous.

79. *Decus datiæ*: a translation of *tanmarkar* : *but* on the Jelling stone 1, cf. p. 117, n. 62 above. What it means has been too long disputed to be discussed here. Saxo may have tried to do better than Sven, with his *Danicæ maiestatis caput* (GD, 274; EC, 10); see the summary in K. M. Nielsen, 155–60, and Moltke, 207.

80. *in fiolis, cytharis*: cf. *Alexandreis*, v 483–5. OFr. *viole* is latinized as *vitula, videla* or *fiola*; see Diefenbach, s.v. *fiala*. The *cithara* is a stringed instrument played with a bow or plectrum; it is associated with *tympana* in Genesis 31: 27, Job 21: 12, Isaiah 5: 12 and 30: 32.

81. *choris et tympanis*: Exodus 15: 20, Judges 11: 34, Psalm 150: 3. Instrumental music is a *topos* of decadence, as in Saxo (cf. Starkather and the flute-player in GD, 168–9; PF, 186); also of enchantment (GD, 63, 335–6; PF, 69; EC, 98–9). When played by *histriones*, as here, the worst can be expected.

82. *renuto . . . recuso . . . devito*: a formula of rejection from the school-book; cf. e.g. *contemnit, renuit, simul abnuit atque recusat* (*Synonyma*, line 536). Gertz preferred the rare *renuto* to *renuntio* in A or *renuo* in S: each is more frequent in the glossaries, and *renuntio* should stand.

83. *parificari non valeat*: *parifico* is used by Suger and by John of Salisbury (*Policraticus*, iii 14; cf. Ducange, s.v.). Gorm's descent from kings 'on either side' of the family is not hinted at earlier; 'on every side' would be better for Sven's *undique*, cf. 'i enhver Henseende er oprunden af Kongers Æt' (Gertz, HS, 55), 'i alle Maader' (LM, 25).

84. Saxo attributes a similarly defiant speech to Archbishop Absalon,

when Landgrave Siegfried of Thuringia made a 'pompous and menacing' request that Knut VI should do homage to the emperor in 1182/3 (GD, 539–40; EC, 606).

85. For *reverentiam et vocem* (A) Gertz read *irreverentiam atrocem* (X): but A will do, '. . . stunned at the awesomeness and tone of this . . . reply'.

86. Prophetic powers were attributed to Thyrwi in *Jómsvíkinga saga* (1962), ch. 3; (1969), ch. 3, and by Saxo when she interprets Gorm's dream (GD, 267; PF, 296).

87. *ad institutionem* (A), *ad internecionem* (S), *ad interstinctionem* (X): Gertz's word is unknown except to Arnobius, who used it to mean a 'distribution'. Paulus Diaconus, HR, 238, used *internecio* for the destruction of the Ostrogothic realm by Narses: this is better.

88. *Blatan*: a by-name which occurs first in CR (before 1150), *cognomine Blatan sive Clac-Harald* (SM, i 17). It was also used in Abbot William's *Genealogy* (1193/4) and explained as *dens lividus vel niger* (SM, i 178).

89. *quasi masoleis illustribus*: 'as if' because *mausoleum* usually meant an ornate burial within a church, as e.g. in William of Malmesbury's *Gesta Pontificum* and Adam of Bremen (AB, ii 82, for St Willehad's tomb at Bremen). On the Jelling burials see K. M. Nielsen (with bibliography).

90. As in Adam of Bremen and CR.

91. The dragging of the rock and the rebellion of the army are elaborated by Saxo in his book ten. The mutiny is attested earlier (EE, 8–9). The supposed cause may be a story invented to explain the siting of two memorials away from Jelling, at Læborg and Bække, to a lady called Thyrwi, who may have been identified as Gorm's queen (cf. Moltke, 228–30).

92. *Æneid*, viii 244, on the flight of Cacus from Hercules.

93. *Hynnisburg(h)* in A and S, *Hyumsburgh* in X: a place implicitly identified by Sven and Saxo with Wolin on the Dziwna, now in Poland. Saxo's detailed narrative of the Danish raids on Wolin in 1170 and 1173(?) suggests that the city was defenceless at the time of the second raid, ruined but not by Absalon (GD, 482, 487, 501; EC, 519, 526, 546). In 1188 the bishop of Pomerania moved his see to Kamien because Wolin 'is deserted on account of war-damage' (Clement III's bull, CPD, no. 63). However, in 1180/1 the Wolinsky had fortified the mouth of the Swina, 23 km west of Wolin, with two forts to keep the Danes out. In August(?) Absalon ordered his brother to burn these

forts, and on the way home the king ordered 'the burnt-out ruins of the forts to be levelled with the ground'—*solo æquari* in Sven's phrase—and the still-glowing foundation stones sunk at sea (GD, 547; EC, 618). This must be the scene Sven remembers; so either he used *moenia* to mean 'defences fifteen miles away', or else Absalon levelled Wolin's walls on an occasion not mentioned by Saxo. According to *Jómsvíkinga saga* (1962), ch. 15; (1969), ch. 13, Pálna-Tóki founded Jómsborg, and Adam of Bremen says that Harald took refuge in *Iumne* (Wolin) when expelled by his son. Sven may have invented the story of a foundation by Harald, and was followed by Saxo. The evidence on the Jómsborg–Wolin question is summarized in *Jómsvíkinga saga* (1962), vii–ix; on the modern myth of the Jómsvikings see Abels, 162–4.

94. *Tygheskeg* (X), *Tycheskeg* (A), *Tiugeskeg*: *Ágrip* (c.1190) and later Icelandic sources have *tjúguskegg*; accurately explained in Abbot William's *Genealogy* as *furcata barba* (SM, i 178). The nickname is not in CR or Saxo.
95. As in Abbot William's *Genealogy* (SM, i 179), but not in Adam of Bremen or CR, where Harald dies a Christian and is buried in Roskilde, 'like a second David' (SM, i 19). However, his ill repute, as a jealous father, appears earlier, in EE, 9. These opposing views endured. Saxo followed Sven but in AR (c.1300) the annalist wrote that Harald was 'blamelessly wounded and made a martyr' (DMA, 255).
96. *freto Grönæsund*: supplied by Gertz from S, where A has a gap after an initial 'r'. Grønsund is the strait between Falster and Møn, where the fleet sometimes assembled for Valdemar I's raids on the Slavs.
97. *binomius extitet* (X): i.e., he could be known by a double name (Paulus Festus gives Numa Pompilius and Tullus Hostilius as examples) or by alternative names (Astyages or Assuerus in Otto of Freising, *Chronicle*, ii 1). In the sagas he is presented as Pálnir son of Tóki but regularly called Pálna-Tóki; but see Kousgaard Sørensen, 104–5, who rejects the possibility of a patronymic. To the Icelanders he was the founder of Jómsborg, the foster-father and ally of Sven Forkbeard, and the slayer of Harald Bluetooth. To Saxo he was just Toko, a retainer of Harald's who was tested to the limits of endurance by the king's malice and deserted to Sven. He eventually killed Harald with an arrow, as Pálna-Tóki did in *Jómsvíkinga saga*. Saxo exonerated him from the kidnapping of Sven Forkbeard; this was attributed to Sigvaldi jarl in the saga, (1962) ch. 25; (1969) ch. 26. It is uncertain how much of this story was invented by Sven. In *Knýtlinga saga*, ch. 40, Sven's great-grandmother Þorgunna is described as the daughter

of a Vagn Ákason; in *Jómsvíkinga saga* Vagn is the son of Pálna-Tóki's son, Áki. Thus, according to mid-thirteenth-century genealogical convention, Sven is here telling the tale of one of his ancestors. However, he gives no sign that he was aware of the connexion. See Appendix, p. 142.
98. *in reclinario*: a contracted form of *reclinatorium* (Song of Solomon 3: 10, where it seems to mean a head-rest). The entry in Ducange is misleading: no one else uses the word, although according to Stephanius, 79, 'the older lexicographers interpret it as 'a place for lying down, or a store-room in a ship'. Thus 'Kahytten' (Fenger, 22), 'Soverum' (HS, 58). The oarsmen, *ordinatis per foros*, 'ranged on deck', could have been 'on their rowing-benches', as in the Gertz translation; but Cicero, *De Senectute*, ch. 106, uses *per foros* for 'deck', and Isidore, *Etym.*, I, xix 2, gives 'hollow sides' for *fori*. Neckam, 166, gives *fori . . . per que remi exire possint*.
99. *subgrunda* (X) is from S; it is not in A. It means the eaves of a house or overhang of a roof in Varro, Vitruvius and the *Digest*, and in medieval usage survived as *subgrundium*, *subrunda*, *subundra* (Ducange). Sven appears to use it for the top strake, thus 'over Skibets Ræling' (HS, 58). The top edge would be reinforced with a *borðstokkr*, with a moulding inside or outside to support a row of shields. Thus there would be a slight overhang, which might suggest the eaves of a house. If he was thinking of a decked ship, then the drainage or scupper-holes in the upper strakes would make *subgrunda* more appropriate; cf. Fenger, 22, 'Kahytslugen' ('cabin-hatch'). In Saxo King Sven puts back the ship's awning and sticks his head out (GD, 278; EC, 16).
100. Cf. the speech Saxo attributed to the Rugian envoy Domborus (GD, 426–7; EC, 438–40), boasting of the prosperity of the Slavs at the expense of the Danes. Capture for ransom was practised by both sides well into Sven Aggesen's lifetime. In the sagas Sven Forkbeard is compelled to marry Gunnhildr, the daughter of their overlord, Búrizláfr, king of the Wends; Búrizláfr himself marries Þyri, sister of King Sveinn. This is an ingenious combination of two fairly certain facts: that at some period Sven Forkbeard was captured and ransomed, and that he married a sister of Boleslaw Chrobry of Poland (Thietmar of Merseburg, vii 36 and 28, viii 39). The combination was probably made by Oddr Snorrason, the first biographer of Óláfr Tryggvason (*c*.1190). Here Sven elaborates one element of the story and avoids the spiritual interpretation of Sven Forkbeard's tribulations found in Adam of Bremen and CR.

101. According to Thietmar, Sven was twice captured by 'Northmen' and twice ransomed 'for an immense price', and thereafter called a slave by ill-wishers. Adam of Bremen calls his captors Slavs. Saxo improves the ransom-story by speculating on the public benefit of Sven's weight-loss in captivity (GD, 278; EC, 18).

102. *in Winningha*: a not uncommon place-name; here either Vindinge, west of Nyborg on Fyn, or, more likely, Neder-Vindinge near Vordingborg in southernmost Sjælland (the royal manor of 'Wynning' in KVJ, i:2, 20). The name means 'reclaimed land, assart' (Houken, 140), which makes it appropriate for this concession of woodlands.

103. *sylvarum et nemorum . . . communia*: common rights in woods and groves are defined by Anders Sunesen (DGL, i:2, 636–8) and Valdemar I's charter for Glumsten wood in Halland (c.1177; DD, i:3, no. 66). Saxo distinguishes between forest rights bought communally in East Denmark and purchased by families in Jutland (GD, 277; EC, 16).

104. *herciscundæ portione* (S), *heresundæ portione* (A): in Roman law the *familiæ herciscundæ actio* was a suit brought by co-heirs for the division of their inheritance (*Institutes*, iv, tit. xvii, div. 4, and tit. vi, div. 20). All Danish codes accept the woman's right to a share in inheritance: 'Sons and daughters shall receive men's shares, but the privilege of sex shall be observed, that the inheritance left to the son shall always be twice as large as the daughter's' (Anders Sunesen's Scanian laws; DGL, i:2, 480).

105. Luke 6: 38. Note that Anders Sunesen saw this system as a male privilege, while Sven (and Saxo) account for it as a concession to women, who had previously got nothing. See B. Sawyer 1985a, 49–50.

106. A longer list than in LC, p. 32 above. Sven adds five countries and substitutes *Samia* for Finland. Knut's conquests are listed in Óttarr svarti's strophe, *Svá skal kveðja* (Skj. i A 299, B 275), in EE, 34 (cf. EE, lxii) and in book six of Henry of Huntingdon's *Historia Anglorum*, whose *gessit eleganter* foreshadows Sven's *eleganter subiugavit*.

107. For the 'calm of peace' see p. 112, n. 46 above; the reference is to LC.

108. From AB, ii, chs. 65 and 74.

109. The tale is an imaginary exaggeration of Knut's journey to Rome to attend the coronation of Conrad II in 1027, which is described by Adam of Bremen. Henry was not married to Gunnhild until 1036, after Knut's death, and was never driven from Rome; nor was Conrad, though he subjugated North Italy in 1026 and the South in 1027. Sven is merely completing a trio of humiliations for the Germans, after Uffi and Thyrwi. See Damsholt 1985, 160.

110. The relics of St Martin helped to repel the Danes from Tours in 841 and 903; they were removed, to escape the Vikings, in 853–4 and 865–77(?); see Gasnault. However, the body was never taken to Rouen, and Knut had no known connexion with Tours. The end of Sven's sentence, *eo quod illam præ ceteris specialiter diligebat*, has usually been interpreted as meaning that Knut translated St Martin's relics to Rouen 'because he loved that city more than others'. Thus Gertz inserted the word *civitatem* into X although it occurs in neither A nor S and makes no historical sense in the context. Rouen was a place of transit on Knut's military expeditions, not a beloved residence, and there is no evidence of any Martin relics there in Sven's time or Knut's. On the other hand, such relics existed at Lund when Archbishop Asser dedicated the altar crypt in 1126 (DD, i:2, no. 48); they may have arrived via Hildesheim, since Bishop Bernward there was given relics of Martin at Tours on a journey to France in 1006 (Thangmar, *Vita Bernwardi*, MGH, *Script.*, iv 776). Thus *illam* must refer not to the city of Rouen but to Gunnhild, the wife-to-be of Emperor Henry, on whose behalf Knut's expedition to Rome and back was conducted. Knut 'carried away'—*asportavit*, not *apportavit*—the relics to the nearest port for England and the North, which was Rouen. This may be nonsense, but it is not quite as nonsensical as the supposed endowment of Rouen, which Saxo, never to be outdone in marvels, made the site of Knut's tomb (GD, 299; EC, 44). Sven may have known that Martin had twice driven Danes away from Tours and that his relics were twice removed to escape them. CR had noted Knut's historical connexions with Normandy (SM, i 20–1).

111. An unlucky gloss, to rectify the explanation of the name in LC: *qui et austerus siue durus est cognominatus* (p. 64 above). Harthaknut just means 'tough-knot'. The conceit that he was born in Harsyssel, N. Jutland, is also found in *Flat.*, i 98, but the Hǫrðaknútr there is King Gorm's father, the supposed son of Sigurðr ormr-í-auga. Harthaknut, Knut's son by Emma, must have been born in England. See EE, 97.

112. The words in parenthesis, missing in A, were supplied by Gertz from S. Sven's fondness for measuring time in *lustra* may reflect his reading of Ovid, who used the word fifteen times in his works to mean a period of five years. The inaccuracy of Sven's regnal chronology was no greater than that of other Danish writers of the period: see the king-lists in SM, i 157, 159. All they had to go on were Adam of Bremen's erratic dates: he claimed that Knut waged war in England for three years and then ruled for twenty-two (AB, ii, chs. 53 and 73), which

make five *lustra* if added together. Adam also said that Knut put three sons in charge of three kingdoms under his rule (AB, ii, ch. 66), but later made it clear that the sons survived their father (AB, ii, ch. 74). It seems that Sven was using a drastic abridgment of Adam's work, or perhaps the Lund king-list, which has only one *Kanutus harthe*, ruling from 1015 (NL, 45).

113. Psalm 143: 12; the commonest cliché of mission history. Adam also introduces his account of Knut's bishops by saying that he returned to Denmark (which he did, in 1019 and 1022), to secure the country after the death not of his son but of his brother, Harald, as in AR (DMA, 161).

114. 'Their sound has gone out . . .' is from Psalm 18: 5. These bishops are mentioned by Adam (AB, ii, chs. 55 and 71) but are not in CR (but cf. SM, i 21, n.). Gerbrand was appointed in the early 1020s, Rudolf in 1026 (not after 1035 as in AB). Sven is more accurate here but he omits Bishop Bernard of Scania and Bishop Reginbert of Fyn.

115. *Ulf . . . Sprakeleg*: Saxo and the sagas agree in giving this nickname to Thrugils/Þorgils, Ulf's father (GD, 288; EC, 30; *Knýtlinga saga*, ch. 5). Ulf is usually called 'jarl', and according to CR and the sagas Knut had him killed in Roskilde church (SM, i 21).

116. An exaggeration of Sven II's own exaggeration of his youthful importance in his conversations with Adam of Bremen. Events are telescoped by the erasure of Harthaknut's reign, 1035–42, which is also omitted in the Lund list and the *Catalogus Regum Danie* (SM, i 157, 159). For 'peace and quiet' see p. 112, n. 46 above.

117. AB, ii, ch. 77, and CR (SM, i 20) both mention the concubine, the Álfhildr of the St Olaf sagas, who according to William of Malmesbury later became a much respected anchoress in England. All sources other than Sven agree that Magnús became king of Denmark in 1041 or 1042 and was confronted by a rebellious Sven the following year. Sven Aggesen cannot accept the legitimacy of Magnús's rule as an elected foreigner with no hereditary title. Saxo can (GD, 301; EC, 48).

118. A compression of events from 1042 to 1046/7 which are copiously and variously recounted by Theodricus and in *Ágrip, Morkinskinna, Fagrskinna, Heimskringla* and *Knýtlinga saga*, mainly on the basis of ambiguous verses by Arnórr Jarlaskáld, Þjóðólfr Arnórsson and Þorleikr fagri. At some point, Magnús won a day-long battle at Helgenæs. Sven's note that he won West Denmark and *Slavia* thereby suggests: (i) that he knew of Magnús's victory over the Wends at Lürschau/Lyrskov and placed it before Helgenæs, unlike Theodricus and Ágrip;

(ii) that he wished his readers to believe that his rival Sven kept control of East Denmark until 1046/7.

119. *subvectoris sternacis* (A): cf. *Æneid*, xii 364, *equus sternax*, and LC, p. 35 above, where *subvectus* is used for 'carried on horseback' (SM, i 72). According to Saxo, Magnús's horse was scared by a hare and ran him into a tree at Alsted (GD, 303; EC, 51). According to Adam of Bremen, he 'died in his ships', while the sagas say he died on land in Jutland.

120. Sven's lust and offspring are mentioned by Ælnoth (VSD, 89); he is called *pater regum* only in Sven's work.

121. *Absalone referente, contubernalis meus Saxo . . . omnium gesta executurus prolixius insudabat*: ambiguous. It could mean that 'Saxo was . . . using . . . Absalon as his source,' but I prefer to follow Gertz (HS, 66), with *prolixius* rendered 'for a long time', as by Friis-Jensen, 334 n. On *contubernalis* see Weibull 1918, 187ff., Christensen in SS, 132–3, 140–2, and pp. 2–3 above.

122. A constitutional theory supported by Saxo (GD, 67, 350, 359; PF, 73; EC, 106, 134) but not by others. Other royal inaugurations, down to 1182, took place at Viborg, or at consecutive provincial assemblies. Saxo may have persuaded Sven of Isøre's prior claim (cf. Hoffmann 1976, 45–60, and Hude, 15), misled by Ælnoth's words (VSD, 90) on Harald's 'election by the whole people' in that place, on the spit west of the Isefjord inlet in N. Sjælland. Sven says the election was *omni(um) convenientia*, but whether he used the noun in Cicero's sense of 'harmony, agreement' or in the later sense of 'pact, contract' is not clear. However, he uses it later to mean 'assent' (SM, ii, Index i), and S has *assentientibus omnium civium suffragiis*. For *ut ipsa omnium convenientia* in X, I read A's *utpote omnium convenientia*.

123. *intronizatur* (X), *successit in regno* (S): absent in A. Latin *Cos* represents ODan. *Hen*, ON *heinn*, 'whetstone'. *Knýtlinga saga*, ch. 23, offers a witty gloss to explain the usage, but cf. *De Profectione Danorum*, ch. 6, where Aki the Crusader is praised because he 'never ceased to play the whetstone by sharpening up all the men he could' (SM, ii 469).

124. *leges Danis tribuit*: from Ælnoth (VSD, 90–1) and CR (SM, i 23) where he is praised highly; but Saxo condemned him as too indulgent. See J. Olrik 1899–1900, Hude, 15–16, Breengaard, 64–5, and Weibull 1986, 24.

125. The Odense view of Knut's sanctity was expressed in the *Passio* of c.1095 and in Ælnoth's work (VSD, 62–136). CR records that 'by a

new and unheard-of law he compelled the people to pay a tribute which our people called the poll-tax' (SM, i 24); however, this writer recognized the king as a martyr (Breengaard, 53–5, 65), and Sven's remarks are probably directed at popular opinion rather than at this text in particular. The cult flourished alongside a strong tradition of disapproval of the martyr's tyrannous rule. In 1186 Knut VI announced his personal veneration in confirming Knut IV's Lund privilege (DD, i:3, no. 134).

126. Knut's 'plenitude of power' is not an allusion to the canonists' *plenitudo potestatis* (*Decretum*, pt 2, causa iii, quaest. vi, c. viii), which defines the pope's power over the church, but a more general usage; see Post. Ælnoth wrote of the Danish fleet waiting for the king at the *occidentalis portus* (VSD, 99), and Sven's Humlum (*in Humla* S) is a village south of Oddesund, fifteen miles from the western outflow of the Limfjord, then open. AR, a Jutland source, puts the muster at Fiskbæk, near Viborg (DMA, 162). *maris continuum* in A is better than *maris contiguum* in X (S has no adj.), 'connecting with the sea' rather than 'next' to it (Weibull 1918, 192).

127. The *Passio* and Ælnoth (VSD, 67, 100) located the conspiracy in the fleet, not at Schleswig. The king's brother Olaf was sent to voice the troops' discontent at the king's delay, arrested at Schleswig and sent to Flanders. Saxo and *Knýtlinga saga* elaborate. Then, according to Ælnoth, the fleet disbanded with the king's permission. Sven may have followed an independent tradition or he may simply have misread his sources.

128. *recumpensatione*: see p. 92 above, n. 43. It refers to the *lethangwite*, reserved as a royal privilege in Knut's 1085 charter to Lund: 'If he shall have neglected the "leding" (*expeditio*), he shall make amends to the king' (DD, i:2, no. 21). Nevertheless, large-scale derelictions of duty occurred under Valdemar I, and the young Knut VI condoned one mutiny just before his accession in 1182 (GD, 535; EC, 598).

129. Interpreted by Gertz, HS, 69–70, as a reference by the king to a maxim against excessive rigour 'which might be found in Roman law'. There was a proverb, 'It is not always worth enforcing the law with rigour . . .' (Walther, no. 18182), which elaborated Proverbs 30: 33, 'the forcing of wrath bringeth forth strife.'

130. Forty-mark fines for the gravest offences were exacted in Sven's own day, and three marks was the conventional payment in lieu of oarsman's service in the thirteenth century (DGL, iv 104). Ælnoth says nothing of the fine and blames the discontent on royal officials who

tried to increase the weight of the *stater* and to 'pervert judgements' at law (VSD, 102). Sven may have invented this story, but he was followed by Saxo. Again, I have followed A and S, *regis rigor*, rather than Gertz, *legis rigor*; cf. Weibull 1918, 186.

131. According to Ælnoth, Knut was on a customary visit to collect his dues (VSD, 104); Sven seems to confuse *census* and *exactio*.

132. *in Vandalis*: Ælnoth says at Børglum, in Vendel 'which means turning'. The Wiener Neustadt *Vita* of St Knut, composed about 1220, adds that he went 'over the river which is called Limfjord, to the island of Vendel. For it was then an island containing two provinces, that is *Thiutha* and *Wendela* [Thy- and Vendsyssel]; today it is called a promontory rather than an island' (VSD, 546). In the next sentence *prerogativam . . . remanendi* is an ironical reference to the right of paying *kuærsæta* instead of doing military service, conceded in some charters from 1146–57 (Skyum-Nielsen, 159).

133. Matthew 10: 23; from Ælnoth, who applies the text to Knut's retreat from Børglum to Aggersborg (VSD, 105).

134. Ælnoth addressed the Devil at this point as 'the most ancient seducer' (VSD, 112), but Sven liked 'prevaricator' enough to repeat it at the end of his work. For Judas as 'prevaricator' see CBP, 1190.

135. *plebs prophana principi letum*: but Ælnoth suggests that nobles and commoners combined against the king (VSD, 103). The 'whispering rumour' of the next sentence recalls Ovid, *Heroides*, xxi 233.

136. For the proverb see Walther, no. 8819.

137. *plebicule rabies furiosa*: a rage described at length by Ælnoth (VSD, 105–6).

138. *Medium Transitum*: literally Middelfart, but the *Passio* and Ælnoth say he sailed from Schleswig; perhaps through rather than over the Belt to enter Odense by the fjord to the north.

139. For a recent evaluation of the lives and cult of St Knut see *Knuds-Bogen*, especially the articles by Breengaard and Meulengracht Sørensen, with bibliography; also Hoffmann 1975, 101–39.

140. *Olavus . . . Famelicum*: the by-name is *Hunger* in AR (DMA, 163), *Fames* in *Vetus Chronica Sialandie* (SM, ii 23), both from *c*.1250. Sven corrects CR, which claimed a nine-year famine (SM, i 24). Ælnoth claimed there was hunger, disease and invasion for eight years and nine months until Knut's remains were elevated (VSD, 129–30). Others blamed the famine on Olaf's failure to ransom his brother Nicolaus, who had taken his place in Flemish custody (Ralph Niger, 86). *Knýtlinga saga*, chs. 64–9, tells of Sven Aggesen's ancestors, the sons of Þorgunna,

undergoing this imprisonment and of their miraculous liberation partly through St Knut's intervention.

141. Spelt *Henricus* in A, *Ericus* in S; in CR he is *Hericus Bonus*. The Ringsted Office (VSD, 189) and other sources give him the surname *Egoth*, 'Ever-good' (cf. *Tilnavne*, s.n.). He was commemorated as a benefactor at Lund on 10 July, chiefly for having obtained the pallium for this see from Paschal II (Weeke, 173).

142. *crucem baiulando*: Luke 14: 27. Erik's 'holy design' of a pilgrimage to Jerusalem was recorded in Robert of Ely's lost *Vita* of Knut Lavard, Erik's son, composed 1135/7, and it was celebrated 30 years before that in Markús Skeggjason's *Eiríksdrápa* (st. 28–31; Skj. i A 450–1, B 419–20). Ralph Niger, 86, styled him 'confessor'. In the next sentence 'from the prison of this life' represents Gertz's final amendment, *vite ex ergastulo* (SM i, 180) of *vitæ segastulo* in A; he had earlier preferred *vite segregatus lute*. S has none of that and states that Erik died on his way back from the Holy Land, presumably misled by Abbot William's *Genealogy* (SM, i 180). The earlier sources make it clear that he died and was buried at Paphos in Cyprus before he reached Jerusalem.

143. *licet variis hymenei successibus*: so S and X; A reads *narus* for *variis*. Variously rendered: 'a high-born posterity of sons, who were the fruit of a series of different alliances' (Olrik, KV, 70); 'a nobly-born brood of sons, although his marital unions were conducted with changeable fortune' (Gertz, HS, 73); 'with various offspring by mating' (Riis, 206). The reference must be to the bastards mentioned in CR (SM, i 25) and later by Saxo, born to different mistresses, rather than to the variable character of the offspring.

144. The words in brackets are not in A but introduced by Gertz from S. Biorn is singled out from his brothers, no doubt because he fought alongside Sven's grandfather at Sønder Onsild in 1132; see pp. 69–70 above.

145. In fact, just over six *lustra*, 1103–34; see pp. 125–6, n. 112. No other source names him *grandevus*; for 'old' Knut Sven uses *vetus*.

146. Samuel 1: 2 and 10: 23. For opposing interpretations of this period see Paludan, and Breengaard, 183–205. Sven stresses Nicolaus's legitimate marriage as a contrast with the union that produced his daughter (*pace* Riis, 216–17).

147. Alias Knut Lavard, 'the Lord'; commemorated as a martyr by papal canonization from 1170, and the subject of a *Vita et Passio*, now lost, written by Robert of Ely 1135/7. Sven draws his account from the later

work, c.1170, represented by the lections of the Ringsted Ofice; see VSD, 189–204, and 175 for borrowings noted by Gertz.

148. Knut bought the crown of the Abotrites from King Lothair and subjugated the Slavs with German assistance; see Helmold, i, ch. 49. Both *strenuitas* and *prudentia* were involved, but *Nam quæ jure strenuitatis prudentia* in A is corrupt, and *singulari fortitudine* in S must be paraphrase. Gertz gives *Nam et mire strenuitatis prevalentia*, but *mire strenuitatis prudentia*, if clumsy, involves less alteration. Saxo invented a 'bequest' of Slavia to Knut by the last Slav ruler (GD, 347; EC, 116–17).

149. *cuius virtutibus [M. eclipsatus] languescere cepit invidia, que caput assolet [in prosperis] alterius [rebus dimittere]*: this may be another proverb, or a maxim distilled from Horace, *Epistles*, i 2, 58: 'The envious man grows lean because his neighbour thrives'; cf. Stephen of Tournai: 'Some men burn at the successes of other men' (*Ep.*, 164; *Lettres*, 191). However, all the words in brackets were invented by Gertz. S merely reads, *Sed conspicuis ejus virtutibus incitata, effervescere coepit invidia*. The following 'with timorous ambition' is good, but not Sven's own: this is nearly all Gertzian fantasy.

150. *regno momentaneo*: the use of *momentaneus*, to distinguish this world from the next, is a common post-Carolingian habit; see NGML, s.v.

151. Lucan, *Pharsalia*, i 92–3; also cited twice by Theodricus (MHN, 10, 25).

152. Statius, *Thebaid*, i 154–5. Theodricus (MHN, 9) cites *Thebaid*, i 151, but attributes the line to Lucan.

153. *Skatelar*: explained in *Tilnavne* as 'magpie-thigh'; in *Knýtlinga saga*, ch. 92, he is called Heinrekr halti. The saga also notes there that 'it is the saying of most people' that he struck the death-blow. He was the son of Sven, an elder brother of King Nicolaus, and so a cousin of Knut Lavard. At this point A is defective and S somewhat abridged, with the names of two other conspirators, Ubbi and Hakon, probably added from Saxo. Sven's source is still the *Passio* known in the Ringsted Office.

154. Added by Gertz from S.

155. *in silva penes Haraldstathæ*: four miles north of Ringsted, in the middle of Sjælland; from Sven's source, see VSD, 197.

156. *Christi athleta*: Ælnoth applied this designation of martyrs, common at least from Cassian and Ambrose onwards (Blaise, 230), to Knut IV and his henchmen, but the surviving hagiography does not use it of Knut Lavard.

157. Matthew 7: 15; the hoods and cloaks are from Sven's source, the text known from the Ringsted Office, but there it is Magnus who holds Knut by the *caputium* of his *cappa* (VSD, 199).
158. John 1: 47.
159. The soul 'imprisoned in the flesh' was identified by Gertz as a loan from the versicles and responses of the Ringsted Office (VSD, 224). On Knut's burial and miracles see the lections from that Office, Alexander III's letter of canonization, and the list in the *miracula* (VSD, 200–2, 246, 242–5). The cult was renewed in 1186 by a joint donation to the Ringsted houses (DD, 1:3, no. 135).
160. *domini instigatus digito*: Exodus 8: 19, *Digitus Dei est hic*, and Augustine, 'The Holy Spirit is called the finger of God' (Sermon 156, 14; PL 38, 857). In his 1135 Lund charter Erik II ascribed his victory in the civil war to God's protection (DD, i:2, no. 65); but CR says that the 'sedition' against Nicolaus and Magnus was merely a pretext for usurpation (SM, i 27), and that God brought about Erik's fall, not his rise (SM, i 31).
161. *Primo in Rinebiergh preliantes*: what Gertz, 186, calls the 'nominative absolute' construction. The battle of 1132 at Rønbjerg, four miles SW of Skive in Jutland, was not the first between them; there had been an earlier clash at Jelling in 1131(?): see e.g. DMA, 17, 56, and GD, 359 (EC, 135). Erik's first assault on Jutland was there repulsed by King Nicolaus and the bishop of Ribe; evidently Sven's family was not involved.
162. *Othenshylle*: in N. Jutland, where Erik's troops were retreating over the Skals river to re-embark for Scania. Note that CR describes these troops as 'a collection of all the oathbreakers and villains' (SM, i 27). Saxo mentioned this battle without alluding to the heroic rearguard action of Aggi and Biorn: 'And several of his [Erik's] troops who were embarking too slowly were slaughtered by the oncoming army of the king' (GD, 361; EC, 136). The Danish annals ignore the episode.
163. *columpnæ . . . immobiles*: an ecclesiastical metaphor, used of St Paul by Clement (inspired by Galatians 2: 9, and 1 Timothy 3: 15), *immobilis columna disciplinæ*, but more widely later. Geoffrey of Monmouth used 'column' of Robert of Gloucester, Waleran of Meulan and King Stephen in his second and third dedications of the British History, and Stephen of Tournai so described Absalon's kinsman, Peter (c.1188; DD, i:3, no. 53). Saxo called Absalon 'column of the fatherland' and Starkather 'column of battle' (GD, 409, 214; EC, 408; PF, 238).

164. Sven leaves out those battles which did not concern his family and friends: the sea-fight off Sejerø in 1132, Nicolaus's reconquest of Sjælland in 1133, and the fights at Værebro and Roskilde described in CR and Saxo.
165. *Lundoniarumque in loco* A: the bay on the SW tip of Scania formed by the Skanör peninsula. Weibull 1918, 185–6, dismissed the reading and argued for *nundiniarum*, 'of the markets', because Skanör did not belong to Lund. The battle was fought on 4 June 1134, and Sven's account can be supplemented by others in CR, Saxo, Helmold and some German annals. It is remarkable that he makes no allusion to the part played in these events by his great-uncle Archbishop Asser, the only prelate to support Erik at this point (so CR; SM, i 28–9).
166. *plebs . . . pollens probitate*: Erik had been proclaimed king in Scania on 11 April 1131, but the Scanians rejected him after he lost Sjælland in 1133, and only 'repented' when he escaped from captivity in Norway in the spring of 1134 (SM, i 27–8); this apparent inconstancy underlies Sven's assertion of Scanian 'probity'. Neither he nor Saxo reveals that Erik was also reinforced by a squadron of 300 German knights, who caught the enemy unprepared while they were disembarking (Erfurt Annals and Annalista Saxo, MGH, *Script.* vi 539, 768). Nevertheless, according to Saxo, Fotavik was a byword for Scanian prowess in the 1180s (GD, 528; EC, 588).
167. *ad tartara trucidantes transmiserunt*: cf. Knut VI's immunity-grant to the bishop of Schleswig, 20 Nov. 1187, *rudentibus inferni detractos in tartarum tradidit* (DD, i:3, no. 143). Sven conveys the triumph of the Scanians, CR the deep dismay of the non-Scanian clergy; see Breengaard, 35–9, on the commemoration of the battle *ad villam hamar* in the Lund *Memoriale Fratrum* and *Liber Daticus*. Sven's two bishops are presumably those of Roskilde and Vestervig commemorated at Lund (NL, 140–1; Breengaard, 222–3), but CR records several more: the bishops of Ribe, Aarhus and Sigtuna, and the bishop of Schleswig who died of wounds later (SM, i 29).
168. *perfide trucidabant*: cf. CR, *infideliter interfectus est*; on 25 June 1134, according to NL; with all his retinue, according to Saxo; Erik II rewarded the citizens for the deed, according to CR (SM, i 30).
169. *Henricus iugi commemoratus memoria* A, *Ericus, æterna dignus memoria* S: *Emun(i)* in AR and *Annales Lundenses* (DMA, 164 and 57). According to CR, Erik was 'always a profligate man, full of rage and deceit', and the text of Knut Lavard's *Passio* in the Ringsted Office described him 'slaughtering and sparing no one in avenging his brother

with lion-like ferocity' (VSD, 202). In Icelandic sources his nickname is *eymuni* or *eimuni*, explained in *Knýtlinga saga*, ch. 99: 'And because many thought they would long have cause to remember his cruelty, he was called Eiríkr the ever-memorable.' Sven and Saxo are more sympathetic, but only Saxo defends his reputation after his triumph in 1134. For a comparison of the sources see Breengaard, 224–36.

170. *intempestæ noctis silentio*: this was a cliché even in the eighth-century Corpus glossary; cf. e.g. Martianus Capella, i 37, and Orosius, 3, 2, 5.

171. *Haraldum kesiæ in curia sua seuiens* A, *Haraldum Kæsiæ in curia sua Jaling* S: Gertz changed *seuiens* to *Scibiensi*, because CR called the place 'Scipying' (SM, i 30); Saxo has 'Scypethorp'. Gertz took it to be Skiby manor, close to Aarhus in NE Jutland, which later in the century was held by King Nicolaus's great-grandson, St Nicolaus (VSD, 399; Gertz, 137). St Nicolaus was not however a direct descendant of Harald Kesia (the by-name means some kind of spear or halberd; it occurs more often in Icelandic than in Danish sources) or of Erik Emune, and it seems that CR's 'Skipying' was probably Skibing in Dover, west of Kolding; see Orluf.

172. *stratu suscitatus . . . sinistri suspicatus*: alliteration heightens the grimness; cf. *nihil sinistri suspicatum*, of St Ethelbert of East Anglia, in the St Albans *Vitæ duorum Offarum* (Chambers, 241). *Catholiciani corripientes caput*: these 'fiscal officers' of the Theodosian Code, Justinian's *Codex* (9, 49, 9, 3), and the Basilics, seem to be needed for the sake of alliteration rather than of precision; but the word recurs (see n. 183 below), and must mean 'henchmen' here. Cf. LMP, ii 251, for later Polish usage.

173. According to CR, Biorn and his brother, Henry the Deacon, were drowned before, not after, the death of their father (SM, i 31). Saxo gives details and blames Sven's grandfather Kristiarn for egging on the king to murder for *raisons d'état* (GD, 367; EC, 350).

174. According to CR, eight of Harald's other sons were killed and buried in a pit; Olaf escaped to Sweden; the Scanians are blamed for the murder. Saxo relates that these other sons were captured with their father in January 1135, and CR tells how they were held in irons in Scania until their deaths in August.

175. *haut patrisando* A: *patrisso* (Plautus, *Pseuodolus*, i 5, 27), 'to take after the father'; thus, unlike Erik I and Sven II, great propagators of sons. In the St Albans *Vitæ* Warmundus says of Offa, *non degener est fili me genealis, sed patrissans* (Chambers, 224).

176. *regulosque pullulantes prorsus extirpasset*: not quite, since Olaf the survivor had escaped in women's clothes (Saxo) or disguised as a beggar or pilgrim (CR) and was to rule in Scania c.1138–41.
177. 2 Thessalonians 2: 8.
178. CR also recognized the hand of God in Erik's assassination, and placed the event near Ribe. The Urne-thing (*in vrnensi placito* A) was the plenary assembly of the South Jutlanders, held on the eastern side of the peninsula, off the Hærvej near Aabenraa; the date was 18 Sept. 1137 (NL). The 'circle of warriors', *militari corona stipatum*, recalls Statius, *virum stipante corona* (*Thebaid*, i 612), and Walter of Châtillon, *iuvenum stipante corona* (*Alexandreis*, iii 128). *Transverberavit*, the word for Plog's deadly thrust, is, if biblical, from Judith 5: 28. Sven ignores Erik II's expeditions to Norway and Rügen, which Saxo noted to the king's credit.
179. He died at Odense on 27 August 1146 (NL, 215). This Erik was the son of Knut Lavard's sister, Ragnhild. He was criticized by the author of CR as undignified and two-faced, apparently because he imposed Bishop Riko on the Roskilde chapter uncanonically. Sven presents the favourable view of all other sources except Saxo: they call him the 'Lamb' or the 'Pacific' (*Spak(e)*, Icelandic *(hinn) spaki*). His hard-fought civil war with Olaf, Harald Kesia's son, is ignored, although Sven's uncle, Archbishop Eskil, was much involved in it (cf. GD, 371–5; EC, 356–61).
180. Two sentences summarize the events of 1146–57, which Saxo treats in detail (GD, 375–412; EC, 362–416). Sven's predecessors (the lections of the Ringsted Office, Helmold) either ignore the election of Knut V or, in the case of the source followed by Ralph Niger, insist that he was 'elected by the whole community at Viborg, where it is the custom for kings to be chosen.' Sven ignores the rivals' parity, and avoids saying that it was Sven III who invested Valdemar with the Schleswig duchy in 1148/9. The word *feodo* in *patris feodo* is lacking in A and Gertz took it from S. If it stood in the original manuscript, it is its first recorded use in a Danish source. Saxo prefers *præfectum* and *beneficium* for the honour. Valdemar appears to have supported Sven III until 1152, and then inclined to Knut. Here Valdemar is described as *sacro cruore oriundus*, perhaps from *Passio Petri et Pauli*, 262, 280 (LHL, i 509), and the stress is on his independence rather than his cunning. According to Ralph Niger, 89, Knut raised Valdemar to the kingship.

181. 25/6 July 1157 in Ralph Niger, 89. Saxo reports that Sven III got Scania, after Valdemar had awarded himself Jutland; Knut was left with the islands, including Sjælland; *Knýtlinga saga* agrees.

182. 8 August 1157. Saxo has a detailed narrative of this episode in GD, 402–8 (EC, 402–10), but he insists that Knut was the host; so does the source used by Ralph Niger (89). The discrepancy with Sven's *apud Suenonem* is seen as highly significant by R. Malmros, who argues that Sven was using an 'unofficial' account of the murder, which predated the attribution of host-betrayal, as well as other infamies, to Sven III; see Malmros 1979 for a full discussion of the sources and their implications. I am not convinced by the argument. Sven Aggesen may just have deduced that Sven III was the host from a careless reading of *hospitem suum* (so in Ralph Niger) as 'his guest' rather than 'his host'—although admittedly this would mean that he ignored the preceding passage. Or he may have used *apud* to mean 'in the presence of'. Saxo says they let Sven as the oldest preside at the feast.

183. *catholiciani*: see p. 134, n. 172, above.

184. *extinctis vero luminaribus*: suggests *luminaria* in the ecclesiastical sense of 'lights, candles' rather than the classical 'windows, shutters'; but cf. Saxo, *fenestras reserantibus* (GD, 405; EC, 406). They would hardly have tried to kill their victims in pitch darkness. Saxo says they opened the shutters to be sure of finishing off their work.

185. *martyrio coronantes interemerunt*: the same phrase was used earlier for the martyrdom of St Knut of Odense; and *Knýtlinga saga*, ch. 114, says, 'The Danes declare him [sc. Knut V] to be a saint.' There is no evidence of a formal cult or of requests for papal canonization. Ralph Niger refers to him as *christianissimus rex*.

186. *stricto mucrone confodere molirentur* X: echoes Valdemar I's foundation charter for Vitskøl abbey (1157–8; DD, i:2, no. 120), *eductis gladiis confodere conati sunt*. The following *coxa* is Late Latin 'thigh' rather than the classical 'hip'; cf. Saxo, *femur quam gravissime sauciatus est*.

187. *divina elapsum conservavit gratia*: again the view expressed in the Vitskøl charter.

188. *secus Gratham*: a large heath sixteen miles south of Viborg, *Grathæheth* in the Ringsted lections *in translacione S. Kanuti* (VSD, 203), where the battle was fought on 23 Oct. 1157.

189. More *lustra* (cf. p. 125, n. 112, p. 130, n. 145, above), and another inaccurate dating. Valdemar ruled for only 25 years after 1157, although he had been styled king since 1155. The calculation may however be

based on a misdated accession, as in the earliest Lund annals, s.a. 1155 (DMA, 18).

190. *persecurizavit* X, *prosiciscatur* A, *pacificavit* S: one of Gertz's less convincing emendations; *persecurizo* is a very rare bird, which occurs in a fifteenth-century note on a manuscript of Annalista Saxo (MGH, *Script.*, vi 550). Even if the word had been abbreviated as Gertz suggests, it could hardly have been misread to give the A or S reading. As early as 1170 the *in translacione* lections of the Ringsted Office included a brief eulogy of Valdemar's rule (VSD, 203); this may have inspired Sven here.

191. Henry of Huntingdon (1153–4), followed by Robert of Torigny, attributed three great achievements to 'old' Knut of England and Denmark. Sven may have known of this. He may also have wished to improve on the passage in the source used by Ralph Niger which attributed two achievements to Valdemar: the conquest and baptism of the Rugians, and the building of a castle 'in the exit of Denmark' so as to block the way in (Ralph Niger, 89–90; see Anne K. G. Kristensen 1968–9, 432, for refs.).

192. Psalm 2: 9 and Ezekiel 20: 33, but the immediate source was Alexander III's bull of 1169(?) putting the newly conquered Rugians under the see of Roskilde (DD, i:2, no. 189).

193. Possibly a reference to *Alexandreis*, ii 351, where the Persian monarch boasts of the 'fired brick' and the 'tower constructed with bitumen' at Babylon. Sprogø is halfway over the Great Belt on the crossing from Nyborg to Taarnborg (where Valdemar also built). The fort on Sprogø has been replaced by a lighthouse.

194. On the Danevirke see p. 120, n. 78, above. Between 1163 and 1182 Valdemar and Absalon fortified about 4 km from Kurburg to the Dannewerk See with a brick wall 22 feet high and 6–8 feet thick; see Neergaard. These achievements are recorded in similar style, but with the mention of Sprogø and the Danevirke reversed, on the lead plate which was discovered in Valdemar's grave at Ringsted in 1855. The inscription appears to have been added, perhaps in 1241 or 1250, by a reader of Sven's work (SM, ii 77–9, 87–8). For a comparison with the X and S texts see Christensen, 28–30.

195. The eulogy repeats the *facetus* and *omni urbanitate* already used to describe Queen Thyrwi. A omits a word after *plus iusto*, and S supplies *crudelior*, which Gertz, 149–50, found difficult to accept, with good reason. A passage in Ralph Niger refers to Valdemar as *crudelis et fortis*, and if Sven knew such a judgment, he may have wished to tone

it down. However, 'just cruelty' is not a quality he commends in other rulers; 'more severe' or even 'more indulgent towards his own' would make better sense. The contrast between cruelty and justice usually needs greater emphasis, as in Geoffrey of Monmouth, 294, on King Morvidus: *Hic nimia probitate famosissimus esset, nisi plus nimie crudelitate indulsisset.* Valdemar certainly imprisoned his cousin Buris in 1167, and was later said to have blinded and castrated him, but he adopted an illegitimate cousin, the orphan Valdemar, son of Knut, 'as if he were his own son' (letter of 1205; BD, no. 41).

196. Sophia, half-sister of Knut V, daughter of Prince Volodar of Minsk and Richiza of Poland, married Valdemar in 1157 at the age of sixteen(?), and in 1184 made a second marriage with Landgrave Lewis III of Thuringia, who repudiated her in 1187. She died in 1198 and is buried in Ringsted church. *Canuti regis Roschildensis* is a title aligning Knut V with the other martyrs, St Knut of Odense and St Knut Lavard of Ringsted; see p. 136, n. 185, above, and Anne K. G. Kristensen 1968–9, 44.

197. *syncoparet*: a grecism which in twelfth-century usage meant 'voicing only part of a word'; see Ducange (who cites St Bernard, Sermon 40), also *Architrenius*, i 484, and Alan of Lille's *De Planctu Naturæ* (PL 210, 454), *locutionis syncopatæ*, a humorous repetition of the word. Gertz supplies 'the skill of the ancients' to fill a gap in A, but S may be better: 'for to describe her would defeat the eloquence of Cicero, would dry up the fluency of Ovid, and tire the ingenuity of Vergil' (cf. Weibull 1918, 187 n.); a usage much favoured by Alan (PL 210, 464, 468, 479–80).

198. *mendicata suffragia*: as in Alan of Lille, *mendicata mei tandem suffragia dentur* (AC, ii 18), and in *De Planctu Naturæ* (PL 210, 470); *formæ preconia*: as in Ovid, *Amores*, iii 12, 9. Behind this courtly praise there is a hint of AC, ii 325–62, where Nature enlists the aid of Sophya, or Fronesis, to form the soul of the New Man: a passage in which Cicero's eloquence and the poetry of Ovid and Vergil are also extolled. Sven's eulogy may be compared to the elegant skull of Queen Sophia photographed and described in F. C. C. Hansen, 50. Her image appeared with Valdemar's on some coins.

199. The claim is not as far-fetched as it sounds. Valdemar became increasingly formidable after 1170. In that year Erlingr skakki, the effective ruler of Norway, became his vassal (GD, 480–1; EC, 517–18), and by 1171 Count Bernard of Ratzeburg was his homager for a fief in Jutland (GD, 496; EC, 540). In 1177 the chief men of Sweden attended his

son's wedding, and his own father-in-law, Volodar of Minsk, sent him a ship laden with gifts (GD, 512, 517; EC, 564, 572). In 1180 Duke Henry the Lion of Saxony crossed into Denmark to ask for his help (GD, 523; EC, 530), and in the winter of 1180–1 the ousted King Magnús Erlingsson of Norway took refuge in Denmark (*Sverris saga*, chs. 48, 50). In 1181 Count Siegfried of Orlamünde sued for and married Valdemar's daughter Sophia at Schleswig (GD, 534; EC, 596). That summer Valdemar arrived in Lübeck to meet Frederick Barbarossa; he came 'with a large retinue, and made a show of himself, boasting loudly of his glory' (*Chronica Slavorum*, ii 21); and made arrangements for two other daughters to marry the emperor's sons (GD, 532–4; EC, 592–6).
200. S includes here a short eulogy on Knut VI, who 'was a religious man, chaste, noble, handsome, an outstanding warrior . . .' The past tense betrays a later hand. According to Saxo's book sixteen, Knut's success in war outdid the achievements of his father, but were attributable mainly to the assistance of Absalon; ignored by Sven. Yet the successful raids of 1184 and 1185 would have been impossible if Absalon's victory over the Pomeranian fleet in May 1184 had not deprived Prince Bugislav of his ships and saved Denmark from invasion. However, this is a book of kings, not of bishops, and Absalon's triumph over Jomsborg has been mentioned above, p. 61.
201. *rostris deauratis choruscabat* : classical *rostrum*, 'ram', was later applied to prows and sterns; cf. *ardebat aurum in rostris*, EE, 18, of Knut's invasion fleet in 1015; *rostrum deauratum*, of Godwin's ship in the B manuscript of Florence of Worcester.
202. Saxo says that Bugislav did homage to Knut after submitting to him outside Kamien, fifteen miles downstream from Wolin (GD, 550–1; EC, 622–3); but neither Saxo nor *Knýtlinga saga*, ch. 129, is precise about the site, and anywhere between the two towns would be *non procul* from Wolin (*non procul* in S, preferred by Gertz; *procul* in A). Sven was an eyewitness, and the other sources agree that the Danes had been ravaging away from Kamien just before the surrender.
203. *ab antiquo preuaricatore*: see p. 129, n. 134, above. Saxo also records the thunder-clap, and comments that 'it was conjectured by the wise that this event portended the downfall of the kingdom of the Slavs.' He preferred to keep the Devil out of history (GD, 551; EC, 624; Blatt, in SS, 12).
204. Conrad, bishop of Pomerania, who had moved his see from Wolin to Kamien in 1176; see p. 121, n. 93, above.

205. Valdemar, second son of Valdemar I and Sophia, was born 28 June 1170, governed Schleswig as duke from 1187 to 1202, and reigned in Denmark from 1202 to 1241. Here he is *iuvenis indolis elegantissimæ*, which may, but need not, suggest that the words were written before 1202.

206. *cunctorum gubernator in sua pace disponat*: the valedictory formula which concludes the prayer after the reconciliation of the dying penitent in the Gelasian and other sacramentaries: *Hanc igitur oblationem Domine cunctæ familiæ tuæ . . . diesque nostros in tua pace disponas* (Wilson, 67); also found in the opening of a blessing by Alcuin which includes the phrase *in pacis tranquillitate* (CBP, 1563a); cf. p. 112, n. 46, above. Saxo appears to answer Sven's prayer at the end of GD, where he records that Bugislav remained loyal to Knut VI until his death in 1187, and that afterwards Knut acted as guardian of his children.

APPENDIX

SVEN'S FAMILY

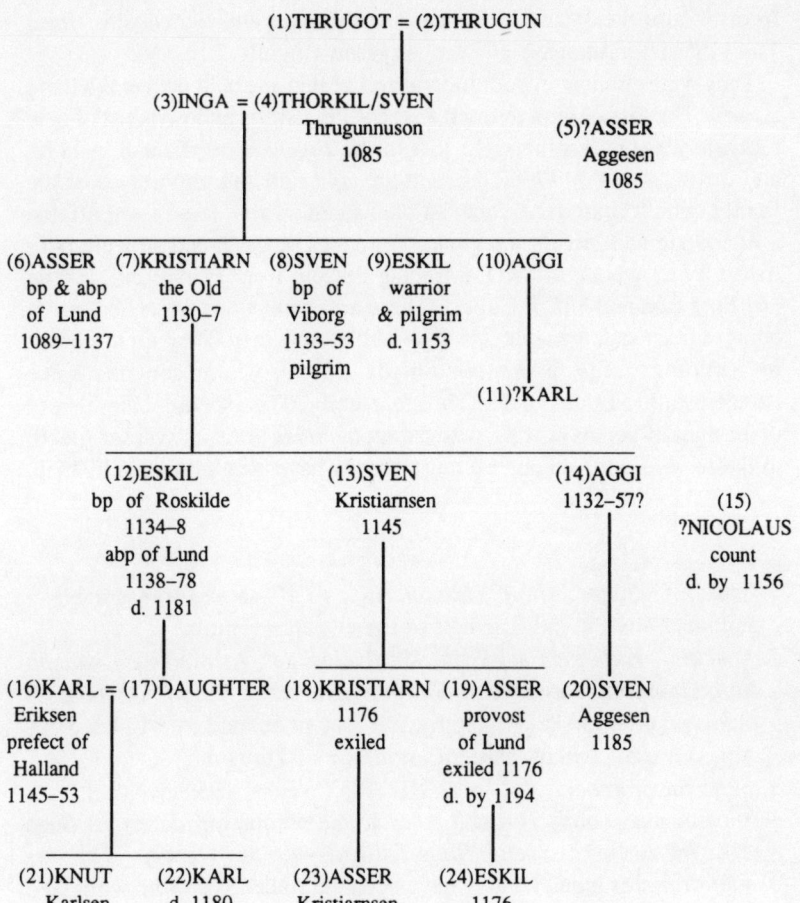

Known as the Thrugot or Thrugun family (Dan. *Trugotslægt, Trundslægt*) by modern historians, they, like other twelfth-century Danish dynasties, had no recorded designation at the time. The identity of the group was asserted by the use of recurrent names (Kristiarn, Asser, Agge, Eskil, Sven) and by public cooperation between kinsmen, usually for or against the king. Descent from a common ancestor also counted for something: from Skialm the White in the case of Absalon and his cousins, from Thorkil/Sven in the case of Sven Aggesen's family.

They were eminent in both Jutland and Scania and held land in Sjælland as well. The loss of land through Archbishop Eskil's endowments of new monasteries and canonries, the loss of the *Eigenkirche* of Lund in 1178, and the purges of 1177–82 reduced the cohesion and importance of the family, which ceased thereafter to play a central role in political affairs.

Elaborate and largely imaginary pedigrees of these people were published by Langebek in SRD, i, tracing descent from Pálna-Tóki, Hákon jarl Eiríksson and Ulf of Galicia. These are connexions wrenched out of context from saga-genealogies and cobbled together. They do not occur in *Knýtlinga saga*, a compilation of *c*.1250, which contains some Lundensian traditions of the Thrugot family. The ascertainable history of the dynasty begins in 1089, with the appointment of Asser Svensen (no. 6) to the see of Lund, although it must already have been important by then.

1. THRUGOT: *Sueno, filius Thrugut* (LC, p. 40 above), presumably a Jutlander alive in the first half of the eleventh century.
2. THRUGUN: *Knýtlinga saga*, ch. 40: Sveinn and Ástráðr *váru kallaðir Þorgunnusynir. Þorgunna, móðir þeira, var dóttir Vagns Ákasonar*. A plausible tradition, supported by WR (see p. 46) and by NL, but Sven Aggesen uses 'son of Thrugut', not 'son of Thrugun'.
3. INGA: *mater venerabilis Azeri*, NL, 105 (Weeke, 195; 19 Nov.).
4. THORKIL/SVEN: *obiit Throckil pater archiepiscopi, qui dictus est Suen* (NL, 78; 20 June). *Sueno, filius Thrugut*—see no. 1 above. If he was *inter primores regni*, he may have been the staller Sven who witnessed the great Lund donation of 1085 (DD, i:2, no. 21). *Knýtlinga saga*, chs. 66–8, tells that he and his brother, Ástráðr, served Knut IV and were imprisoned in Flanders as hostages for the release of King Olaf Hunger until freed by the intercession of the martyred Knut. The story seems to reflect later links between the descendants of St Knut and of Thorkil/Sven; see no. 16 below.

5. ASSER: an *Ascer Akonis filius* witnessed the 1085 Lund charter after Sven (no. 4 above), and the recurrence of these names among Thorkil/Sven's descendants suggests kinship.
6. ASSER: bishop of Lund from 18 Nov. 1089, archbishop from 1103, died 5 May 1137: *vir acer et amarus, et sapiens et nullius constancie* (CR; SM, i 28). If he was of canonical age at his election, he must have been born *c.*1050, but he remained politically active to at least 1134.
7. KRISTIARN: *Christiarn pater domini arch. Eschili* (Weeke, 128; 20 May); *Christiernus, Suenonis filius* (LC; p. 39 above). Surnamed *Gamlæ*, 'the Old', in annals (DMA, 319, 320). According to Saxo, born to high status in Jutland and politically active against King Nicolaus and later in the election of Erik III (GD, 360, 361, 371; EC, 135–6, 356). (The two brothers, Asser and Kristiarn, flourished in the period down to 1137; the other brothers were active in the 1140s and 1150s and may not have been sons of Inga.)
8. SVEN: canon of Lund, provost and bishop of Viborg 1133–53, died in Palestine 3 March 1153/4 (NL, 63 n.) on pilgrimage with his brother Eskil, no. 9 below (SM, ii 437–41). Famous for his piety and high birth, with St Kjeld as his provost from *c.*1147.
9. ESKIL: also *inter primores regni* according to Sven in LC (p. 40 above); described in SM, ii 437, as 'warlike and carnal, swollen with power... ferocious and fearsome'; died in Palestine on pilgrimage with his brother, Bishop Sven, on 3 March 1153/4 (SM, ii 437–9; NL, 63 n.). Not mentioned by Saxo, but he could be the *præfectus* of Erik III who witnessed DD, i:2, no. 85 (1142/6) and the *villicus* of Roskilde in 1145 (DD, i:2, no. 91).
10. AGGI: mentioned in LC (p. 40 above); he could be the chamberlain *Ago* of DD, i:2, no. 76 (1104/17), and possibly the father of no. 11.
11. KARL: Karl *agisun* attested the 1145 Lund charter, DD, i:2, no. 86.
12. ESKIL: provost of Lund *c.*1131, bishop of Roskilde 1134–8, archbishop of Lund 1138–78; died at Clairvaux 6 Sept. 1181. Apparently married when young; see no. 17 below.
13. SVEN: attested DD, i:2, no. 88 (1 Sept. 1145) as *Swen Christians sun*; mentioned by Saxo as the father of Kristiarn and Asser, nos. 18–19 below (GD, 511, 512; EC, 562, 563).
14. AGGI: *patre meo Aggone* in HC (p. 69 above); fought with Biorn Haraldsen for Erik II at Onsild in 1132, and for Sven III at Grathe Heath in 1157 (GD, 410; EC, 414). Possibly the brother who died unreconciled to Archbishop Eskil (SM, ii 436–7).
15. NICOLAUS: *comes, carne et sanguine michi proximus* in Archbishop

Eskil's 1158 charter for Esrum (DD, i:2, no. 126). He became a monk there and left land to the brothers at Tjæreby and Veksebo in N. Sjælland (DD, i:2, no. 127). The *Vita Prima* of St Bernard (iv, ch. 26) records that he was *propinquus* to Eskil, but a great sinner, and dead (Weeke, 102; 30 April) by the time of Eskil's visit to Clairvaux in 1156. As he held the rare new title of 'count' (*greve*) and was still *adolescens* at his death, he must have been the son of a powerful man or woman, perhaps of Count Erik (fl. 1130–45), whose son Karl married Eskil's daughter (no. 17 below), or of Count Ubbi Esbiornsen (DD, i:2, nos. 32, 34), who married King Nicolaus's daughter, Ingerd (Ingigerth) and was hanged in 1133 (GD, 364; EC, 140). His connexion with Eskil was presumably through Eskil's mother or sister. See McGuire, and Szacherska 1977, 140 n., for further refs.

16. KARL: the 'Lord Karl' was a charter witness 1145–57/8 (DD, i:2, nos. 88, 102, 121); son of Cecilia, daughter of Knut IV; Saxo says he was governing Halland for Sven III in 1153 (GD, 388; EC, 382).
17. ESKIL'S DAUGHTER: Saxo says that the sons of Karl, the conspirators of 1176/7, had Eskil as their maternal grandfather (GD, 503; EC, 549), although he fails to mention the fact earlier, when he describes how in 1153(?) Karl's wife (unnamed) was abducted by Jon Sverkerson of Sweden and later returned to him (GD, 388; EC, 382). This alliance of the Thrugot family with Knut IV's descendants through Cecilia created a yet more powerful group, perhaps in response to the growing power of the Skialm family under Ebbi Skialmsen in Sjælland and Toki Skialmsen, who married Knut Lavard's daughter, also in the 1140s, and got land in Jutland.
18. KRISTIARN: a 'Kristiarn, whose father was Sven' was exiled after confessing complicity in Magnus Eriksen's plot in 1176/7 (GD, 511–12; EC, 562–3).
19. ASSER: canon and provost of Lund by 1171 (DD, i:3, no. 19), exiled for conspiracy 1176/7 (GD, 512; EC, 564); at Magdeburg 1185–6 (DD, i:3, nos. 119, 125); died before 1194 (Weeke, 62; 25 March), and left land at Venestad and Bjæverskov to his chapter (Weeke, 70–1). He may have had a sister, *Gunnild doter Suens* (Weeke, 89), and he left heirs who sold more land at Bjæverskov to the brothers of Sorø c.1200 (SRD, iv 36 and 470).
20. SVEN: for his biography see pp. 1–4 above.
21. KNUT: son of Karl; an extremely well-connected but unlucky nobleman, who was implicated in the conspiracy of 1176/7, fled to Sweden, invaded Denmark 1179/80, was wounded, imprisoned and disinherited

by Valdemar I (GD, 502–23; EC, 549–80). According to Saxo, he was grandson of Eskil, *cognatus* with Absalon (through Absalon's mother, Inga, perhaps a sister of Count Erik, Knut's paternal grandfather?), and *propinquus* to Birger jarl of Sweden (also a great-grandson of Knut IV, through his daughter Ingerd/Ingigerth). Date of death unknown; no known descendants.

22. KARL: shared his brother Knut's fortunes but was mortally wounded in the invasion of 1179/80, and his corpse later found in a wood on the Halland-Götaland frontier (GD, 523; EC, 580). These brothers were aided by a half-brother, a bastard son of Karl Eriksen called Benedikt (GD, 506–9; EC, 554–9), and the appearance of a *Bendict Karlssun* among the twelve Scanian worthies who swore to the boundaries of the Lund estate at Bällingslev (1202/41; DD, i:4, no. 72) raises the possibility either that Benedikt the bastard lived to be very old, or that a son of Karl Karlsen was named after his uncle Benedikt.

23. ASSER: *Ascer Cristiarnsun* appears in a brotherhood associated with Harsyssel, NW Jutland, in the Brother-list (KVJ, i:2, 84, ii:2, 550); presumably a descendant, alive in the 1190s, of old Kristiarn, no. 7 above.

24. ESKIL: *Asceri hic filius erat* wrote Saxo of a conspirator unmasked in 1176/7 (GD, 511; EC, 562), and the only Asser he mentions in the context was Provost Asser (no. 19 above). It is possible that Archbishop Eskil had an otherwise unmentioned brother called Asser, who could have been this Eskil's father.

Thus within four years, 1176–80, six members of the most powerful group of kinsmen in Denmark were dead or exiled or imprisoned. Eskil the former archbishop was preparing for death as a monk at Clairvaux; and the way was clear for the dominance of Archbishop Absalon and his kinsmen: Esbiorn Snara, Alexander Petersen, Ebbi Olafsen, Suni Ebbesen and his seven sons, Aki Stighsen and Provost Toki Stighsen, and the four sons of Ingerd/Ingigerth Petersdottir.

However, the records of Lund, the Brother-list, and the *Avia Ripensis* suggest that descendants of Sven Aggesen's family survived as local 'gentry' in both Scania and Jutland. A Benedikte Kristiarnsdottir married Thorkil Bille *c*.1230 (Weeke, 203–4); Peter Aggesen and Kristiarn and Nicolaus, Aggi and Kristiarn, formed brotherhoods in Omersyssel and Almindsyssel; Kristiarn Benediktsen lived near Aarhus in 1243 (SM, ii 223); and Kristiarn Aggesen was alive in 1275 (*Avia Ripensis*, 20).

ABBREVIATIONS AND BIBLIOGRAPHY

Note. The following is a finding-list, complete or virtually so, for the authors and titles mentioned in the Introduction and Notes other than works by classical authors which are readily found in series of standard editions. Place of publication is noted only in the case of sixteenth-century prints.

A	The text of AM 33 4to in Gertz 1915/16 and SM, i.
Aarbøger	Aarbøger for nordisk Oldkyndighed og Historie.
AB	Adam of Bremen, *Gesta Hammaburgensis ecclesiae pontificum.* Ed. B. Schmeidler. 1917.
Abbot William's *Genealogy*	*Wilhelmi Abbatis Genealogia regum Danorum.* SM, i 176–85.
Abels	R. P. Abels, *Lordship and Military Obligation.* 1988.
AC	*Anticlaudianus.* See Alan of Lille.
Adam (of Bremen)	See AB.
Ælnoth	*Gesta Svenomagni regis et filiorum eius et passio gloriosissimi Canuti regis et martyris.* VSD, 77–136.
Ágrip	*Ágrip af Nóregskonunga sǫgum.* Ed. Bjarni Einarsson. ÍF xxix. 1985.
AJ	*Danasaga Arngríms lærða [Jónssonar].* In *Danakonunga sǫgur,* 3–38.
Alan of Lille	*Anticlaudianus.* Ed. R. Bossuat. 1985.
	De Planctu Naturæ. In PL 210.
	Summa de Arte Prædicatoris. In PL 205.
Albøge, Gordon	'Til Vederloven', *Festskrift til Kristian Hald* (1974), 293–318.
Alexander Jóhannesson	*Isländisches etymologisches Wörterbuch.* 1956.
Alexandreis	See Walter of Châtillon.
Alfræði	*Alfræði íslenzk.* Ed. Kr. Kålund and N. Beckman. 1908–18.
Ancher, P. K.	*En Dansk Lov-Historie fra Kong Harald Blatands Tid til Kong Christian den Femtes.* 1769.

Anders Sunesen, Hex. *Andreæ Sunonis Filii Hexaemeron.* Ed. S. Ebbesen and L. B. Mortensen. 1985-8.

Anders Sunesen's Scanian laws *Anders Sunesøns latinske Parafrase af Skånske Lov.* In DGL, i:2.

Andersen, N. K. 'Kanonisk Rets Indflydelse paa Jydske Love', *Med Lov skal Land bygges* (ed. E. Reitzel-Nielsen, 1941), 84–120.

Anderson, H. 'Hovedstaden i Riget', *Nationalmuseets Arbejdsmark* (1960), 13–35.

Ann. Fuld. *Annales Fuldenses.* Ed. R. Rau. 1969.
Annales 1095–1194 In DMA, 307–9.
Annales Bartholiniani In SRD, i.
Annales Lundenses In DMA, 21–70.
Annales Ripenses In DMA, 254–67.
Annales Ryenses In DMA, 149–75.
Annales Valdemarii In DMA, 75–9.
Annalista Saxo In MGH, *Script.*, vi.
Annals of St Bertin *Annales Bertiniani et Annales Vedastini.* Ed. R. Rau. 1969.

Appuleius *Opuscules philosophiques.* Ed. J. Beaujeu. 1973.

APS *Acta Philologica Scandinavica.*
AR See *Annales Ryenses.*
Arbusow, L. *Colores rhetorici.* Second ed. 1963.
Architrenius *Johannis de Hauvilla Architrenius.* Ed. P. G. Schmidt. 1974.

Arnold (of Lübeck) *Chronica Slavorum.* Ed. G. H. Pertz. 1868.

Arup, E. *Danmarks Historie,* i. *Land og Folk til 1282.* 1925.

Augustine, St, *Ep(istolæ)* In PL 33.
Augustine, St (and Pseudo-Augustine), *Sermones* In PL 38.
Avia Ripensis *Samling af Adkomster . . . og kirkelige Vedtægter for Ribe Domkapittel og Bispestol . . . kaldet 'Oldemoder'.* Ed. O. Nielsen. 1869.

Azo	*Summa Azonis*. Basel 1563.
BD	*Bullarium Danicum*. Ed. A. Krarup. 1932.
Bernard of Pavia	*Bernardi Papiensis Summa Decretalium*. Ed. E. A. T. Lespeyres. 1860.
Bernard Silvestris	W. Wetherbee, *The Cosmographia of Bernardus Silvestris*. 1973.
Bjarni Guðnason	*Um Skjöldungasögu*. 1963.
Blaise	A. B. Blaise, *Dictionnaire latin-français des auteurs chrétiens*. 1954.
Blaise, *Vocab.*	A. B. Blaise, *Le vocabulaire latin des principaux thèmes liturgiques*. 1967.
Blatt, in SS	Franz Blatt, 'Saxo, en repræsentant for et 12. århundredes renæssance', SS, 11–19.
Blom, G. Authén	*Kongemakt og privilegier i Norge inntil 1387*. 1967.
Boberg	Inger M. Boberg, 'Die Sage von Vermund und Uffe', APS, xvi (1942), 129–57.
Bolin, S.	*Ledung och frälse*. 1934.
Bonizo, *Liber de vita Christiana*	Ed. E. Perels. Second ed. 1930.
Bosworth–Toller	J. Bosworth, T. N. Toller, *An Anglo-Saxon Dictionary*. 1898–1921.
Breengaard, C. B.	*Muren om Israels Hus: Regnum og Sacerdotium i Danmark 1050–1170*. 1982.
(the) Brother-list	In KVJ, i:2, 164–6; cf. ii 544–66.
Bruylants, P.	*Concordance verbale du Sacramentaire Léonien*. 1945.
Brøndum-Nielsen, J.	'Om Sprogformen i de Sjællandske Love', APS, xxix (1973), 81–110.
Bø, Olav	'*Hólmganga og einvígi*', MSc., ii (1969), 132–48.
Carpenter, D.A.	*The Minority of Henry III*. 1990.
Cary, G.	*The Medieval Alexander*. 1956.
Catalogus Regum Daniæ	In SM, i 159–60.

CBP	*Corpus benedictionum pontificalium.* Ed. E. Moeller, OSB. CCSL, 162. 1971–3.
CCSL	Corpus Christianorum Series Latina.
Chadwick, H. M.	*The Origin of the English Nation.* 1907.
Chambers, R. W.	*Beowulf. An Introduction.* Third ed. 1959.
Aksel E. Christensen 1945	*Kongemagt og Aristokrati.* 1945.
Aksel E. Christensen 1978	*Ret og Magt i dansk Middelalder.* 1978.
Christensen	Karsten Christensen, *Om Overleveringen af Sven Aggesens Værker.* 1978.
Christensen, in SS	Karsten Christensen, 'Forholdet mellem Saxo og Sven Aggesen', SS, 128–37 (and 'Diskussion', 137–42).
Christiansen, Tage E.	*'Isti tres fratres.* Broderlisten i Kong Valdemars Jordebog', *Middelalder Studier tilegnede Aksel E. Christensen* (1966), 77–112.
Chronica Slavorum	See Arnold.
Chronicon Lethrense	In SM, i 43–53.
Chronicon Roskildense	In SM, i 14–33.
CL	See *Chronicon Lethrense.*
Cleasby–Vigfússon	R. Cleasby, Gudbrand Vigfusson, *An Icelandic-English Dictionary.* 1874.
Cohen	G. Cohen, *La 'Comédie' latine en France au xiie siècle.* 1931.
Cons. Lund.	*Consuetudines Lundenses. Statutter for Kannikesamfundet i Lund c. 1123.* Ed. E. Buus. 1978.
Consiliatio Cnuti	In Liebermann, i.
Corpus iuris civilis	Ed. P. Krueger, Th. Mommsen, R. Schoell, W. Kroll. 1888–95.
CPD	*Codex Pomeraniæ Diplomaticus.* Ed. K. F. W. Hasselbach and K. G. L. Kosegarten. 1843–62.
CR	See *Chronicon Roskildense.*

Curtius, E. R.	*European Literature and the Latin Middle Ages*. Tr. W. R. Trask. 1953.
Damasus	*Damasi . . . Regulae Canonicae*. Cologne, 1564.
Damsholt 1978	Nanna Damsholt, 'En studie i Valdemars-tidens kvindesyn', *Kvindestudier*, ii (1978), 117–44.
Damsholt 1985	Nanna Damsholt, *Kvindebilledet i dansk højmiddelalder*. 1985.
Danakonunga sǫgur	Ed. Bjarni Guðnason. ÍF xxxv. 1982.
Danevirke	Ed. H. Andersen, H. J. Madsen, O. Voss. 1976.
Danmarks Historie, i	I. Skovgaard-Petersen, Aksel E. Christensen, Helge Paludan, *Tiden indtil 1340*. (Gyldendals) *Danmarks Historie*, i. 1977.
DD	*Diplomatarium Danicum*. I. Række, i–iii. 1963–77.
Decretum	*Corpus iuris canonici. Pars prior, Decretum Magistri Gratiani*. Ed. A. Friedberg. 1879.
DGK	*Danmarks gamle Købstadslovgivning*. Ed. E. Kroman. 1951–61.
DGL	*Danmarks gamle Landskabslove*. Ed. J. Brøndum-Nielsen and P. J. Jørgensen. 1933-41.
Diamond, A. S.	*Primitive Law*. 1971.
Diderichsen, P.	*Dansk Prosahistorie*. 1968.
Diefenbach, L. D.	*Glossarium Latino-Germanicum*. 1857.
Digest	In *Corpus iuris civilis*.
DMA	*Danmarks middelalderlige Annaler*. Ed. E. Kroman. 1980.
DR	*Den danske Rigslovgivning indtil 1400*. Ed. E. Kroman. 1971.
Ducange	C. du Fresne du Cange et al., *Glossarium Mediæ et Infimæ Latinitatis*. 1883.
Ebbesen	*Anders Sunesen. Stormand, teolog, administrator, digter*. Ed. Sten Ebbesen. 1985.

(Saxo) EC	Saxo Grammaticus. *Books X–XVI*. Tr. Eric Christiansen. 1980–1.
Edda Snorra	*Edda Snorra Sturlusonar*. Ed. Finnur Jónsson. 1931.
EE	*Encomium Emmæ Reginæ*. Ed. A. Campbell. 1949.
Einhard, *Vita Karoli*	*Einhardi Vita Karoli Magni*. Ed. G. Waitz. 1911.
Ellis Davidson, H.	*The Sword in Anglo-Saxon England*. 1962.
EHD	*English Historical Documents*, i, *500–1042*. Ed. Dorothy Whitelock. 1955.
Ep., Epp.	*Epistola, Epistolæ*.
Erfurt Annals	In MGH. 1844.
De Eskillo archiepiscopo et duobus Eskilii patruis narratio [from *Exordium Magnum*, Distinct. III, cc. xxv–xxvi]	In SM, ii 428–42.
Etym.	See Isidore.
Fagrskinna	*Fagrskinna. Nóregs konunga tal*. Ed. Bjarni Einarsson. ÍF xxix. 1985.
Faulkes, A. R.	'The genealogies and regnal lists in a manuscript in Resen's library', *Sjötíu ritgerðir helgaðar Jakobi Benediktssyni* (1977), 177–90.
Fenger	R. Th. Fenger, *Svend Aagesens Danmarks Krøniker, oversat og oplyst*. 1842.
Fenger 1989	O. Fenger, *Kirker rejses alle vegne*. (Gyldendal og Politikens) *Danmarks Historie*, iv. 1989.
Flahiff, G. B.	'Ralph Niger: an introduction', *Medieval Studies*, ii (1940), 104–26.
Flat.	*Flateyjarbók*. Ed. Guðbrandur Vigfússon and C. R. Unger. 1860–8.
Florence of Worcester	*Chronicon ex Chronicis*. Ed. B. Thorpe. 1848–9.
Foote, P.	'Things in early Norse verse', *Festskrift til Ludvig Holm-Olsen* (1984), 74–83.

Foote, P., and Wilson, D. M.	*The Viking Achievement.* 1970.
Forcellini	J. Facciolati, E. Forcellini, *Totius Latinitatis Lexicon.* Ed. J. Bailey. 1826.
Frank, Tenney	'Some classical quotations from the middle Ages', *Classical Philology*, iv (1909), 82–3.
Fredegar's *Chronicle*	*The Fourth Book of the Chronicle of Fredegar.* Ed. J. M. Wallace-Hadrill. 1960.
Friis-Jensen, K.	'Was Saxo a Canon of Lund?', *Cahiers de l'Institut du Moyen-âge Grec et Latin*, lix (1989), 331–57.
Fritzner, iv	J. Fritzner, *Ordbog over Det gamle norske Sprog*, iv. Rettelser og Tillegg ved Finn Hødnebø. 1972.
Frosell, B.	'En gejstlig stormand ser på retten i Skåne,' in Ebbesen, 243–53.
Fundinn Nóregr	In *Flat.*, i 219–21.
Den Gamle Gaardsret	In KR, v 23–46.
Garmonsway, G. N., and Simpson, J.	*Beowulf and its Analogues.* 1968.
Gasnault, P.	'Le tombeau de Saint Martin et les invasions normandes dans l'histoire et dans la légende', *Revue d'histoire de l'église de France*, xlvii (1961), 51–66.
(Saxo) GD	*Saxonis Gesta Danorum.* Ed. J. Olrik and H. Ræder. 1931.
The Gelasian Sacramentary	Ed. H. A. Wilson. 1894.
Genealogy of the Kings of Denmark by an Unknown Author	See *Incerti Auctoris Genealogia.*
Geoffrey of Monmouth	*The Historia Regum Britanniae of Geoffrey of Monmouth.* Ed. A. Griscom. 1929.
Gertz; Gertz 1915/16	M. Cl. Gertz, *En ny Text af Sven Aggesøns Værker genvunden paa Grundlag af Codex Arnæmagnæanus 33, 4to.* 1915/16.

Gierke, O.	*Political Theories of the Middle Ages.* Tr. F. W. Maitland. 1900; repr. 1958.
Giles	*William of Malmesbury's Chronicle.* Tr. J. A. Giles. 1847.
Glaber	See *Rodulfi Glabri Historiarum libri quinque.*
Godefroy	*Corpus Iuris Civilis accesserunt commentarii D. Gothofredi.* 1624.
Graham-Campbell, J.	*Viking Artifacts.* 1980.
Gransden, A.	*Historical Writing in England c.550 to c.1307.* 1974.
Gratian	See *Decretum.*
Gregory, St	*Moralia in Iob.* Ed. M. Adriaen. CCSL, cxliii. 1979.
Grundtvig, N. F. S.	*Danmarks Krøniker.* 1818–22.
Haastrup, W.	'Bøger i Danmark på Anders Sunesens tid', in Ebbesen, 99–114.
Hálfs saga	*Hálfs saga ok Hálfsrekka.* Ed. A. Le Roy Andrews. 1909.
Hamsfort	*Chronologia... secunda,* in SRD, i.
F. C. C. Hansen	*De ældste Kongegrave og Bispegrave i Roskilde Domkirke.* 1914.
N. C. Hansen	'Nogle Navne fra Vederloven', APS, xi (1936–7), 82–90.
Jens S. Th. Hansen	'Theodoricus Monachus and European literature', *Symbolae Osloenses,* xxvii (1949), 70–127.
HC	See *Historia Compendiosa.*
Heimskringla	Snorri Sturluson. *Heimskringla.* Ed. Bjarni Aðalbjarnarson. ÍF xxvi–xxviii. 1941–51.
Helmold	*Chronica Slavorum.* Ed. B. Schmeidler. 1937.
Henry of Huntingdon	*Historia Anglorum.* Ed. T. Arnold. 1879.
Ad Herennium	*Ad C. Herennium de ratione dicendi.* Ed. and tr. H. Caplan. 1954.
Hex.	*Hexaemeron.* See Anders Sunesen.
Hirðskrá	In NGL, ii 387–450.

Historia Compendiosa   In Gertz 1915/16 and SM, i.
Historia Norwegiae   In MHN, 70–124.
Historia de Profectione Danorum   In SM, ii 443–92.
Hjärne, E. H.   'Vederlag och sjöväsen', *Namn och Bygd*, xvii (1929), 83–116.
Hoebel, A. Adamson   *The Law of Primitive Man*. 1954.
Hoffmann 1975   E. Hoffmann, *Die Heiligen Könige bei den Angelsachsen und den skandinavischen Völkern*. 1975.
Hoffmann 1976   E. Hoffmann, *Königserhebung und Thronfolgeordnung in Dänemark bis zum Ausgang des Mittelalters*. 1976.
Hofmann, D.   *Nordisch-englische Lehnbeziehungen der Wikingerzeit*. 1955.
Holberg, L.   *Dansk Rigslovgivning*. 1889.
Hollister, C. W.   *Anglo-Saxon Military Institutions*. 1962.
Hooper, N.   'The housecarls in England', *Anglo-Norman Studies*, vii (1984), 161–76.
Houken, Aage   *Håndbog i danske Stednavne*. 1975.
Hrólfs saga   *Hrólfs saga kraka*. Ed. D. Slay. 1960.
HS   *Sven Aggesøns historiske Skrifter*. Tr. M. Cl. Gertz. 1916/17; repr. 1967.
HT(D)   (Dansk) *Historisk Tidskrift*.
Hude, Anna   *Danehoffet og dets Plads i Danmarks Statsforfatning*. 1893.
Hugh of St Victor, *De Bestiis*   In PL 177.
Hversu Nóregr byggðisk   In *Flat.*, i 21–4.
Hyndluljóð   In *Norrœn fornkvæði . . . Sæmundar Edda*. Ed. S. Bugge. 1867.
Hørby, K.   In Niels Lund og Kai Hørby, *Samfundet i vikingetid og middelalder*. (Gyldendals) *Dansk social historie*, ii. 1981.
ÍF   *Íslenzk Fornrit*, i– . 1933– .
Incerti Auctoris Genealogia (Regum Danie)   In SM, i 186–94.
(Justinian's) *Institutes*   In *Corpus iuris civilis*; and in *Justinian's Institutes*. Tr. P. Birks and G. McLeod. 1987.

Isidore, *De ecclesiasticis officiis*	In PL 83.
Isidore, *Etym.*	*Isidori . . . Etymologiarum libri XX.* Ed. W. M. Lindsay. 1911.
Isidore, *Sententiæ*	In PL 83.
Ivo of Chartres, *Decretum*	In PL 161.
Ivo of Chartres, *Panormia*	In PL 161.
Jacobsen, Lis	*Svenskevældets Fald.* 1929.
Jaeger	C. S. Jaeger, *The Origins of Courtliness.* 1985.
Jerome, *Commentary on Jeremiah*	*S. Hieronymi . . . Opera . . . In Hieremiam.* Ed. S. Reiter. CCSL, lxxiv. 1960.
Jakob Benediktsson	'Icelandic traditions of the Scyldings', *Saga-Book,* xv:1 (1957), 48–66.
Johannesson, Kurt	*Saxo Grammaticus.* 1978.
John of Genoa	*Catholicon.* Rouen 1515.
John of Hauteville	See *Architrenius.*
John of Salisbury, *The Letters*	*The Letters of John of Salisbury.* Ed. W. J. Millor, SJ, and C. N. L. Brooke. 1955-86.
John of Salisbury, *Metalogicon*	Ed. C. C. I. Webb. 1929.
John of Salisbury, *Policraticus*	Ed. C. C. I. Webb. 1909.
Johnsen, A. O.	*Om Theodricus og hans Historia de antiquitate regum Norwagiensium.* Avh. utg. av Det Norske Videnskaps-Akademi. II. Hist.-filos. Klasse, 1939, No. 3.
Jómsvíkinga saga (1962)	*The Saga of the Jomsvikings.* Ed. and tr. N. F. Blake. 1962.
Jómsvíkinga saga (1969)	*Jómsvíkinga saga.* Ed. Ólafur Halldórsson. 1969.
Jones and Jones, *Commentary*	*Commentary on the First Six Books of the Æneid* [attr. to Bernard Silvestris]. Ed. J. W. Jones and E. F. Jones. 1977.
Justinian	See *Institutes.*
Jutland Law	In DGL, ii–iv.
Jørgensen	P. J. Jørgensen, *Dansk Retshistorie.* Sixth ed. 1974.
A. D. Jørgensen 1876	'Bidrag til Oplysning om Middelalderens Love og Samfundsforhold. III. Witherlogh. Worthhæld', *Aarbøger* (1876), 56–92.

A. D. Jørgensen 1879	*Valdemar Sejr. Udvalgt Samling af ... Kildeskrifter ... i dansk Oversættelse.* 1879.
Kalkar, O.	*Ordbog til det ældre danske Sprog (1300–1700).* 1881–1918; repr. 1976.
Kemble, J.	*The Saxons in England.* 1876.
Kinch, J.	'Om den danske Adels Udspring fra Thinglid', *Aarbøger* (1875), 247–350.
KL	*Kulturhistorisk leksikon for nordisk middelalder.* Ed. L. Jacobsen, G. Rona et al. 1956–78.
Knuds-Bogen	*Knuds-Bogen 1986. Studier over Knud den Hellige.* Ed. T. Nyberg, H. Bekker-Nielsen, N. Oxenvad. Fynske Studier, xv. 1986.
Knýtlinga saga	In *Danakonunga sǫgur*, 93–321.
Kock, A.	'Etymologiska anmärkningar om nordiska ord', *Arkiv för nordisk filologi*, xxiv (1908), 179–98.
Konungs skuggsiá (Konungsskuggsjá)	Ed. L. Holm-Olsen. Second ed. 1983. *The King's Mirror.* Tr. L. M. Larson. 1917.
Kormáks saga	In *Vatnsdœla saga.* Ed. Einar Ól. Sveinsson. ÍF viii. 1939.
KR	J. L. A. Kolderup-Rosenvinge, *Samling af gamle Love.* v. *Danske Gaardsretter og Stadsretter.* 1827.
Anne K. G. Kristensen 1968–9	'Knud Magnussens Krønike', HT(D), 12. Række, 3 (1968–9), 431–52.
Anne K. G. Kristensen 1969	*Danmarks ældste Annalistik.* 1969.
Kroman 1973	E. Kroman, 'Danmarks gamle Love', APS, xxix (1973), 111–26.
KV	*Krøniker fra Valdemarstiden.* Tr. J. Olrik. 1900–1.
KVJ	*Kong Valdemars Jordebog.* Ed. Svend Aakjær. 1926–43.
Lagerbring, S.	*Monumenta Scaniensia.* [Lund disputations publ. by S. Bring] 1744–51.
Lange, Gudrun	*Die Anfänge der isländisch-norwegischen Geschichtsschreibung.* Studia Islandica, 47. 1989.

Langebek	See SRD.
Langfeðgatal	In *Alfræði*, iii 57–9.
Larson 1904	L. M. Larson, *The King's Household in England before the Norman Conquest*. 1904.
Larson 1912	L. M. Larson, *Canute the Great*. 1912.
Lausberg	H. Lausberg, *Elemente der literarischen Rhetorik*. Sixth ed. 1979.
Law of the Retainers	See *Lex Castrensis*.
LC	See *Lex Castrensis*.
Leges Henrici Primi	Ed. L. J. Downer. 1972.
Lejre Chronicle	See *Chronicon Lethrense*.
Lex Castrensis	In Gertz 1915/16 and SM, i; cf. DR, 6–34.
Lexicon Poeticum	Sveinbjörn Egilsson, *Lexicon poeticum antiquæ linguæ septentrionalis*. Ed. Finnur Jónsson. Second ed. 1931.
LHL	O. Schumann, *Lateinisches Hexameter Lexicon*. 1979–82.
Liebermann	*Die Gesetze der Angelsachsen*. Ed. F. Liebermann. 1903–16.
Liedgren, J.	'Gårdsrätt', KL, v 645–7.
Lindow, J.	*Comitatus, Individual and Honor*. 1975.
LM	See Læssøe Müller.
LMP	*Lexicon Mediae et Infimae Latinitatis Polonorum*. Ed. M. Plezia. 1953– .
Lukman 1976	N. Lukman, 'Ragnar loðbrók, Sigifrid, and the Saints of Flanders', MSc., ix (1976), 7–50.
Lukman, in SS	See Christensen, in SS . . . 'Diskussion'.
Lund *Liber daticus*	In NL and Weeke.
Lund king-list	In NL.
Lund *Memoriale fratrum*	In NL.
Lund necrology	In NL.
Lund Pontifical	See Strömberg.
Læssøe Müller, P.	[Sven Aggesen's] *Kortfattet Historie om Danmarks Konger*. 1944.
Löfstedt, E.	*Arnobiana*. Lunds Universitets Årsskrift, NF, Avd. 1, xii 5. 1917.

Maldon	*The Battle of Maldon.* Ed. E. V. Gordon. 1937.
Malmros 1979	R. Malmros, 'Blodgildet i Roskilde historiografisk belyst', *Scandia,* xlv (1979), 43–66.
Malmros 1985	R. Malmros, 'Leding og Skjaldekvad', *Aarbøger* (1985), 89–139.
Map, Walter	*De Nugis Curialium.* Ed. T. Wright. 1850.
Martínez-Pizarro, J.	'Sven Aggesen', (Scribner's) *Dictionary of the Middle Ages* (ed. J. H. Strayer, 1988), xi 322–30.
Maurer, K.	*Das älteste Hofrecht des Nordens.* 1877.
McGuire, B. P.	'Politics and Property at Esrum Abbey: 1151–1251', MSc., vi (1974), 122–50.
MGH (*Ep., Leg., Poet., Script.*)	*Monumenta Germaniæ Historica.* Ed. G. H. Pertz et al. 1826– .
MHN	*Monumenta historica Norvegiæ.* Ed. G. Storm. 1880.
Moltke, E.	*Runes and their Origin.* 1985.
Morkinskinna	Ed. Finnur Jónsson. 1932.
Mortensen, L. Boje	'Hvem var Anders Sunesens muse? En undersøgelse . . .', in Ebbesen, 205–19.
MSc.	*Mediaeval Scandinavia.*
Neckam	*De nominibus utensilium.* Ed. A. Scheler, *Jahrbuch für Romanische und Englische Literatur,* vii (1866), 155–73.
Neergaard	C. Neergaard, 'Teglstensmuren, Kong Valdemar den Stores Værk', *Nordiske Fortidsminder,* i (1890–1903), 283–97.
NGL	*Norges gamle Love indtil 1387.* Ed. R. Keyser et al. 1846–95.
NGML	*Novum Glossarium Mediae Latinitatis.* Ed. F. Blatt, Y. Lefèvre. 1957– .
H. Nielsen	'Hird: Danmark', KL, vi 577–9.

K. M. Nielsen	'Jelling Problems. A Discussion', MSc., vii (1974), 156–79.
Niermeyer, J. F.	Mediæ Latinitatis Lexicon Minor. 1954–76.
Niger, Ralph	Radulphi Nigri Chronica. The Chronicles of Ralph Niger. Ed. R. Anstruther. 1851.
Nightingale, P.	'The origin of the court of Husting . . .', English Historical Review, 102 (1987), 559–78.
NL	Necrologium Lundense: Lunds Domkyrkas Nekrologium. Ed. L. Weibull. 1923.
Nyrop, C.	Danmarks Gilde og Lavsskraaer fra Middelalderen. 1895–1904.
Oddr Snorrason	Saga Óláfs Tryggvasonar af Oddr Snorrason munk. Ed. Finnur Jónsson. 1932.
Ohley, F.	'Die Pferde im "Parzival" Wolframs von Eschenbach', Settimane di Studio del Centro Italiano di Studi sull'alto Medioevo, xxxi:2 (1985), 849–927.
Óláfs saga helga	See Heimskringla and Den store Saga.
A. Olrik	The Heroic Legends of Denmark. Tr. Lee M. Hollander. 1919.
Olrik 1899–1900	J. Olrik, 'Harald Héns Love', HT(D), 7. Række, 2 (1899–1900), 177–212.
Olrik, J.	See KV.
Olsen, B. Munk	'Anders Sunesen og Paris', in Ebbesen, 75–97.
Orluf, F.	'Hvor dræbtes Harald Kesia?', Danske Studier (1953), 54–64.
Otto of Freising, Chronicle (of Two Cities)	Ottonis . . . Chronica, sive Historia de duabus civitatibus. Ed. A. Hofmeister. 1912.
Ousager, B.	'Gorm Konge', Skalk, Nr 2 (1957), 19–30.
Paludan, H.	'Flos Danie', in Jyske Samlinger, Ny Række, vii (1966–7).

Paulus Diaconus, *Historia Langobardorum*	Ed. L. Bethmann and G. Waitz, in MGH. 1878.
Paulus Diaconus, HR	*Pauli Diaconi Historia Romana*. Ed. A. Crivelluci. 1914.
Personbinamn	E. H. Lind, *Norsk-isländska personbinamn från medeltiden*. 1920–1.
Peter of Blois	*Petri Blesensis Epistolæ*. In PL 207.
(Saxo) PF	See SG, i.
PL	*Patrologia Latina (Patrologiæ cursus completus series secunda)*. Ed. J.-P. Migne. 1844–1905.
Post, G.	'Plena potestas and consent in medieval assemblies', *Traditio*, i (1943), 355–408.
Quicherat, L.	*Addenda Lexicis Latinis*. 1862.
Rahewin, *Gesta Friderici*	*Ottonis et Rahewini Gesta Friderici I Imperatoris*. Ed. G. Waitz. 1884.
RB	*Regula Benedicti*. Ed. and tr. D. Hunter Blair. 1906.
Regino of Prüm	*Chronicon*. Ed. F. Kurze in MGH. 1890.
Ribe Annals	See *Annales Ripenses*.
Rickert, E.	'The Old English Offa Saga', *Modern Philology*, ii (1904–5), 29–76, 321–76.
Riis	T. Riis, *Les institutions politiques centrales du Danemark 1100–1322*. 1977.
Riis 1982	T. Riis, 'Autour du mariage de 1193', *La France de Philippe Auguste* (ed. R. H. Bautier, 1982), 341–62.
(the) Ringsted Office	In VSD, 189–204.
Robert of Torigny	*Chronique de Robert de Torigni*. Ed. L. Delisle. 1872.
Rodulfi Glabri Historiarum libri quinque	Ed. J. France. 1989.
Roger of Wendover	*Flores Historiarum*. Ed. H. O. Coxe. 1841–4.
Roskilde Chronicle	See *Chronicon Roskildense*.
Rüde Annals	See *Annales Ryenses*.
S	The text from Stephanius in Gertz 1915/16 and SM, i.

The Saga of King Heidrek the Wise	Ed. and tr. C. Tolkien. 1960.
Salvian of Marseilles, *De Gubernatione Dei*	In PL 53.
Sawyer 1985a	Birgit Sawyer, 'Saxo—Valdemar—Absalon', *Scandia*, li (1985), 33–60.
Sawyer 1985b	Birgit Sawyer, 'Valdemar, Absalon and Saxo', *Revue Belge de Philologie et d'Histoire*, lxiii (1985), 685–705.
Sawyer, P.	*Da Danmark blev Danmark*. 1988.
Scanian Law	In DGL, i:1.
Schwerin, C. von	*Dänische Recht*. Germanenrechte, viii. 1938.
Seip, D. A.	'Hirdskrå', KL, vi 580–2.
Series ac Brevior (Historia Regum Danie)	In SM, i 161–6.
Servius	*Servii Grammatici . . . commentarii*. Ed. G. Thilo, H. Hagen. 1881–4.
SG, i	Saxo Grammaticus. *The History of the Danes*. Tr. Peter Fisher (= [Saxo] PF). Ed. H. Ellis Davidson. 1979.
SG, ii	H. Ellis Davidson and P. Fisher. Saxo Grammaticus. *The History of the Danes. Books I–IX. Commentary*. 1980.
(A) Short History (of the Kings of Denmark)	See *Historia Compendiosa*.
Simon	Gertrud Simon, 'Untersuchungen zur Topik der Widmungsbriefe mittelalterliche Geschichtsschreiber bis zum Ende des 12. Jahrhunderts', *Archiv für Diplomatik*, iv (1958), 52–119, v (1959), 73–153.
Sjælland Law (Valdemar's)	In DGL, vii–viii.
Sjælland Law (Erik's)	In DGL, v–vi.
Skj.	*Den norsk-islandske Skjaldedigtning*. Ed. Finnur Jónsson. 1912–15.
Skjoldungernes Saga	Ed. C. Lund and K. Friis-Jensen. 1984.
Skjǫldunga saga	In *Danakonunga sǫgur*, 3–90.

Skyum-Nielsen, N.	*Kvinde og Slave.* 1971.
Skyum-Nielsen, in SS	N. Skyum-Nielsen, 'Saxo som kilde til et par centrale institutioner i samtiden', SS, 174–86.
SM	*Scriptores minores historiæ Danicæ medii ævi.* Ed. M. Cl. Gertz. 1917–22.
SRD	*Scriptores Rerum Danicarum medii ævi.* Ed. J. Langebek et al. 1772–1878.
SS	*Saxostudier.* Ed. I. Boserup. 1975.
St Albans *Vitae (duorum Offarum)*	In Chambers, 217–43.
Steenstrup 1896	J. C. H. R. Steenstrup, *Danmarks Riges Historie*, i. 1896.
Steenstrup, *Normannerne*	J. C. H. R. Steenstrup, *Normannerne.* 1876–82.
Stenton 1932	(Sir) Frank Stenton, *The First Century of English Feudalism.* 1932.
Stenton 1950	(Sir) Frank Stenton, *Anglo-Saxon England.* 1950.
Stephanius	*Svenonis Aggonis Filii . . . quæ extant Opusculi.* Ed. Stephanus Johannis Stephanius. 1642.
Stephen of Tournai, *Lettres*	*Lettres d'Etienne de Tournai.* Ed. J. D. Desilve. 1893.
Den store Saga	*Den store Saga om Olav den Hellige.* Ed. O. A. Johnsen and Jón Helgason. 1941.
Strand	B. Strand, *Kvinnor och män i Gesta Danorum.* 1980.
Strömberg, B.	*Den pontifikale Liturgi i Lund och Roskilde.* 1955.
Suger, *Vita Ludovici Grossi*	*Vie de Louis VI le Gros.* Ed. and tr. H. Waquet. 1929.
Sven Aggesen	*Historia Compendiosa* (HC, Short History), in Gertz 1915/16 and SM, i.
Sven Aggesen	*Lex Castrensis* (LC, Law of the Retainers), in Gertz 1915/16 and SM, i.
Sverris saga	Ed. G. Indrebø. 1920.

Synonyma	*Opus synonymorum*. Ed. P. Leyser, in *Historia Poetarum medii aevi* (1721), 312–20.
Szacherska 1977	S. M. Szacherska, 'The Political Role of the Danish Monasteries in Pomerania 1171–1223', MSc., x (1977), 122–55.
Szacherska 1988	S. M. Szacherska, 'Valdemar II's Expedition to Pruthenia and the Mission of Bishop Christian', MSc., xii (1988), 44–75.
Søndergaard, G.	'Canutus—historien om et navn', *Knuds-Bogen*, 157–80.
Sørensen, J. Kousgaard	*Patronymer i Danmark*. 1984.
Thangmar, *Vita S. Bernwardi*	In MGH. 1841.
Theodricus, *Historia de antiquitate regum Norwagiensium*.	In MHN, 3–68.
Thesaurus Novus	*Thesaurus Novus Latinitatis*. Ed. A. Mai. 1836.
Thietmar	*Thietmari Merseburgensis Episcopi Chronicon*. In MGH. 1889.
Tilnavne	*Danmarks gamle Personnavne*. II. *Tilnavne*. Ed. G. Knudsen, M. Kristensen, R. Hornby. 1949–64.
Vedel	A. S. Vedel, *Den danske Krønicke som Saxo Grammaticus screff*. Copenhagen 1575.
Velschow	*Saxonis Grammatici Historia Danica*. Ed. P. E. Müller and J. M. Velschow. *Pars posterior, Prolegomena et Notæ uberiores*. 1858.
Vita Ædwardi	*Vita Ædwardi Regis. The Life of King Edward*. Ed. and tr. F. Barlow. 1962.
Vita Prima (of St Bernard)	In MGH. 1882.
Vita of St William of Æbelholt	In VSD, 300–69.
VSD	*Vitae Sanctorum Danorum*. Ed. M. Cl. Gertz. 1908–12.
Waitz, G.	'Zur Kritik Dänischer Geschichtsquellen', *Neues Archiv der Gesellschaft für ältere deutsche Geschichtskunde*, xii (1887), 25–39.

Walter of Châtillon	*Galteri de Castellione Alexandreis.* Ed. M. L. Colker. 1978; *The Alexandreis.* Tr. R. Telfryn Pritchard. 1986.
Walther, H.	*Lateinische Sprichwörter und Sentenzen des Mittelalters.* 1963–9.
Weeke, C.	*Lunde Domkapitels Gavebøger.* 1884–9; repr. 1973.
Weibull 1918	Curt Weibull, 'Saxoforskning', *Historisk Tidskrift för Skåneland,* vii (1918), 181–241.
Weibull 1986	Curt Weibull, 'Ny och äldre historieskrivning om Danmark under tidig medeltid', HT(D), lxxxvi (1986), 1–25.
L. Weibull	'Tyre Danmarkar bot', *Scandia,* i (1928), 187–202.
Widsith	Ed. Kemp Malone. 1936.
William of Blois, *Alda*	In Cohen.
William of Jumièges	*Gesta Normannorum Ducum.* Ed. J. Marx. 1914.
William of Malmesbury, *Gesta Pontificum*	*De Gestis Pontificum Anglorum.* Ed. N. E. S. A. Hamilton. 1870.
William of Malmesbury, *De Gestis Regum*	*De Gestis Regum Anglorum.* Ed. W. Stubbs. 1887–9.
Wilson	See *The Gelasian Sacramentary.*
Wolff, Odin	*Den förste Danske Historieskriver Svend Aagesens kortfattede Danmarks Historie.* 1807.
WR	*Witherlax ræt* (see Introd., p. 5).
X	The reconstructed text in Gertz 1915/16 and SM, i.
Ynglinga saga	In *Heimskringla,* i.

INDEXES

I. Persons (other than authors). II. Authors, ancient and modern. III. Places and peoples. IV. Laws, sources, texts. V. Institutional and legal matters. VI. Various topics; style; realia. VII. Some words commented on in the Notes.

In the following indexes page-references to the translated texts are printed bold. The Notes are only selectively indexed; the words 'Denmark' and 'Danes', which occur *passim*, are not included at all. Abbreviations used are: abp = archbishop; bp = bishop; d. = daughter; E = Emperor; f. = father; K = King; KD = King of Denmark; KN = King of Norway; m. = mother; P = Pope; Q = Queen; s. = son.

I. *Persons (other than authors)*

Abel, KD 10, 97
Abraham 27
Absalon, abp 1–6, 9–11, 13, 17, **31, 44, 61, 65,** 108, 120, 132, 139, 142, 145
Aggi (brotherhood member) 145
Aggi Svensen **40, 46,** 143
Aggi Kristiarnsen 1–2, **69–70,** 143
Aggi Thver **41, 46**
Aki (the crusader) 127
Alexander (the Great) **32,** 88, 94, 95, 110
Alexander III, P 132, 137
Alexander Petersen 145
Álfhildr, m. of Magnús the Good 126
Alfred, K 10
Anders (Andrew) Sunesen, abp 15, 91, 94, 95, 96, 99, 100
Andrew, deacon of Lund 3
Angantýr, K 113
Asser Aggesen 143
Asser Kristiarnsen 145
Asser Svensen, abp **40, 46,** 142, 143
Asser Svensen, provost 1, 3, 144
Ástráðr Þorgunnuson 142
Athisl, K 107
Augustus, E 120
Benedikt Karlsen 145
Benedikte Kristiarnsdottir 145
Bernard of Ratzeburg, Count 138
Berno (a viking) 114
Bernward, bp of Hildesheim 125
Biorn Ironside, s. of Harald Kesia **68, 69–70,** 143
Birger jarl 145
Bo Hithinsen **40, 46**
Bo Ketilsen **41, 47**
Bugislav I, Duke of Pomerania 22, 25, **73,** 139
Bugislav II 26, 140
Buris Henriksen 138
Byrhtnoth 111
Canute — see Knut
Cecilia, d. of Knut IV 144
Charlemagne 25
Chnob, KD 115
Conrad II, E **63,** 124
Dan the High-minded, s. of Uffi, KD 19, **54,** 112
Dannia 112
Dido 117
Dodona **32**
Domborus 123
Ebbi Olafsen 145
Ebbi Skialmsen 144
Edward the Confessor, K 112, 118
Eiríkr (Blood-axe), KN 24
Elef jarl 100
Ennignup (*Sealendensis bondo*), regent in Denmark **55,** 75
Erik, Count 144, 145
Erik I, the (Ever-)Good, s. of Sven II, KD **39, 46, 67–8,** 130
Erik II, the Ever-memorable, KD 9, 22, **68–71,** 84, 96, 143
Erik III, the Lamb, KD 8, 9, 22, **71,** 92, 143
Erik V, Glipping, KD 10
Erlingr skakki 138
Esbiorn, archdeacon 3
Esbiorn Snara 145
Esger Ebbesen **41, 46**
Eskil Assersen 145
Eskil Kristiarnsen, abp 1–4, 78, 142,

143, 144, 145
Eskil Svensen **40, 46,** 143
Eskil, s. of Øpi 14, **34, 44**
Estrith, Old Knut's sister, m. of Sven II 65
Ethelred, K 12
Eysteinn, abp 23, 76, 82
Frederick Barbarossa, E 21, 26, 90, 108
Frithlefer, s. of Frothi the Old, KD **54**
Frothi the Bold, s. of Rokil, KD, **50**
Frothi *Frithgothæ*, KD 11, **54,** 101
Frothi the Old, s. of Dan, KD **54**
Frothi, s. of Skiold, KD **49**
Gerbrand, bp of Roskilde **64**
Geryon of Hesperus **32,** 87
Gorm *Løghæ*, s. of Klak-Harald, KD **56,** 117
Gunhild, d. of Old Knut **63**
Gunnhildr, Q in Norway 24
Gunnild, d. of Sven 144
Hadrian I, P 16
Hákon Aðalsteinsfóstri, KN 11
Hákon jarl Eiríksson 142
Hakon *malus* (Hlaðajarl) 24
Halfdan, s. of Skiold, KD **49**
Harald Bluetooth, s. of Gorm, KD **61–2, 73,** 117
Harald Kesia, s. of Erik I **68, 70**
Harald, s. of Sven Forkbeard, KD 126
Harald Whetstone, s. of Sven II, KD 7, **39, 46, 65–6**
Haraldr harðráði, KN 25, 80
Harthaknut (*Canutus austerus sive durus*), s. of Old Knut, KD 25, **39, 46, 64,** 115
Helghi, s. of Halfdan, KD **49**
Henrik the Lame **68**
Henry the Fowler, K 115, 118
Henry (III), E **63**
Henry the Lion, Duke 21, 26, 139
Hercules 87, 121
Herioldus, K 116 (cf. Klak-Harald)
Jon Sverkerson, K in Sweden 144
Judas 16, **42, 44,** 100
Kamien, bp (Conrad) of **73,** 121
Karl *Agisun* (= s. of Aggi [Svensen]?) 143
Karl Eriksen 144, 145

Karl Karlsen 145
Kazymar II, Duke of Pomerania 26
Keti and Vigi 107
Kjeld, St 112, 143
Klak-Harald, s. of Snio, KD **56,** 116–17
Knut, kings of Denmark so named 115
Knut (I), s. of Sighwarth, KD **55–6**
Knut (II), Old Knut (*vetus Kanutus, Kanutus Senis*), s. of Sven Forkbeard, KD 9, 10–12, 13–17, 25, 30, **32–39, 40, 45–6, 63–5,** 89
Knut (III) — see Harthaknut
Knut IV, St Knut of Odense, s. of Sven II, KD 18, **39, 46, 66–7,** 82, 100, 128–30, 142
Knut V, s. of Magnus, s. of Nicolaus, KD 9, 19, 22, **71–2, 73** (*Canutus rex Roschildensis*), 136
Knut VI, s. of Valdemar I, KD 1, 3, 5, 7–9, 12, 13, 17, 20–2, 26–7, **31, 44, 73,** 82, 89, 107, 109, 111
Knut Karlsen 144–5
Knut Lavard, Duke, St Knut of Ringsted, s. of Erik I 20, 22, **68–9, 71,** 100, 144
Kristiarn (two brotherhood members) 145
Kristiarn Aggesen 145
Kristiarn Benediktsen 145
Kristiarn Svensen 1, 13, 15, **39–40, 41, 46, 47, 69–70,** 78, 119, 143, 145
Kristiarn Svensen (conspirator) 144
Kristofer I, KD 10, 86, 97
Lothair, K 131
Magnus the Good, s. of St Olaf, KN & KD, 24, 25, **39, 46, 65**
Magnus, s. of Nicolaus 22, **68–71**
Magnus Eriksen 10, 144
Martin, priest 3
Martin, St **64,** 125
Nestor **56**
Nicolaus (brotherhood member) 145
Nicolaus, Count 143–4
Nicolaus the Old, s. of Sven II, KD 1, 9, **39, 41, 46, 68–70,** 82, 130, 143, 144
Nicolaus, St 134
Offa 21, 30

Olaf (*Olaus*), KD 27, **55**
Olaf (*Olaus Famelicus*), s. of Sven II, KD **39, 67,** 142
Olaf Haraldsson, St, KN 11, 24, **65,** 79
Olaf, s. of Harald Kesia 134–5
Otto, E 24, **56–60**
Palna-Toki (*Palna Tokki*), Pálnatóki 11, **62,** 142
Peter Aggesen 145
Peter, bp of Roskilde 112
Philip II Augustus (married to Ingeborg, d. of Valdemar I), K 20
Plogh the Black **71**
Ragnar — see Regner
Raki, Dog-king 19
Regner *Lothbrogh* 11, **55,** 114
Ro 19, 105, 112
Rodulf, bp of Schleswig **64**
Rokil Slagenback, s. of Rolf Kraki, KD **49**
Rolf Kraki, s. of Helghi, KD **49,** 116
Romulus 105
Saul, K **68**
Schleswig, bp of 133; Duke of 110, 140
Semiramis 117
Sheba, Q of **56**
Siegfried, Landgrave of Thuringia, Count of Orlamünde 121, 139
Sigefridus (= Sigurðr ormr-í-auga?) 114
Sighwarth, s. of Regner *Lothbrogh*, KD 27, **55**
Skiold, KD 20, 27, **49,** 105
Snio, s. of Knut, KD **56**
Solomon, K **56**
Sophia, d. of Volodar of Minsk, half-sister of Knut V, wife of Valdemar I 4, 22, 26, **73,** 117, 138
Sophia, d. of Valdemar I 139
Suni Ebbesen 145
Sveinn Þorgunnuson — see Sven, s. of Thrugot
Sven Aggesen 1–4 (*Sveno archidiaconus* 3), **61** (*ego Sueno*), family 142–5
Sven I, Forkbeard, KD 11, 21, **32, 61–3,** 78
Sven, s. of Old Knut, KN **64**
Sven II, Estrithsen, KD 25, **39, 46, 65,** 81

Sven III, Grathe, s. of Erik II, KD 1, 2, 9, 22, **68, 71–2,** 88, 143, 144
Sven Kristiarnsen 2, 143
Sven Svensen, bp of Viborg **40, 46,** 143
Sven, s. of Thrugot **40** (= s. of Thrugun **46**) (*alias* Thorkil 142)
Theseus 94, 110
Thorkel (the Tall, s. of Strút-Harald) 11
Thorkil — see Sven, s. of Thrugot
Thorkil Bille 145
Thrugot **40,** 142
Thrugun **46,** 142
Thuri Doki **39, 46**
Thuringia, Landgrave (Lewis III) of 26, 84, 117, 138; and see Siegfried
Thyrwi, Ornament of Denmark, Q 21, 24, 26, **56–61**
Toki Skialmsen 144
Toki Stighsen 145
Tomyris, Q 117
Ubbi Esbiornsen, Count 144
Uffi, s. of Wermund, KD 26, 30, **50–4**
Ulf of Galicia 142
Ulf of Ribe 9
Ulf Sprakaleg **65,** 95
Úlfr Óspaksson 80
Ulysses **56**
Vagn Ákason 142
Valdemar I, s. of St Knut of Ringsted, KD 1, 2, 7–9, 19–22, **31, 68, 71–3,** 91, 92, 122, 137, 145
Valdemar II, s. of Valdemar I, KD 7–8, 15, 26, **74,** 88, 91, 97, 110
Valdemar IV (Atterdag), KD 92
Valdemar Knutsen, bp of Schleswig 19, 26, 82, 84, 109, 114, 138
Volodar, Prince of Minsk 139
Wermund the Wise, s. of Frothi the Bold, KD **50–4**
William, abbot of Æbelholt 20, 90, 92, 112, 115, 121, 130
Withi the Staller (*Guido Stabularius*) **41, 46**
Ælfheah (Alphege), abp of Canterbury, St 11, 91
Øpi the Wise (*Snialli*) 14, **34, 44,** 94

II. *Authors, ancient and modern*

Abelard 28
Abels, R. P. 79
Adam of Bremen 18, 19, 114, 115–16, 118, 121–7
Alan of Lille 23, 87, 109, 112, 114, 118, 119, 138
Albøge, G. 6
Alcuin 112, 140
Aldhelm 92, 119
Ancher, P. Kofod 16–17
Appuleius 109
Arnold of Lübeck 23, 83, 117
Arup, E. 76
Augustine, St (& Pseudo-Augustine) 89, 100, 105
Azo 81, 94
Bering, V. 28
Bernard of Chartres 101
Bernard of Clairvaux, St 100, 138, 144
Bernard of Pavia 81
Bernard Silvestris 87, 118
Boethius 84
Bonizo 91
Brøndum-Nielsen, J. 76
Chadwick, H. M. 20, 107, 111
Christensen, A. E. 76, 77–8
Christensen K. 7, 76
Cicero 81, 108, 118, 123, 127, 138
Damasus 15, 92, 95
Damsholt, N. 76, 119
Diderichsen, P. 6
Dorotheus 14
Fenger, R. T. 28–9, 123
Festus, Paulus 122
'Florence' of Worcester 88, 107, 139
Friis-Jensen, K. 3
Garmonsway, G. N. 30
Geoffrey of Monmouth 23, 102, 132, 138
Gertz, M. Cl. 2, 5; translation by 29, 105, 123; notable emendation by 84–5, 87, 89, 91, 92, 99, 102, 108–9, 114, 118–19, 125, 131
Gísl Illugason 79
Glaber, Rodulfus 26, 108
Godefroy, D. 91
Gregory, St, P 94, 104
Grundtvig, N. F. S. 29
Helmold 135
Henricus Septimellensis 112
Henry of Huntingdon 124, 137
Holberg, L. 16–17, 29, 82, 102
Horace 109, 119, 131
Hyginus 110
Hørby, K. 16, 78
Isidore of Seville, St 80, 91, 92, 123
Ivo of Chartres 93
Jaeger, C. S. 102
Jocelyn of Brakelond 89
Johannesson, K. 14
John of Genoa 87
John of Hauteville 118
John of Salisbury 92, 101, 108, 109, 120
John of Wallingford 112
Joseph of Exeter 23
Justin 105, 117
Justinian 14–15, 134
Jørgensen, A. D. 29
Jørgensen, P. J. 5
Kemble, J. 30, 79
Kristensen, A. K. G. 3
Kroman, E. 5, 6
Lagerbring, S. 3
Lange, G. 25
Langebek, J. 3, 5, 28, 108, 142
Larson, L. M. 30, 79
Lehman, O. 28
Liebermann, F. 10
Lindow, J. 77
Lucan 23, 131 (cf. **68**)
Lyschander, C. 4
Læssøe Müller, P. 29
Malling, O. 28
Malmros, R. 136
Malone, K. 107–8
Martianus Capella **48,** 84, 89, 104, 107, 112, 114, 134
Martínez-Pizarro, J. 4
Martinus, jurist 119
McGuire, B. 144
Niger, Ralph 19, 129, 130, 135–7
Oddr Snorrason 123
Olrik, A. 20
Olrik, J. 29, 76, 104, 130

Orosius 119, 120, 134
Óttarr svarti 124
Otto of Freising 76, 101, 122
Ovid 23, **37**, 83, 94, 105, 125, 138
Paulus Diaconus 121
Peter of Blois 95, 101
Plautus 107, 111, 119, 134
Priscian 101, 110
Quintilian 102
Radulphus Diceto 18
Regino of Prüm 104
Riis, T. 5, 6, 85, 93, 100, 130
Robert of Ely 18, 130
Roger of Wendover 18, 112
Salvian of Marseilles 108
Sawyer, B. 14–15, 76
Sawyer, P. 80
Saxo (Grammaticus) 1–3, 5–11, 13, 14, 16, 18–19, 22, 23, 26–9, **65**, 143–5
Servius 87
Simon, G. 104
Simpson, J. 30
Skyum-Nielsen, N. 17, 76, 94
Snorri Sturluson 11, 79, 119
Statius 23, 83, 109, 111, 135 (cf. **68**)
Stephanius, St. J. 4, 18, 27–8, 95, 97, 108, 123
Stephen of Tournay 90, 114, 131, 132
Suger 120
Sven Aggesen 1–4 (*Sveno archidiaconus* 3), **61** (*ego Sueno*), family 142–5
Szacherska, S.M. 144
Sæmundr hinn fróði 20, 82, 112
Tertullian 86
Theodricus Monachus 23–5, 108, 131
Theophilus 14
Thietmar of Merseburg 123
Tribonian 14
Úlfr Óspaksson 80
Vedel, A. S. 28
Vegetius 86
Velschow, J. M. 3
Vergil 23, 83, 87, 111, 113, 115, 121, 138 (cf. **33, 51, 58, 61**)
Waitz, G. 5
Walter of Châtillon 23, 87, 106, 110, 112, 137
Walter Map 108

Weibull, C. 75, 133, 138
William of Blois 118
William, abbot of Æbelholt 20, 90, 92, 112, 115, 121, 122, 130
William of Jumièges 112
William of Malmesbury 18, 105, 121, 126
Wolff, O. 28
Þórðr Kolbeinsson 12
Ælnoth 18, 127–9, 131

III. *Places and peoples*
Aachen 114
Aarhus 145
Almindsyssel 145
Ascanians 21
Bällingslev 145
Bjæverskov 75, 144
Borg **41, 46**
Bremen 84, 121
Børglum 129
Canterbury 18
Clairvaux 1, 143–5
Copenhagen 4
Cyprus **68**
Danube, R. **55**
Dingsbüll 110
Eider, R. 26, **52, 60**
Elbe, R. **50**
England 10, 11, 25, **32, 34, 38, 44, 63, 64, 66,** 78, 89, 108
Esrom (abbey) 2, 92, 144
Finland **32,** 87–8
Fiskbæk 128
Flanders 142
Flensburg 97
Fotavik **70**
France 2, 14, 20, 21, 23
Fyn **65,** 126
Gaul **64**
Germans (*Alamanni, Teotonici*) 18, 21, 29, **50–54, 58, 61, 63**
Grathe (Heath) 1, **72,** 143
Greeks **32, 63**
Grønsund **61**
Götaland (*Gotia*) **64,** 145
Haraldsted **68**
Harsyssel **64,** 145

Helgenæs 65
Hohenstaufen 21, 26
Holstein (*Holzatia*) 26, **52**, 84
Holy Land 26
Humlum (*Humla*) 66
Iceland, Icelanders (*Tyle, Islandia, Islandenses*) 23, **32**, **49**, **63**, **64**, 105-7, 112-13
Ireland (*Hybernia*) 63
Isøre (*Hysøre*) 65
Italy 26, **63**, **64**
Jelling (*Ialang*) 21, **61**, 132
Jerusalem 67
Jómsborg (*Hyumsburgh*) 11, **61**, **62**, **73** ('the city ... founded by ... Harald')
Jómsvíkingar 11, 21, 78
Jutland (*Iucia, Iutia*) 8, 15, **65**, **72**, 93, 120, 142, 144, 145
Kamien **73**, 121, 139
Kampen 110
Knýtlingar 20
Kolbacz 19
Lejre (*Letra*) **49**, 112
Lime **41**, **47**
Limfjord 128, 129
Little Belt (*Medium Transitum*) 67
Lolland (*Lalandia*) **71**
Lombardy (*Langobardia*) **63**, **64**
London 11, 93
Lund 1, 3, 4, 19, **40**, **70**, 128, 142, 145
Læborg 121
Magdeburg 75, 144
Mecklenburg 26
Norway (*Noruegia*) 11, 24, 25, **32**, **44**, **63**, **64**, 93, 95, 110, 138
Norwegians 8, 23, 82
Oddaverjar 20, 113
Odense (*Othonia*) 8, 18, **39**, **46**, **66-7**, 98, 115
Omersyssel 145
Onsild (*Othenshylle*) **69**, 143
Palestine 143
Paris 2, 23, 75, 114
Pomerania, Pomeranians 1, 3, 19, 22, 25, **73**, 108
Ribe 132
Ringsted (*Rinstadia*) 8, **68**, **71**, 92
Roman Empire **50**, **56**

Romans, city of **64**
Roskilde (*Roschildensis civitas*) 19, 21, **49**, **64**, **71-2**, 95, 112, 126, 137, 143
Rouen (*Rotomagus*) 64
Rugia, Rugians 25, **72**, 123
Rønbjerg (*Rinebiergh*) **69**, 96
Samland (*Samia*) **44**, **63**, 87-8
Saxons, Saxony (*Saxonia*) 8, **58**
Scania, Scanians 1, 3, 6, 7, 9, 10, **65**, **70-2**, 134, 142, 145
Schleswig (*Slesuik*) 9, 19, 26, **58**, **64**, **66**, **68-70**, 129, 139
Sejerø 133
Sjælland (*Sialandia*) **34**, **44**, **55**, **65**, 127, 133, 142, 144
Skialm family 142, 144
Skibing (?) **70**, 134
Skioldunger 49
Skjǫldungar 20-1
Skåne — see Scania
Slavia, Slavs 9, 25, **32**, **61-3**, **65**, **68**, **72**, **73**
Sorø 4, 75, 144
Sprogø (*Sproua Insula*) **72**
Sweden (*Suetia*) **50**, **64**, 107, 116, 138, 144, 145
Teutons — see Germans
Thule — see Iceland
Tjæreby 144
Tommerup (abbey) 7
Tours (*Turones*) **64**
Trondheim 23
Urne (Urnehoved) **71**, 135
Varde (*Warwath*) **41**, **46**, 98
Veksebo 144
Vendel(-dweller, -dwellers) (*Wandalus, in Vandalis*) **40**, **46**, **67**
Venestad 75, 144
Viborg **40**, **46**, **71**, 143
Villingerød 99
Vindinge (*Winningha*) **63**
Vitskøl 136
Wends 25

IV. *Laws, sources, texts*
Annalists (Danish) 3, 19, 76, 83, 84, 96, 122, 132, 133
Avia Ripensis 145

Beowulf 105, 106
Books (ancient) **48**
Brother-list 78, 145
Canon law 14–15, 77, 80, 86
Charters (of Valdemar I) 8, 92
Chronicles (Danish) — see Lejre and Roskilde
Cistercian sources 81, 96
CL — see Lejre Chronicle
Codex Resenius 114
Compendiums (historical) 18
Consiliatio Cnuti 11, 89
CR — see Roskilde Chronicle
Draco Normannicus 23
Eiríksdrápa 12
(Den gamle) Gaardsret 14
(Lost) Genealogy (by Sven Aggesen?) 26–7
Genealogy by Abbot William 20, 112, 115, 121, 130
Genealogy of the Kings of Denmark by an Unknown Author 27
Gesta Suenomagni regis 18
Gulathing Law 11, 93
HC — see Short History
Hexaemeron 15 (see Anders Sunesen, Index I)
Hirðskrá 8
Historia de antiquitate regum Norwagiensium 23
Historia compendiosa — see Short History
Historia Norwegiæ 83
Historia de profectione Danorum 84, 102, 104, 127
Justinian (Codex, *Institutes*) 14–15, 134
King-lists 115, 125–6
Knýtlinga saga 126, 129–31, 136, 142
Konungs skuggsjá 8, 90
Law of the Retainers 2, 4, 5, 6, 7–17, 25, 26, 28–30; translated 31–43; cf. *Vederlov*, *Witherlax ræt*
Laws: of K. Abel 10, 97; II Cnut 10; of Erik V 10; of Forest 11; of Frederick Barbarossa 90; of Harald Whetstone 7, **65;** of Henry I 12, 99; of Jutland 8, 15, 93, 97, 120; of Knut VI (decree for Scania) 7, 10, 17, 89; of Kristofer I 10, 86, 97; of Lombardy 82; of Norway 11, 93, 95; of St Olaf 79; of Regner 11; of Scania 94, 97, 98, 99, 100, 101, 124; of Schleswig 93, 97; of Sjælland 7, 97, 98, 101; of Valdemar I 7; of Valdemar II 7–8, 15, 97. Cf. *Consiliatio Cnuti, Gaardsret*, Gulathing Law, *Hirðskrá*, Justinian, *Lex Castrensis*, Roman law, *Vederlov, Witherlax ræt*
Lejre Chronicle (CL) 19, 20, 23, 111
Lex Castrensis (LC) — see Law of the Retainers
Lund annalists 3, 19, 137, 145
Lund *Consuetudines* 91
Lund king-list 115, 126
(Ringsted) Office of St Knut Lavard 131–2
Old men as sources 20–1, **32, 40, 43, 48,** 83, 104
Roman law 13, 80–1, 91, 94, 128
Roskilde Chronicle (CR) 19, 21, 112, 122, 132–5
Short History (Sven Aggesen's) 2, 5, 14, 18–26, 27, 30; translated 48–74
Sven Aggesen's works 4–7 (texts of), 27–30 (translations of)
Vederlov 5, 9, 15, 17; cf. Law of the Retainers, *Witherlax ræt*
Vetus Chronica (of Sjælland) 129
Vita Ædwardi regis 112, 118
(St Albans) *Vitae duorum Offarum* 21, 107, 111, 134
Vulgate 88, 108, 109, 110, 113, 135 (cf. **32, 53, 55, 57, 59, 63, 64, 67, 68, 69, 71**)
Witherlax ræt (WR) 5, 6; translated 44–7; cf. Law of the Retainers, *Vederlov*

V. *Institutional and legal matters*
Bishops 14, **46, 64, 70, 73,** 101, 133
Boran **37,** 99
Bot 16, **39, 40–2, 57,** 78, 98
Catholiciani, 'commissioners' **70, 72,** 134
Crimen laesae maiestatis — see Treason
Fjarthing, 'quarter' **37, 44, 46**
Frithkøp 7

Forest rights 63
Government (of Denmark) 8–10
Gyrsum (gørsum) 41, 46, 97
Hird, hirð 8–10, 44
Hirðstefna 93
Hof, hofmæn 10, 14
Homage 36, 121
Homicide 38, 39, 49, 50, 60–1, 67, 69, 71, 72, 89
Hostages 58, 60–1
Humiliations 35, 38–9, 39–40, 41, 81, 124
Huskarlastefna 10, 12, 15, 37, 44, 45
Huskarlar, housecarles 45–6, 89–90
Husting, húsþing 11–12
Høfthinge(r) 10
Kings 48, 49, 51, 58, 63, 66, 68, 72
Knights 8–9, 34, 59, 133
Kværset 129
Lething 8, 128
Málamaðr, máli 80, 103
Monday Court (in London) 11
Nithing (nithingsorth, 'name of nithing') 9, 39, 45, 46
Nobility, rank 32–3, 49
Oaths 37–8, 41, 42, 45
Officials 8, 78, 98
Ordeal 45, 78
Outlawry 39, 43
Pay 36, 44
Penance 16
Queens 56–61, 73
Remedies 15, 34–7
Satisfactio 16, 97
Summonsing 44–5
Staller(s) 8, 41, 46
Tinglith — see Þingalið
Treason 9–10, 13, 42–3, 44–5, 66, 70
Urne-thing (in Vrnensi placito) 71, 135
Witherlagh, -logh 31, 37, 44, 45, 46
Viborg assembly (Viburgense placitum) 71
Worthæl (varðhald) 10
Þegn 12
Þeningmenn 12
Þing 11–12
Þingalið (þingamenn, þingamannalið) 11–12, 33 (Tinglith)

VI. *Various topics*; *style*; *realia*
Adam (debt of) 64, 73
Axes, gilded 33
Beating 14, 41, 98
Bricks 72
Cheerfulness, duty of 36 (cf. 44)
Contubernalis, contubernium 2
Cross of Christ 61, 67, 69
Danevirke 58–9, 72, 112, 120
Devil (Enemy of Peace, Old Prevaricator, Old Serpent) 15, 22, 38, 42, 67, 73, 94, 139
Dishonour (shame, disrespect) 42, 43, 49, 50, 54, 56, 57, 60
'Distribution' 54, 111
Dwarves (on shoulders of giants) 43, 101–2
Epicureans 51, 56
Fortune 54, 112
Gilds 11, 97
Gluttony 51, 56
Horses 8, 34–5, 65
Imitatio Christi 27
Irony 17, 53, 57, 59
Labyrinth (of forgetfulness) 27
Ladder (of undutifulness) 42
Latin 31, 102
Lion 32, 53, 134
Lustra (quinquennia) 64, 68, 72, 125
Music 8, 59, 120
Nature 49, 56, 73, 118
Organological politics 34, 94
Orthodoxy 56, 61
Pedigree, lineage 20, 24, 26–7, 32, 48; (Icelandic) 105–7, 112–3, 115, 123; (Sven Aggesen's) 141–5
Pilgrimage 67, 96, 143
Plebeians 49 (*agrestes*), 61 (*vulgaris tumultuatio*), 65 (*turba agrestis*), 66 (*plebs*), 67–8 (*popularis turba*; *plebicula*), 70 (*plebs Scanensium*)
Plenitudo potestatis 66, 128
Propaganda 4, 22, 28–9
Ransom 62–3, 77, 123
Rhetoric 27, 31, 43, 108
Schools (of Paris) 2, 23, 75
Seating (in king's hall) 35, 37, 45

Indexes

Style 15, 18, **43, 48, 65,** 83
Swords 33 (hilts); **38, 39** (drawn swords); **52, 53, 54** (swords of champions); **71, 72** (sword-blows)
Tranquillity (*pacis, quietis tranquillitas*) 22, **38, 54,** 63
Tribute **50, 56–7, 60, 62**
Vernacular (*[sermo] vulgaris noster*; *vulgaris assertio*) **41, 50, 67**
Women 24 (folly and wisdom); **56** (virtues); **59–60** (cunning); **63** (inheritance rights)

VII. *Some words commented on in the Notes*
(a) *with reference to the Law of the Retainers*
aconite 94
ascella 98, 103
boran 93–4
caballus 90
calumnia 91, 99
castrenses 86
catholiciani 134
classicum 101
condicio humana 88
constitutio 93
contectales 89
contubernium 86
curiales 89
dextrarius 90
discissio 100
doki 96
faleratus 102
'famulariter' 88
Favonius 101
fjarthing 94
geniculor 98–9
gyrsum, gørsum 97
huskarlar 89–90
huskarlastefna 93
incantatio 92
inconsequentia 95
insidiator 94
matricula 86
nithingsorth 95
nutricius 86
palefridus 90
patronisare 91
prescriptio 94

recumpensantes 92
runcinus 90
secretarii 89
stangehug 98
stemmata 88
subputo 88
sveet, sveit 94
taxatio 96
thver 97
vapnatak 101
witherlogh 86

(b) *with reference to the Short History*
Alamanni 111
ampullositas 109
asporto 125
binomius 122
blatan (blátǫnn) 121
bondo 116
catholiciani 134
columpna 132
comminitatio, comminatio 109
convenientia 127
cos 127
coxa 136
cythara 120
discrimen 118
distribuo 111
ecclipsus 114
elegantissimus 111
expientissimus, experientissimus 109
eymuni 134
feodum 135
fiola 120
forus 123
gentiles 107
hen (heinn) 127
herciscunda 124
indago 120
internecio 121
intersignium 110
interstitium 114
iugi memoria 133–4
kesia 134
klak 116–17
knut 114–15
lethangwite 128
løghæ 117

luminaria 136
masoleum 121
mediamnia 110
momentaneus 131
monarchia 106
nepos 113
nodus 115
novercalis 112
parifico 120
patrisso 134
perspicior 104
persecurizo 137
plenitudo potestatis 128
præcluis 112
prerogativa remanendi 129
prolixius 127
pugillatorius 111

purpureus 118
reclinarium 123
recumpensatio 128
renuto, renuntio 120
retexere 105
rigor regis 129
rostrum 139
Sealendensis 116
skatelar 131
spiculatores 108
subgrunda 123
subvector 127
syncopare 138
Tartara 133
tranquillitas pacis 112
turgiditas 108, 109
tygheskeg 122